THEN COMES
MARRIAGE

More Praise for

THEN COMES MARRIAGE

"Compelling. . . . Kaplan deftly uses [Thea Spyer and Edie Windsor's] story as a lens through which to consider a broader set of inequities, less about marriage than common human decency. . . . [A] deeply moving book."　　　—David L. Ulin, *Los Angeles Times*

"Written with a passion that comes right off the page, renowned litigator Roberta Kaplan testifies to the trials and tribulations she endured arguing for Windsor before the Supreme Court, which ultimately led to the dissolution of DOMA and paved the way for the embrace of same-sex marriage in the United States."
　　　　　　　　　　　　　　　　　　—*Ms. Magazine*

"A nail-biting journey. Few people expect a book about the law or a specific case to be a scintillating read. Yet in *Then Comes Marriage* Roberta Kaplan [has] done just that and given readers a story worthy of their time. . . . Kaplan [has] accomplished what many legal writers strive for and fall short of achieving: a book that lawyers and non-lawyers alike can enjoy. This book deserves a place on everyone's shelf."　　　—Joan M. Burda, *New York Journal of Books*

"*Then Comes Marriage* is breathtaking. We laughed. We cried. We were made angry and hopeful and full of gratitude all over again. Mostly, we were reminded of the heroism of two strong women who wouldn't take no for answer. Roberta Kaplan and Edie Windsor changed the world. In her book, Roberta Kaplan seamlessly marries her personal story with her historic journey to the Supreme Court. The book is a must-read both for its historic account of a landmark case and as a portrait of family values."
　　　　—Terrence McNally, Tony Award–winning playwright,
　　　　　　　　　　　　and Tom Kirdahy, Broadway producer

"[A] gripping historic story. . . . Absolutely astounding are the moments of profound kismet, of the cosmic intersection between the lives of Kaplan and Spyer that invariably led Kaplan to Windsor and created in her the deep personal commitment to defeat DOMA." —Karen Ocamb, *Frontiers Media*

"Prominent litigator Kaplan—the architect of the 2013 Supreme Court case that brought down the Defense of Marriage Act and compelled the federal government to recognize same-sex marriages—weaves legal drama with personal narrative for a behind-the-scenes look that is both inspiring and genuine." —*Jewish Telegraphic Agency*

"I thought I knew the *Windsor* case chapter-and-verse. As if! *Then Comes Marriage* will forever change the understanding of this landmark case—its genesis, its outside-the-box strategy and its tactical brilliance. This is the can't-put-down, emotional, funny, essential explanatory text that makes sense of *Windsor*, not just as law but as life." —Rachel Maddow, television host

"*United States v. Windsor* was a landmark ruling, and the case's architect, Roberta Kaplan, emerged as a true American hero. *Then Comes Marriage* is a riveting account of a watershed moment in our history, and the strategy, ingenuity, and humanity that made it happen." —President Bill Clinton

"Roberta Kaplan makes questions of constitutionality and the intricacies of legal strategy read like a John Grisham thriller. *Then Comes Marriage* explains how we arrived at this surprising moment in history, but it's also a testament to the persuasive, transformative power of a good story." —Alison Bechdel

THEN COMES MARRIAGE

How Two Women Fought for and Won
Equal Dignity for All

ROBERTA KAPLAN

with Lisa Dickey

Foreword by Edie Windsor

W. W. NORTON & COMPANY

Independent Publishers Since 1923

New York | London

Excerpt from "'It is marvellous to wake up together . . .'" from *Edgar Allan Poe &
The Juke-Box* by Elizabeth Bishop, edited and annotated by Alice Quinn.
Copyright © 2006 by Alice Helen Methfessel. Reprinted by permission
of Farrar, Straus and Giroux, LLC.

"The Prophets" from *W. H. Auden Collected Poems* by W. H. Auden, copyright ©
1976 by Edward Mendelson, William Meredith, and Monroe K. Spears, Executors
of the Estate of W. H. Auden. Used by permission of Random House, an imprint
and division of Penguin Random House LLC. All rights reserved. Any third-party
use of this material, outside of this publication, is prohibited. Interested parties
must apply directly to Penguin Random House LLC for permission.
Copyright © by W. H. Auden. Reprinted by permission of Curtis Brown Ltd.

For information about permission to reproduce selections from this book,
write to Permissions, W. W. Norton & Company, Inc.,
500 Fifth Avenue, New York, NY 10110

For information about special discounts for bulk purchases, please contact
W. W. Norton Special Sales at specialsales@wwnorton.com or 800-233-4830

Manufacturing by Quad Graphics, Fairfield
Book design by Chris Welch
Production manager: Anna Oler

The Library of Congress has cataloged the hardcover edition as follows:

Kaplan, Roberta A., author.
Then comes marriage : United States v. Windsor and the defeat of DOMA /
Roberta Kaplan with Lisa Dickey ; Foreword by Edie Windsor.
pages cm
Includes index.
ISBN 978-0-393-24867-8 (hardcover)
1. Windsor, Edie—Trials, litigation, etc. 2. United States. Defense of Marriage Act.
3. Marriage law—United States. 4. Same-sex marriage—Law and legislation—
United States. 5. Gay couples—Legal status, laws, etc.—United States. I. Title.
KF229.W56K37 2015
346.7301'68—dc23
2015023636

ISBN 978-0-393-35336-5 pbk.

W. W. Norton & Company, Inc.
500 Fifth Avenue, New York, N.Y. 10110
www.wwnorton.com

W. W. Norton & Company Ltd.
15 Carlisle Street, London W1D 3BS

1 2 3 4 5 6 7 8 9 0

For Rachel and Jacob—the family I never dreamed I would ever have and for whom I am grateful every single minute of every single day. Neither United States v. Windsor *nor this book would have happened without you.*

CONTENTS

Foreword 11

Chapter 1. GAY PRIDE 17

Chapter 2. PARENTS AND SECOND PARENTS 32

Chapter 3. THE BEGINNINGS OF A NEW PERSPECTIVE 48

Chapter 4. BE BRAVE—DO THE RIGHT THING 64

Chapter 5. A VERY LONG ENGAGEMENT 85

Chapter 6. THE REST WAS JUST DANCING 103

Chapter 7. IT'S ALL ABOUT EDIE, STUPID 117

Chapter 8. SOMETIMES, PRAYER WORKS 131

Chapter 9. SUPERIOR DANCE 148

Chapter 10. PROFESSOR DIAMOND AND CAPTAIN UNDERPANTS 166

Chapter 11. PERFECTLY PLEASED 183

Chapter 12. BE OUR GUEST 203

Chapter 13. TO DE-GAY OR NOT TO DE-GAY 223

Chapter 14. ALREADY MARRIED, ALREADY GAY 242

Chapter 15. SKIM MILK 261

Chapter 16. EQUAL DIGNITY 289

Epilogue 315
Acknowledgments 325
Index 331

The world might change to something quite different,

As the air changes or the lightning comes without our blinking,

Change as our kisses are changing without our thinking.

—*Elizabeth Bishop*, "It Is Marvellous to Wake Up Together"

FOREWORD

When I first met Robbie Kaplan in 2009, she asked me to go over to the computer in the living room of my apartment and watch a video clip of her arguing a case three years earlier seeking marriage equality in the state of New York. Then Robbie explained to me that she had lost the case. That impressed the hell out of me. It obviously takes enormous guts to show a potential client a video clip of you arguing a case that you had lost.

But Robbie was right, of course. I was so impressed with the way that she argued that case in 2006. And I was even more impressed that she had the courage and integrity to show me that clip. In fact, that was what convinced me on the spot that I wanted her to represent me in my legal challenge to the constitutionality of section three of the so-called "Defense" of Marriage Act a few months after the death of my spouse, Thea Spyer.

After that, everything having to do with the case of *Windsor v. United States* (which later became *United States v. Windsor*) was only a plus for me. I appeared at Paul, Weiss and was introduced to what turned out to be an incredibly multitalented, smart, and energetic group of lawyers. James Esseks of the ACLU and Pam Karlan of Stanford were welcome and indispensable additions to the Windsor team. I remember thinking to myself, *"Wow! There is someone on this team who can answer every single question that I have."* As time went on, I never encountered a situation—legal or

otherwise—without feeling completely supported and validated
by Robbie and the other members of her team. And we all really
liked and respected each other a lot. In retrospect, I cannot imagine that I could have endured that three and a half years, nor that
I could have succeeded with any other lawyers. We were a great
match. It was a long, joyous, and exhilarating ride.

The truth is, I love this book. It's a wonderful explanation of
what happened every step of the way, including every decision we
made, every roadblock we faced, and every joke we laughed at.
It also explains complicated legal arguments in a way that all of
us nonlawyers can understand and learn from. And even though
I obviously know what is going to happen in the end, it's a real
page-turner to boot.

It gives me such joy and gratitude to know that the case I
brought with Robbie has proven to be such a powerful precedent that dozens of courts (fifty-eight and counting) throughout
our nation have relied on it to grant equal rights to LGBT people under the law, including the right to marry. But even more
importantly, I hope that our case, our story, and this book will
help to serve as a strategic roadmap of how to litigate and win an
LGBT civil rights case going forward, a strategy that other advocates, activists, and clients will follow in the years ahead.

Because I was the youngest in my family, justice has always
mattered a lot to me. What this book shows is that what I learned
in my elementary school civics class was absolutely true—this is
a great country, we do have a Constitution that should be cher-
ished, and abstract phrases like "due process" and "equal protection" continue to have real meaning and power as interpreted by
the courts.

It is often said that as gay people, we get to choose our own
families. Those words could not be truer for me. Not a single day
goes by when I don't think about my parents or about Thea—the
love of my life—and while no one could ever replace them in

my heart, I have also fallen in love with Robbie's family, most especially her son, Jacob. As a result, I have spent a lot of "family time," including holiday meals and celebrations, with the whole Robbie crew. Robbie; her wife, Rachel; and Jacob will always be a part of my family.

Edie Windsor, Plaintiff
New York, New York
May 2015

THEN COMES MARRIAGE

I

GAY PRIDE

In the spring of 2009, I knew three things about Edith Windsor. First, she was a math geek, an apparent computer genius who had worked for many years as a software programmer at IBM. Second, she had been hit with a huge estate tax bill after her spouse, Thea Spyer, had died. And third, she was hard of hearing.

That third fact was the reason I walked four blocks from my West Village apartment to hers on the morning of April 30. Edie and I had never met, but we had spoken the day before about whether I would be willing to help her file a lawsuit to get those estate taxes back. She was having trouble hearing me over the phone, so I said, "Why don't I just come over and see you tomorrow? We can talk about it in person."

The next morning, I walked to her building, one of Manhattan's massive 1950s white-brick complexes just north of Washington Square Park. The doorman sent me up, and as I knocked, I was expecting to be greeted by a nerdy elderly lesbian in a flannel shirt and comfortable shoes. But when Edie opened the door, I stared at her, dumbfounded. She was a knockout—a slender, impeccably dressed woman with a blond bob, a string of pearls, and perfectly manicured nails. It took me a moment to compose myself, but after Edie's "Come in," I followed her into the apartment.

And then I was dumbfounded all over again. The apartment

looked exactly as I remembered it from the summer of 1991, the first time I had been there.

I was twenty-four then, just starting to come out as a lesbian, and for the first time in my life, I was seriously depressed and anxious. I had asked around for therapist recommendations, and one name kept popping up: Thea Spyer. I didn't know Thea from a hole in the wall, but she had a reputation as a talented and caring psychologist who understood "gay issues," so I called her to set up an appointment. I saw Thea for only two sessions, right in that very apartment, before moving to Boston later that summer.

Eighteen years had passed since then. But when I walked into Edie's living room, it was exactly the same as I remembered it from those two therapy sessions so long ago. And as I looked at the chair where Thea had sat while I, sitting across from her, had poured out my fears, my heart began to pound.

"I'm sorry," I told Edie. "I need a minute." I had known, of course, when I was walking over that this was the same apartment where I had met with Thea, but I did not expect to feel it so viscerally; walking into that room felt like returning to the scene of an accident, and I experienced emotions that I had not felt in years. I took a deep breath and told Edie, "I've actually been here before"—and then I told her why.

In the summer of 1991, I had just graduated from law school at Columbia University and was living in a tiny one-room studio apartment at 80th and Amsterdam while studying for the bar exam. My parents had flown in for a visit from my hometown of Cleveland on the last weekend in June—coincidentally, the weekend of New York's Gay Pride Parade (as it was then called). On that Sunday morning, as my parents made their way through Manhattan to my apartment, they found themselves having to navigate around the parade.

My mother happened to see then–Manhattan Borough President Ruth Messinger, the mother of one of my college roommates, riding in the parade in support of gay rights. By the time she and my father got to my apartment, she was in quite a state about the whole thing.

"I can't believe Ruth Messinger would actually join in a gay parade," she said.

"Okay, Mom," I said. "Enough." For about a thousand reasons, this was not a conversation I wanted to have with her.

My mother ignored me and kept going, criticizing the very idea of a "pride" parade: "It's just horrible seeing all these mobs of gay people marching openly in the streets."

"Mom, enough already," I told her. "I don't want to hear this."

But she continued, "Well, I'm just saying, I think it's horrible." And that was about all that I could take.

"Stop!" I snapped. "Just stop it! Enough already!" Now she turned to look at me, her eyes narrowing.

"*Why* do you want me to stop?" she asked. "What's the matter? Are you *gay* or something?"

I stared at her, shaking. I had started seeing my first girlfriend only a few months earlier, but I had known for much longer that I was a lesbian, so this was a moment I had been dreading for years. I was trembling, scared of how my parents might react, but now I was angry as well.

"Yes," I told her. "I'm gay."

My mother did not say a word. She simply walked to the edge of the room and started banging her head against the wall. *Bang. Bang. Bang.*

I watched for a moment in complete shock, and then somehow, in one of the saner moments of my life, I managed to turn and walk out of my own apartment. My mother's reaction was so over the top that there was no way to engage with her. So I left and went to a friend's place a few blocks away to try to calm down. I had known that my mom would not be happy about this news, but her reaction was even worse than I had expected. And it only served to confirm my fears about what my life would be like now that I had finally admitted out loud that I was gay.

For a newly out gay person in 1991, there was little reason to expect that a normal life was possible. This was pre-Ellen, pre–*Will & Grace*—a time when most gay characters in Hollywood movies tended to be sad, lonely, or dying, or all of the above. The AIDS epidemic was raging, the antigay Religious Right was gathering steam, and laws still on the books in many states made sexual relationships between gay people a criminal offense.

Ever since high school, I had suspected that I might be gay, but I couldn't really confront the issue until my third year of law school, in part because I was terrified of the very reaction that my mother had just had. The consequences seemed clear: Being gay meant losing the love and support of your family. It meant never being able to get married or to start a family of your own. It meant living a covert life on the fringes of society, a life where none of the promises of a happy, secure adulthood applied. I didn't feel empowerment or relief when I came out, I felt depression and despair. And my mother's reaction sent me into a downward spiral.

And then I went to see Thea Spyer.

When I walked into her apartment for our first session, just a few weeks after the incident with my mother, I was immediately struck by Thea's commanding presence. She had a Hepburn-esque high-cheekboned beauty and a regal bearing. She was also a quadriplegic. Thea had been diagnosed with a particularly virulent form of multiple sclerosis back in 1977, and by 1991 she was using a wheelchair and had only limited use of her hands. Yet even though her body was weak, she exuded strength, calm, and self-assurance, three qualities I had in very short supply at that time.

In that first session, I told Thea about my deepest fears: that I would never have a normal life, a successful relationship, close ties with my family, or a family of my own. For years, my mother and I had talked almost every day, but since the episode in my apartment, we had not spoken at all. I missed her terribly, but there did not seem to be any way to bridge the enormous rift my coming out had created between us. And even though I had finally allowed myself to become involved with a woman, I had no expectation that my current relationship would last. It seemed self-evident that by admitting I was gay, I had scuttled any chance of ever being at peace with myself. I had never felt so alone, and I saw no way to make it better.

And then Thea told me about her own long-term relationship with a brilliant mathematician named Edie. She and Edie had been together for twenty five years by then, living together as a committed couple through thick and thin, in sickness and in health. Their relationship had started in the 1960s, pre-Stonewall, at a time when it was even more difficult to be gay. But they had persevered and continued to love each other through the decades, building a stable and joyful life together. It is unusual for a psychologist to talk so much about herself or her spouse during a therapy session, but Thea's message to me was clear: it was possible to have a fulfilling relationship and a happy life, even if you happened to be a lesbian. She and Edie were the proof.

Thea's words gave me the comfort I desperately needed. I only saw her for one more session before moving to Boston, but I never forgot the sense of relief I felt after talking with her. At last I had heard from someone who knew and could prove that it was possible to create the kind of life I wanted, one that included a lifelong partner, strong family ties, and maybe even children of my own one day.

Eighteen years later, when I walked into Edie and Thea's apartment, I had created that life for myself. I had a fascinating job, a close relationship once again with my parents, a loving wife named Rachel, and our amazing son, Jacob—my life was full of fulfillment and purpose. I had everything that I had ever wanted, and Thea Spyer was the one who had first given me the strength to think it was possible.

So that morning in 2009, as Edie Windsor described her situation to me—her forty-four-year relationship with Thea, the marriage they had celebrated when they were in their seventies, and the federal government's refusal to acknowledge that relationship—all I could think was, *I will do this for Thea*. In Yiddish (which I had grown up with since my maternal grandmother, Belle, was fluent), the word *bashert* means, in its most basic sense, "it was meant to be." In other words, it was as if God had dropped this case in my lap as a way to pay Thea back for helping me so much through some of my darkest days.

GROWING UP IN Cleveland, Ohio, in the 1970s, I never thought that I would turn out to be gay. In fact, for a long time I did not even know what gay meant. But I did always know that I would become a lawyer.

For one thing, from the moment I started talking, I apparently never stopped. When I was very young, my mother wrote letters to her brother, Benjie, who was then serving in the Peace Corps in India. Her descriptions of me tended to focus, with love and pride, on my loquaciousness and assertiveness. From July 1969, when I was three, she *kvelled*: "Robbie can recite the alphabet as well as give a rousing rendition of 'Ducky Duddle.' . . . She plays with five-year-old kids and all I ever hear her say is, 'Now it's my turn.'"

August 1969: "Robbie, especially, enjoys being in the limelight. . . . She thinks she's a real big shot and her mouth supports her."

July 1970: "Robbie is a real doll. You have to converse with her to appreciate [it]. . . . If she lets you get a word in, that is."

Grandma Belle noticed this too: "Robbie is a doll and bright as a whip. I asked her to please stop talking for fifteen minutes, and she answered, 'I can't, Grandma. I'm a big talker.' And she surely is. On & on & on."

So I liked to talk. And I had heard that lawyers got to talk a lot as part of their jobs. With that in mind, at the mature age of twelve, I plotted out the rest of my life. We then lived in a suburb of Cleveland, but my mom had a subscription to *New York* magazine, and after flipping through the latest issue one day, I became a girl on a mission—I decided that I would move to New York City one day and become a lawyer.

Actually, I was pretty logical about it. First, I decided that I would have to go to an Ivy League college, and then I would move on to law school in New York. Twelve-year-old kids—especially those who talk as much as I did—come up with a lot of silly ideas. But what is more than a little frightening is that this is exactly what I ended up doing. (The fact that Sandra Day O'Connor was appointed by President Reagan to be the first woman Supreme Court justice three years later when I was in high school only strengthened my resolve.)

I am sure my parents did not expect me to follow through on my grand pronouncement, but they did encourage my brother, Peter, and me to think independently. My mother especially was very curious about the social issues of the day. Mom was involved in the women's movement of the 1970s and belonged to a consciousness-raising group. She also wanted to expose us to as much art, music, and culture as she could. One day in 1981, she exposed me to something I'm sure neither of us expected.

I was fourteen that spring, and Mom brought me along to a former synagogue in Cleveland Heights, where a group of women were installing the feminist artist Judy Chicago's famous piece *The Dinner Party*. The installation is huge—a triangular banquet table measuring forty-eight feet long on each side, with dozens of place settings and hundreds of engraved floor tiles all representing different women throughout history. Whenever it was exhibited in a new venue, Chicago enlisted numerous local feminist volunteers to help set it up. My mom is not exactly a do-it-yourself type, but she was eager for us to participate in what was a great artistic happening.

The only thing I remember from that day is all the butch women wearing tool belts (literally). Everywhere I looked, there were women carrying hammers, pulling wrenches out of leather pouches, whipping out tape measures. I had never seen anything like these women. I was definitely exposed to something new that day, and it made me self-conscious, uncomfortably so.

From that point on, I was aware that there was something different about me, something that needed to be hidden. By the time I was in high school, a lurking fear had taken root: *What if I turn out to be gay?* I could not bear that thought, so I just kept pushing it down as deep as it would go. Even though my parents never made negative comments about gay people, I knew that they would not be happy if I turned out to be a lesbian. So I tried to change and I tried to hide. I dated guys throughout high school. Ironically enough, my high school prom date, a guy named Aaron Belkin, would also turn out to be gay. Later, he became an activist for LGBT rights, one of the key players behind the 2010 repeal of the U.S. military's Don't Ask, Don't Tell policy. There must have been something in that prom punch. Or maybe it is not surprising that two of the few gay kids in a graduating class of ninety students would be drawn to each other. Unconsciously, perhaps, we sensed each other's secrets.

Despite my fear of exposure, or maybe because of it, I was even more driven to succeed academically, to be part of the exciting world I had dreamed of since I was young. And just as I had planned so carefully at the age of twelve, I set off for Harvard in the fall of 1984. Upon arriving in Cambridge from the hinterlands of Cleveland, however, I initially found myself intimidated by the hordes of East Coast private-school girls—one of whom, a young woman from New York City, asked me in all innocence whether Woody Allen films ever made it to Cleveland movie theaters. My new classmates all seemed able to read Kant in the original German, planned someday to be president or secretary of state, and seemed not to have an iota of self-doubt. Navigating my new social life was difficult enough, even without the additional layers of confusion and anxiety about the possibility that I was gay.

Every time that I had a crush on a girl, my fear about my mother's reaction to my lesbianism intensified, even though I still did not have the nerve to actually go out on a date with a woman. If only I could have worried less about what others, even my mother, thought of me and more about learning who I was. If I had expended half the energy on dating women that I did on fearing what my mother might say about it, I would have had a much better time in college. But I was paralyzed not only by my own shame but also by a realistic assessment of the consequences that could result when a gay person was honest about who she was.

There was one story going around campus that epitomized my fears. I knew a sophomore who had lived a seemingly charmed life, attending Manhattan's best private schools while growing up in a wealthy, sophisticated New York family. Yet during her freshman year at Harvard, when she told her mother she was a lesbian, her mother (with whom she had been very close) responded by disowning her, cutting her off both emotionally and financially. Several people told me this story, and each time it intensified the sick feeling that I had in my stomach whenever I thought about telling my own mother. I also heard of other students who had been forced into so-called reparative therapy by their parents to "cure" them of their homosexuality. Most of those people had not chosen to come out, had not shoved their "lifestyle choice" into other people's faces. They had hidden, like me, and still they had been found out. In other words, there were very real reasons to be afraid.

In fact, my anxiety during college became so acute that I was not sure I would ever tell anyone I was gay. I wondered whether it might be possible just to marry a nice man and make do. But in my heart of hearts, I knew such a false marriage would not only be terribly unfair to my theoretical husband but also doomed to failure.

I could not think my way into a solution, my first and favorite way of dealing with problems. And following my feelings to solve the issue was completely unacceptable. The trade-off of certain social jeopardy versus possible emotional fulfillment and love was simply not worth it for me. Instead, I chose my familiar habits of caution and repression. I just boxed up my feelings and hoped they would somehow disappear. They did not, of course. Instead, I fell in love with a classmate I'll call "Kate."

Kate and I met freshman year, and there was an instant connection between us. We spent hours together—talking, studying, arguing politics, and figuring out the world's woes. By the end of freshman year, we knew that we wanted to room together as sophomores. I was falling hard for Kate but could not admit it, even to myself. Instead, I would lie awake at night thinking, *If only Kate were a guy, everything would be so much easier.* That is as close to self-awareness as my mind could manage.

Throughout my sophomore year, my feelings for Kate deepened as we lived and studied together, becoming almost inseparable. In the spring of my junior year, having declared Russian history and literature as my major, I spent a semester studying in Moscow. Being in the Soviet Union at that time was an incredible experience. Perestroika was just beginning and I had a front-row seat to history in the making. I was lucky enough to become friends with extraordinary members of the Russian intelligentsia—dissidents, artists, and Jewish refuseniks. It was heady stuff for a young woman who had grown up in the Cleveland suburbs.

When I came back to the States, I could not wait to see Kate.

I was so excited to reconnect with her, but when we met again she broke my heart. That first evening as we sat on the roof of her building, Kate told me she was dating someone. And that someone was a woman.

I listened to Kate's news and felt my heart shatter. And the worst part was I could not even let myself, much less Kate, understand that my heart was breaking. Yet even if I did not understand what I was feeling, I nonetheless felt it: wave after wave of grief, rage, disappointment, and frustration. It is hard to explain to people who have never had to hide a key element of themselves how corrosive it is. It is not simply that you do not allow others—your family, your friends, your neighbors—to truly know you. It is also that you give up on knowing yourself. And you give up on that which makes you most human: your capacity to give and accept love. From that hurt and corroded place in my soul, I only knew that I had come back from the Soviet Union to find Kate and that she had rejected me. Or at least that is how it felt to me at the time—not that she had found love, but rather that I had lost it.

And, in that vein, I retaliated. The Cold War might have been thawing internationally but, on a personal level, I chose the nuclear option. On some level I must have believed that Kate and I had a tacit agreement. We would be each other's primary person but we would pretend otherwise, dating boys neither of us took seriously. Kate had unilaterally violated that agreement. She had chosen someone else—someone female who was not me.

Rather than acknowledge that truth, I attacked. All my years of anger and frustration became focused on one target: Kate. My feelings were not wrong, hers were. Sobbing and screaming, I told her that what she was doing was wrong, hurtful, and incredibly damaging. What I did not do was explain *why* I was so upset. I could not name or face the sickening jealousy that surged through me, because there was no reason for me to be jealous. So instead of honesty, I went for moral disapproval.

Kate, in turn, was enraged. Her response to my litany of criticisms was to conclude, not unfairly, that I was homophobic. We had been planning to room together again for our senior year, but she told me flatly that there was no way she could live with a person like me. Our friendship was over. Back on campus, we had to switch around our rooming arrangements—and that's how the rumor spread throughout Cambridge that Robbie Kaplan was a neoconservative, reactionary homophobe. What else could explain the explosive reaction I had had to the news that my old friend Kate had a girlfriend?

So my final semesters at Harvard were not the best period of my life. Kate and I did not reconcile until two decades later when I ran into her in New York and brought her home to meet my wife and son. I graduated in 1988 never having revealed my secret. I still did not know if I could live as a lesbian, and I felt less inclined than ever to try to find out. My life plan was still on track, however: just as I had envisioned, I enrolled in law school at Columbia University in New York City.

I had a better time at Columbia, making great friends whom I remain close to even today. Yet I still could not admit that I was gay—not even to my gay friends. I was so tightly wound, so self-hating, that nothing happened until almost the end of my third year of law school—and even then only with the aid of copious amounts of alcohol. At long last, while drunk with a friend one night, I finally let myself kiss a girl. I knew immediately that it felt right. I was twenty-four years old and still petrified of coming out publicly, but after a decade of struggling with my feelings, my longing finally outweighed my fear. Once that happened, I knew that there was no going back.

I RELATE ALL this now because, given the dramatic sea change in American attitudes toward LGBT people over the last few decades, it is easy to forget how difficult it was for gay people to come out in the 1980s and early 1990s. It is still very difficult for many people today, of course, especially those who live in more conservative parts of the country. But there is no doubt that times were different back then.

In 1991, the year my mother banged her head against the wall, the AIDS epidemic was raging through the gay community. NBA superstar Magic Johnson announced he was HIV-positive, and Freddie Mercury of the rock group Queen (who was hugely popular among my Russian friends during the time I spent in the Soviet Union) died of AIDS-related complications, having concealed that he had AIDS until the very end of his life. The antiretroviral drug treatment that would make AIDS survivable for many people was still several years away, making the disease essentially a death sentence, and as the number of cases worldwide hit ten million, much of the national discussion about gay people was tinged with ignorance and hysteria.

That same year, a poll conducted by the University of Chicago's National Opinion Research Center asked whether sexual relations between two adults of the same sex were always wrong, almost always wrong, wrong only sometimes, or not wrong at all. In 1973, the first time the poll was conducted, 73 percent of respondents answered that it was always wrong. By 1991, the year I received my JD from Columbia, that number had actually risen to 78 percent. In most of the United States, gay people had no rights or legal protections.

L.A. Law—a program my roommates and I watched obsessively in our first year of law school—showed the first lesbian kiss ever broadcast on network television, to a mixed response: the show's ratings soared, but numerous advertisers pulled their ads. Very few high-profile people came out publicly that year, though some, like then–Pentagon spokesman Pete Williams (now the Supreme Court reporter for NBC), were outed by gay journalist Michelangelo Signorile out of a sense of growing impatience with closeted people in powerful positions. One could argue (and many did) that outing fellow gay men and lesbians was not simply exposing hypocrisy, it was being complicit in bigotry. But some LGBT activists, watching their friends and lovers die by the thousands, felt that desperate times called for desperate measures. At that time, the U.S. military could and did dishonorably discharge soldiers simply for being gay. As Signorile has since written, "Pete Williams was not personally responsible . . . for ruining the lives of over ten thousand discharged queer servicepeople; he was a spokesperson for an organization that was."

On May 1, 1991, three same-sex couples in Hawaii attempted to change that. The couples—Ninia Baehr and Genora Dancel, Tammy Rodrigues and Antoinette Pregil, and Pat Lagon and Joseph Melillo—had applied for marriage licenses at the state's Department of Health the previous December. When the Department of Health turned them down, the couples decided to sue the state for the right to marry. Neither the American Civil Liberties Union nor Lambda Legal Defense and Education Fund would agree to represent the couples, despite the efforts of Evan Wolfson, then a staff attorney at Lambda Legal. The couples retained a local civil rights lawyer and litigated the case all the way to the Hawaii Supreme Court. The ripples from that case would eventually grow into a tidal wave, altering the course of gay rights in this country forever. Conservative fear over what was happening in Hawaii would lead not only to a backlash against President Bill Clinton's stated goal in 1993 of opening the military to gay men and lesbians but also to the passage of the Defense of Marriage Act in 1996.

At the same time that these determined couples were fighting for their legal rights, I was going back into the closet. In the late summer of 1991, I moved to Boston to clerk for United States District Court Judge Mark Wolf. When a young male attorney clerking for another judge asked me out, I said yes. He and I dated on and off, despite the fact that I was involved in a long-distance relationship with a woman in New York. I never told him the truth about my New York girlfriend, because I still could not admit to others what I could barely admit to myself. There is no doubt in my mind that the struggles in the LGBT rights movement of the 1990s, and the brave gay activists who fought those battles, laid the foundation for the battles and victories to follow, including marriage equality. While I wish now that I, too, could have been one of those courageous pioneers, I was definitely not ready.

When my clerkship ended, I went to work full-time at Paul, Weiss, Rifkind, Wharton & Garrison, the New York firm where I had been a summer associate during law school. At Paul, Weiss, I knew I would finally get to fulfill my dream of litigating high-profile, cutting-edge commercial cases. (Yes, that was actually my dream.) I settled into the usual routine of a first-year attorney in a big firm, working ninety hours a week, and I loved it. Pretty soon, my girlfriend and I moved in together—not that I told anyone at work, of course. I was content being a closeted New York corporate lawyer with a nineties haircut and an actual closet full of dark suits with padded shoulders.

And that is how things might have stayed if it were not for a particular New York judge, who had something different in mind for me.

2

PARENTS AND SECOND PARENTS

It was about a year and a half into my time at Paul, Weiss that I met Judith Kaye. She had recently been named chief judge of the New York Court of Appeals, the state's equivalent of the U.S. Supreme Court, but instead of resting on the laurels of her new position, she immediately assigned herself the task of reforming New York's broken jury system. At that time, almost anyone with or without a brain could get out of jury service in New York merely by citing any one of nearly two dozen automatic exemptions, such as declaring that they were an embalmer or a Christian Science practitioner. Judge Kaye sought to fix that problem, among many others in the court system, so that New Yorkers could truly be tried by a jury of their peers.

Judge Kaye tapped Paul, Weiss partner Colleen McMahon to lead the Jury Project, and Colleen invited me to work with her on it as a junior associate. Colleen had become the first woman litigation partner at Paul, Weiss in 1984, and she and I had bonded almost immediately from the minute I came to the firm. One afternoon in 1993, we walked into Judge Kaye's chambers for our first meeting. Apparently Judge Kaye liked me, because at the end of the meeting, she pulled Colleen aside and told her that she wanted me to come clerk for her. Colleen did not tell me this until months later when the Jury Project's work was completed. By then, I had already finished one clerkship with Judge Wolf in Boston, so I was not exactly eager for another. On top of that, several partners at Paul, Weiss advised me against taking the clerkship, saying it was time for me to get down to the business of litigating cases. But not only was Judith Kaye the highest-ranking judge in New York State and the first woman to achieve that position, I also really liked her. So when she asked me to begin clerking for her after the Jury Project's report came out, I enthusiastically said yes.

Most of the cases I worked on in the year and a half I spent clerking for Judge Kaye were interesting though uneventful. But near the end of my clerkship, the court got a case that would change the lives of gay couples and their families in New York—including, ultimately, my own.

The case was about adoption. Under New York law at that time, any person married to a biological parent could easily adopt his or her spouse's child. If you weren't married, however, you could adopt your partner's child only if your partner's own parental rights were terminated. So for unmarried couples, either straight or gay, there was no way to create a two-parent family through adoption short of marriage. And because marriage equality was a distant dream in 1994, this essentially meant that gay and lesbian partners could never legally become coparents to their children.

Two cases challenging this policy had made their way through the New York courts: *Matter of Jacob* had been brought by a straight couple, and *Matter of Dana* by a lesbian couple. I was dismayed when the court decided to hear the two cases together because the stakes were clearly so different. It was one thing to tell straight couples that they must marry before adopting each other's kids, since at least they had that option. But it was quite another thing to have the same requirement for gay or lesbian couples since it was impossible for them to get married. Unlike the straight couple, if the lesbian couple were to lose the case, their family would be at risk, with no legal protections, and there would be absolutely nothing they could do about it.

For the first time, I found myself taking part in a case that could affect me as a lesbian. I did not have kids and did not know if I ever would, but I desperately wanted the seven-member court to rule in favor of the couples. I knew Judge Kaye would vote for the single parent's ability to adopt, but I was not sure whether she knew just how personal my interest in this decision was. I was still so deeply closeted that I had told only a few people I worked with that I had a girlfriend, and Judge Kaye was definitely not one of them.

Even so, in the time I had been clerking for the judge, she and I had grown very close. We often drove to and from Albany together, talking the whole way while taking occasional detours to the Woodbury Common discount shopping center, where she would inevitably urge me to buy more colorful clothes. We worked well together and had similar opinions on most legal issues, including those having to do with the rights of gay people.

In fact, four years earlier—the same year that my mother banged her head against the wall—Judge Kaye had bravely cast the sole dissenting vote in favor of a lesbian parent in a case before the New York State Court of Appeals. In *Matter of Alison D.*, a lesbian sued for visitation after she and her partner, the biological mother of their son, split up. Six judges voted to deny Alison D. visitation rights, while Judge Kaye, in her dissent, noted that "as many as eight to ten million children are born into families with a gay or lesbian parent" and observed that the decision "falls hardest on the children of those relationships, limiting their opportunity to maintain bonds that may be crucial to their development." She did not see gay and lesbian parents as being any different from straight parents, which was a pretty radical view in 1991.

Working with Judge Kaye was a wonderful experience professionally, but it was also meaningful to me personally. She was about my mother's age and she really understood and valued what drove me. She also had a daughter about my age who already had children. One afternoon, I joked to her, "You know, I think my mother wishes I were more like your daughter." The judge just laughed and said, "Oh, Robbie, your mother could never say such a thing about you."

Even though Judge Kaye once tried to fix me up with a guy she knew in the mayor's office, I still had this odd suspicion that she knew I was gay. Which just goes to show, as a closeted lesbian, how incredibly sensitive I was to this whole issue at that time. As I later learned, Judge Kaye had no idea I was gay, and even if she had, I sincerely doubt she would have cared. But that is the problem with having a secret—you are always afraid it will be exposed. Colleen McMahon, who had become a close friend, told me, "You're not giving Judith enough credit." Looking back, I can see that, as usual, Colleen was right.

At the time, though, Judge Kaye was both a maternal figure to me and a professional role model. I could not bear the idea that I might once again experience the same rejection I had gone through with my own mother. It might have crushed me.

ORAL ARGUMENTS IN the *Jacob* and *Dana* case took place on June 5, 1995. The next day the seven judges voted and the split was 4–3, with Judge Kaye on the losing side.

Typically, after a vote is taken, the court hands down its opinion within a few weeks—certainly by the end of the session. As Judge Kaye's clerk, my task was to help her write her dissent, but I refused to accept that the decision was going against the couples—and their children. I knew it was wrong, as a matter of both constitutional and family law, where the standard is the best interest of the child. So I asked the judge if she could arrange to have the case held over the summer to the following session, which is almost never done. Judge Kaye asked me why, since it seemed highly unlikely that we could convince one of the other four judges to switch sides. "It's not about getting the fourth vote," I told her. "We just need time to write a better dissent."

In fact, I did hope that Judge Kaye might be able to persuade one of the other judges to change his vote. But in order to do that, we needed more time, thanks to a judicial scandal that was playing out that summer. A prisoner released by a trial court judge on bail had committed a horrific crime, and the New York tabloids were gleefully pillorying the state's judges and Judge Kaye in particular for being too soft on criminals. As the chief judge, the top judicial official in New York, Judge Kaye spent a lot of time responding to the media attacks, and I was the one she tapped for the time-consuming task of helping her draft her speeches.

So Judge Kaye agreed to the unusual step of holding the case over to the next session. And then I went to work.

One particular judge, Howard Levine, had started his career as a Family Court judge in upstate New York, and he seemed more likely than the others to switch his vote. I really believed that he wanted to vote our way, but he just hadn't found the right way to do it. I started lobbying his clerk, a friend of mine named Alicia Ouellette, hammering on a somewhat obscure point about the interpretation of statutes that potentially raise constitutional concerns. It was a technical argument, but it did not matter how we got the vote. We had to get it.

I became obsessed with winning Judge Levine's vote, talking with Alicia as often as possible while opinions were being drafted and circulated among the judges. Everyone in the office knew how badly I wanted this decision, but no one knew why except for the only other lesbian who worked at the Court of Appeals, a woman who was as closeted as I was. She saw what I was doing, and one afternoon she told me she did not think it was appropriate that I was pushing so hard to win the vote. The statute was the statute, and I had no business overstepping just because I happened to be gay myself.

We got into a very heated argument, which, as I recall, ended in my inviting her to commit an anatomically impossible act. It was definitely not my politest moment, but I really believed that she was wrong. She was, in my opinion, coming at the argument from a place of internalized self-loathing as a lesbian that blinded her to looking at the issue on the objective merits of my argument: that gays and lesbians were equally good parents and that their children needed and were entitled to the same legal protections as all other children. And that self-righteous claim to impartiality pushed all my buttons—in part because I was still struggling with self-loathing myself. But despite my lingering shame about being gay, I knew that fighting for this vote was the right thing to do, no matter what.

In August, more than two months after the initial 4–3 vote, I received a call from Alicia Ouellette. "We're on board," she told me. "Congratulations. Chief Judge Kaye is now writing the majority opinion."

I started whooping and screaming right there in my office, a wild banshee in low-heeled black pumps. Judge Kaye was having a meeting with some other appellate judges in the conference room next door, and someone asked, "What's going on?"

"Oh, don't mind that," Judge Kaye apparently replied. "That's just my law clerk, Robbie." Judge Kaye had no idea what I was carrying on about, but it was obviously good, and she knew that I would tell her soon enough. When I did, she was thrilled and I knew that my deep respect for her was well founded. For the first time ever in New York State, gay and lesbian partners would be free to adopt each other's children, giving their families desperately needed legal protections.

The way that the majority opinion written by Judge Kaye framed the inquiry produced the answer to the question in the case:

> Under the New York adoption statute, a single person can adopt a child. . . . Equally clear is the right of a single homosexual to adopt. . . . These appeals call upon us to decide if the unmarried partner of a child's biological mother, whether heterosexual or homosexual, who is raising the child together with the biological parent, can become the child's second parent by means of adoption.

Ultimately, Judge Kaye's opinion for the court held that individuals who were participating in raising their partner's child should be permitted to become a second parent:

> To rule otherwise would mean that the thousands of New York children actually being raised in homes headed by two unmarried persons could have only one legal parent, not the two who want them.

Judge Kaye's opinion actually says very little about the rights of gay people; rather, it focuses almost exclusively on the rights of the children. The truth is, in 1995, we would never have found the votes for this case by arguing for the rights of gay people. At that point, most people did not believe that gay people deserved the same rights as straight people. Judith Kaye and her colleagues needed to make a different argument, essentially saying that these kids were being born whether society liked it or not, and that it was obviously in their best interest to have two parents, rather than one. As Judge Kaye put it, to deny children:

> the opportunity of having their two de facto parents become their legal parents, based solely on their biological mother's

sexual orientation or marital status, would not only be unjust under the circumstances, but also might raise constitutional concerns in light of the adoption statute's historically consistent purpose—the best interests of the child.

If Judge Kaye had not made her bold decision to carry the case over to the next session, the decision in *Jacob* and *Dana* would have gone the other way, with disastrous consequences for gay families throughout New York State. On a purely personal note, I would not have been able to adopt my own son, Jacob, in 2006. And without the ability to marry, we would have had no standing to defeat the Defense of Marriage Act, the odious law passed the very next year by a panicky Congress and signed into law by President Bill Clinton.

IN THE SUMMER of 1996, marriage equality was not a reality anywhere in the United States, but the state of Hawaii was coming way too close for many conservatives' comfort. The Hawaii marriage case, filed by those three pioneering couples, had made its way up to that state's Supreme Court, which in 1993 declared for the first time that denying gays the right to marry was a discriminatory act. The Hawaii court then sent the case back down to a trial court to determine whether such discrimination was justifiable under the state constitution.

This sent the right wing into a frenzy. Not only was Hawaii flirting with marriage equality, but President Clinton—the first Democratic president in twelve years—had declared his intention to end the ban on gay men and lesbians serving openly in the military. Conservatives fought back, forcing Clinton into a box with the Don't Ask, Don't Tell policy, which had been instituted in February 1994. And in midterm elections that same year, the Republican Revolution swept into Washington, with the GOP winning control of both the House and the Senate, Newt Gingrich claiming the gavel of Speaker of the House, and the Christian Right reaching new heights of power.

The culture wars were on. In 1995, President Clinton signed an executive order declaring that gay men and lesbians could not be denied security clearances due to sexual orientation, and Hawaii's Commission on Sexual Orientation and the Law became the first state body to recommend that gay men and lesbians be given the right to marry. That same year, a gay man named Scott Amedure was murdered after he revealed his crush on a straight man on *The Jenny Jones Show,* and Ralph Reed, the head of the Christian Coalition, appeared on the cover of *Time* magazine alongside a headline dubbing him "The Right Hand of God."

Amid all this crossfire, the Hawaii case marched on. Fearful that Hawaii might actually legalize marriage equality, Georgia Representative Bob Barr introduced the Defense of Marriage Act in the House in May 1996. The purpose of DOMA was to define marriage as being between a man and a woman, thereby denying federal rights to any gay married couples, regardless of what certain states might choose to do. And the House Judiciary Committee's report made the reasoning behind DOMA clear: "to reflect and honor a collective moral judgment and to express moral disapproval of homosexuality"—a phrase that would later be used as a powerful tool to defeat DOMA.

President Clinton signed the law in the dead of night, at 12:50 a.m. on September 21, 1996, with no fanfare or cameras present, no ceremonial handing out of pens. LGBT activists bitterly protested the law, but I was not in the United States to watch those protests play out. Instead, I was in Tokyo working on a corporate case for Paul, Weiss, having returned to the firm after finishing my clerkship with Judge Kaye.

Martin London, a powerful Paul, Weiss litigation partner, had invited me to work on the Tokyo case, which involved a Japanese executive who had lost more than a billion dollars through rogue trading in copper. As Marty recalls, he was basically commuting to and from Tokyo at that time, and he decided that the project needed more than one-week "drop-ins" from him. It needed a full-time head of the PW-Sumitomo office. So Marty called me up at my parents' house in Cleveland, where I was visiting my family, and asked if I could come back to the "mother ship" and work on this case. I called Judge Kaye for advice and she immediately said, "Robbie, if Marty London wants you, you go!" I ended up working interminable hours, corralling huge teams of lawyers and paralegals reading through literally rooms of documents, enduring long dinners of countless glasses of sake and still-wiggling pieces of raw fish, while dealing with the stark cultural differences between Japan and the United States in terms of the role of women, all the while jetting back and forth every six to eight weeks between New York and Tokyo. Marty himself later commented that I hadn't just "smashed a glass ceiling"; I had "smashed a concrete cultural ceiling that had existed for thousands of years." He said, "I never had a doubt, or I would not have asked Robbie to come." And it all paid off in 1998 when I became a partner at Paul, Weiss at age thirty-one. Whatever was happening in the LGBT civil rights movement, my priorities were elsewhere.

Then I met Rachel Lavine. And that changed everything.

RACHEL AND I met when my old friend Amy Rutkin organized a group of friends to go to Rosh Hashanah services at Congregation Beit Simchat Torah, New York's gay and lesbian synagogue, in September 1999. I had recently broken up with my long-term girlfriend, and Amy had a sense that Rachel and I would like each other, so she tried to get us both to go to services with her.

I did not sit next to Rachel at the service, but walking out afterward, we bonded over the fact that we both thought the sermon (which had focused on Judy Garland) did not have the depth we expected for one of the most important Jewish holidays. Or as Rachel said, to the bemusement of the rest of the group, "Just because I'm gay doesn't mean that I can't think about nongay things." I was intrigued by Rachel's intelligence and candor, and by the time we arrived at the dinner Amy had arranged, I was angling to sit next to her. Rachel and I talked a lot that night, and I was impressed by how smart and funny she was, not to mention beautiful and warm. I wanted to see her again, but apparently Rachel had come away from our evening with a different thought: she wanted to set me up with a friend of hers. Amy would have none of it. When Rachel called her to suggest the idea, Amy said, "You know, I think Robbie would rather go out with you." So that is how it started, with Amy the crazy genius yenta matchmaker plotting to get us together.

On one of our early dates, Rachel, who was extremely active in local politics, took me to a political fund-raiser, which is when I began to understand just how deeply involved she was. She was on a first-name basis with all the elected officials there, people I had only read about in the newspapers. It soon became clear that Rachel had been walking the walk for a very long time, devoting herself to the causes that she cared about.

And Rachel cared passionately not just about social change but also about the history of social change—one of my fascinations as well. Unsurprisingly, we often had different interpretations of key moments of history. For example, later that year we went out for dinner at a small, charming bistro in Chelsea and spent a romantic evening heatedly arguing about the relative political power of the Mensheviks versus the Bolsheviks during the Russian Revolution and whether peaceful revolution was ever possible.

At one point Rachel (who had studied Russian history in graduate school) told me that had we both been alive in Russia at the time, I surely would have been a Bolshevik since I always like "to be on the winning side." Horribly offended, I told Rachel that was the most insulting thing anyone had ever said to me. As the other people in the restaurant looked on as if we were completely nuts (which, perhaps, we were), I told Rachel that she was completely wrong: I too would have been killed because I would have remained loyal to her and would have been dragged along when she and all the other overly idealistic Mensheviks were murdered in the Bolshevik-led purges that followed. And yes, in case you are curious, Rachel and I still have debates like this to the present day.

When I was ten, I was busy planning my legal career. By contrast, when Rachel was ten, she had long been involved in her father's campaigns to get reelected to the Connecticut state legislature. After getting into an argument with her parents one summer morning about rules and chores, Rachel staged her first political protest: she drew three big posters saying "Children Are People Too" and recruited her little brother and sister to march around the living room, protesting with her. In the 1980s, when I was a freaked-out, closeted college student, Rachel was protesting the shutdown of the lesbian co-op at Smith College and getting quoted as the movement's leader in the *New York Post*.

Rachel has always been, in her own words, someone who believes that the world should—and could—be a fairer place. From her participation in New York's Gay & Lesbian Independent Democrats to her work helping some of the first openly gay New York candidates like Deborah Glick, Tom Duane, and Christine Quinn get elected to public office, she has always been at the forefront of LGBT political activism. By the time we met, in 1999, I was out of the closet at Paul, Weiss, but only in that tiptoeing, nothing-to-see-here, don't-ask-don't-tell kind of way. I had brought my former girlfriend to a firm dinner, but otherwise did not really talk about her or our relationship. Being involved in a relationship with Rachel, I soon realized, would require stepping further outside the closet. In fact, it would mean burning down the closet door altogether.

I was drawn to Rachel's fearless, outspoken nature, but it also made me anxious—especially when it brushed up against my own lingering internalized homophobia. The first time Rachel met my parents was a classic example.

For months after the head-banging incident, my mother and I did not speak at all. Gradually, with the help of my father and Grandma Belle, we were able to bridge that gap, and eventually we resumed our old habit of talking almost daily. My parents had made a lot of progress since that time in tolerating the idea that I was a lesbian, though we still had our rough spots.

I first introduced my parents to Rachel over dinner at a steak-house in Grand Central Station. Right from the start we had a culture clash, with Rachel's directness and strong sense of fairness bumping up against my parents' Midwestern sense of reticence and stoicism. During the course of dinner, my mother asked me about an old law school friend, a woman who had had a discon-certing response to my breakup with my girlfriend of seven years. I had been pouring my heart out about the split to this friend, and she had responded by completely ignoring what I was say-ing, oddly changing the subject to the topic of a lace tablecloth her mother had recently given her. And this was a close friend, a well-educated woman who had gay friends besides me and who had known my ex-girlfriend. She was either unable or unwill-ing to discuss the end of my relationship, much less give me any comfort, since she clearly thought the subject was either trivial or something best kept quiet about, and that had hurt me still further.

After I finished telling this story, my mother said that she did not see what my friend had done wrong and that I should not be so touchy.

"What do you mean?" Rachel responded. "Robbie and her girlfriend were together seven years. This was like a divorce. It's really homophobic that her friend did not acknowledge that."

My parents were shocked. This was not the way they communicated with me or with anybody in their social circle, much less with someone they had just met. But that is Rachel's way. She believes in being a truth-teller. At that moment, I was simultaneously freaked out and a little bit thrilled. Rachel was sticking up for me. No one had done that for me in that way before. But Rachel was and would always be on my side, and if she saw me being the victim of any kind of unfair or unkind treatment, including homophobia, she was going to speak up even if I was afraid to. Or perhaps *especially* when I was afraid to. (I should also add that my parents eventually came not only to accept Rachel's approach but to embrace it. When the woman in question encountered my mother years later while putting together her wedding registry, she pretended that she had invited me and that the invitation had been returned with a bad address! Since the wedding had yet to occur, my mother whipped out a piece of paper and wrote down my home address—with Rachel's full name on it. "Try again," my mom advised. Needless to say, we never received that invitation.)

It was not always easy for me to get used to Rachel's fearlessness and her willingness to challenge what she saw as wrong, no matter what. She, in turn, had a hard time with what she saw as my more diplomatic—or perhaps conciliatory—need to defer to social convention, so we had our share of heated conversations in those early years. And when we clashed, Rachel wanted to discuss it, to talk about our feelings and where they came from and why. Since feelings were messy, sometimes painful, and often not subject to rational control, I did not always want to go there. There were days when I wanted to let things go. But with every discussion and argument we had, I was learning not to repress myself so much. And over the years as I have changed, those around me have changed and grown as well, including Rachel, who is now more patient with people who may have different views.

Even so, there was no escaping the complicated feelings we both had about taking our relationship to the next level: becoming domestic partners.

Marriage still was not available to gay Americans in 2002. Rachel and I had decided to become domestic partners, in large part for health insurance reasons, so it was a practical as much as a romantic endeavor. Unexpectedly, I found myself beset by a complicated array of feelings about the whole thing as we drove down to the New York City Clerk's Office to complete the paperwork. We had to stop at a bank to get some forms notarized, and I was overcome by a mixture of anxiety and frustration.

As lesbians growing up in the 1970s and 1980s, Rachel and I had no out and open role models to follow in creating a committed relationship or to support us as a couple. Of course, we knew older lesbian and gay couples, but often those relationships were an open secret at best. And their relationships were never seen as equivalent to those of straight married couples— significant, perhaps, but not equal. One of the great benefits of marriage is that it gives couples the opportunity to experience their community rallying around them, to feel the support of loved ones who pledge to celebrate the joyous moments but also to be there for them during the dark times as well. Gay people were never allowed to have that community support, and I think it wounded many of us in many ways. Because we had always been excluded from marriage, many of us had never fully understood what is at the core of the marriage experience—that it is not simply a relationship between two people, but also a relationship between a couple and their larger community. I think I felt in my bones the limits of what domestic partnership would grant to us in those moments before we registered. It bothered me that we were denied a right that any random straight couple had. The fact that two drunk heterosexual strangers could get hitched in ten minutes in Vegas, while committed gay couples were denied that right in every state, created a lot of deep-seated resentment and sadness for many gay people, even if we did not always consciously realize it.

So when we had to make an extra stop to get the papers notarized, all my irritation came to the forefront. "What is the *point* of this?" I asked Rachel. "I mean, it's not like we're getting *married*."

Rachel turned around to look at me, her eyes blazing. "Well, just forget about it, then!" she said. She, too, had conflicted feelings but felt hurt that I was being dismissive of what was in fact an important step for our relationship. So it was no surprise that my casually glib dismissal set her off.

"No, no," I said. "We're already here, let's just get it done." This was hardly a romantic or soothing gesture on my part, and Rachel, understandably, remained hurt. We both were seething by then, but we got the paperwork notarized.

We became domestic partners that day, although we were barely speaking to each other by the end of the process. As we left the City Clerk's Office, we saw that there was some sort of political protest taking place on the nearby steps of City Hall. Rachel, of course, knew the people who were protesting, and when we told them why we were there, they erupted in shouts of "Mazel tov!" and "Congratulations!" Our straight progressive friends were ecstatic for us. All I could think was, there was not much to celebrate. Who knew when there ever would be?

As it turned out, the answer would come the very next year, thanks to a tireless advocate named Mary Bonauto.

3

THE BEGINNINGS
OF A NEW PERSPECTIVE

You may not know this, but if you are a married gay person in the United States of America today, Mary Bonauto actually helped walk you down the aisle. For the last quarter of a century, this no-nonsense, publicity-shunning, get-the-job-done attorney has been fighting the fight for all of us. Former Massachusetts Representative Barney Frank once called Mary the "Thurgood Marshall of our movement," and I agree. I would say that she's all that plus our own Wonder Woman, except that as a sensible New Englander, she would never countenance wearing bright red and blue spandex.

Mary began working with Gay & Lesbian Advocates & Defenders (GLAD) in 1990, back when the notion of marriage equality was derided not only by conservatives but by those within the LGBT rights movement as well. In the mid 1980s, Evan Wolfson was one of the first to start advocating for marriage equality, but most other LGBT activists dismissed the idea. In August 1989, when Andrew Sullivan published a groundbreaking *New Republic* cover story, entitled "Here Comes the Groom," advocating for marriage equality, the response was even harsher: many gay activists and organizations lashed out, arguing that he was pursuing a path that was not only wrong but had the potential to set the movement back.

Sullivan had anticipated the backlash to his article, writing that "Much of the gay leadership clings to notions of gay life as essentially outsider, anti-bourgeois, radical. Marriage, for them, is co-optation into straight society"—a co-opting that many felt would eviscerate, rather than empower, the gay community. As the filmmaker John Waters famously put it, "I always thought the privilege of being gay is that we don't have to get married or go into the Army."

I remember reading Sullivan's article as a deeply closeted freshman at Harvard, where Sullivan had been a graduate student. He begins by referencing a significant gay rights case that had just been decided by the New York Court of Appeals, *Braschi v. Stahl Associates*. *Braschi* involved what was then a very pressing issue in the LGBT community—whether the lover of a man who had died of AIDS could remain in their rent-controlled New York City apartment. The court held that he could, observing that a family for these purposes could include "two adult lifetime partners whose relationship is long and is characterized by an emotional and financial commitment and interdependence." *Braschi* was written by Judge Vito Titone, who was still on the Court of Appeals when I clerked for Chief Judge Kaye years later. One of my favorite parts of the clerkship was sitting in Judge Titone's Albany chambers late in the evening listening to him tell stories about New York politics. Sullivan predicted in his article that "legal gay marriage could also help to bridge the gulf between gays and their parents"—something that certainly proved to be true with respect to my own family. In fact, Judge Titone's own son Matthew went on to become the first openly gay elected official from Staten Island.

During Mary Bonauto's early years at GLAD, gay people faced so much legalized discrimination that it seemed entirely beside the point to pursue marriage, which clearly was not going to happen anytime soon. We could be fired from jobs, denied custody of our own children, lose our housing, and be thrown in jail for having sex, *simply because we were gay.* The list of horribles went on and on. Why chase after the pipe dream of marriage when we had so many other urgent problems to solve? For all these reasons, Mary initially declined to take on any marriage equality cases.

Mary also understood, however, that once gay people were allowed to marry, we would achieve a different stature in society's eyes—and that alone would go a long way toward solving the other problems we faced. Marriage, after all, is the mechanism by which our legal system recognizes our relationships with the people we love. As a result, marriage is not only legally and practically important but symbolically important as well. If gay people were to achieve equality in marriage, it would mean that they would be considered equal in other facets of life. So a few years into her tenure at GLAD, as American attitudes began changing in the mid 1990s, Mary decided it was finally time to take the plunge. She developed a brilliant, careful, concerted state-by-state strategy for bringing marriage cases to the courts, and then she started filing complaints. "I said no to many people over the years," she would later tell the *New York Times.* "And then I finally said yes."

The first case that Mary brought for marriage equality was in Vermont in 1997. That case, *Baker v. Vermont,* made it all the way to the Vermont Supreme Court, which managed to simultaneously delight and dismay gay advocates with its ruling. The good news was that the court said gay people should have the right to have their relationships recognized under the law. The bad news was that it dodged the important step of deciding how to implement its own decision, instead tossing the issue of the appropriate remedy back to the Vermont legislature. Vermont lawmakers responded by creating civil unions, essentially giving gay Vermonters separate but equal status. Since we had never been seen as equal before, this was a huge step forward.

But it definitely wasn't good enough. So in 2001, Mary filed her next suit, on behalf of seven gay couples in Massachusetts. That case, *Goodridge v. Department of Public Health*, wound its way through the court system up to the highest court in Massachusetts, the Supreme Judicial Court. In March 2003, Mary argued the case for the plaintiff couples, insisting to the justices that "civil unions" were not sufficient:

> [W]hen it comes to marriage, there really is no such thing as separating the word "marriage" from the protections it provides. The reason for that is that one of the most important protections of marriage is the word, because the word is what conveys the status that everyone understands as the ultimate expression of love and commitment.

The Supreme Judicial Court was not expected to hand down its decision until the fall of 2003, but in the interim two things happened that gave hope to marriage equality supporters. In early June, the Canadian province of Ontario legalized marriage equality. And on June 26, in its landmark *Lawrence v. Texas* decision, the U.S. Supreme Court struck down a Texas law criminalizing sexual relationships. As Justice Anthony Kennedy put it, "When sexuality finds overt expression in intimate conduct with another person, the conduct can be but one element in a personal bond that is more enduring. The liberty protected by the Constitution allows homosexual persons the right to make this choice." This decision reversed one handed down just seventeen years earlier, in 1986, when the Court had upheld an analogous Georgia anti-sodomy law in *Bowers v. Hardwick*.

Winning *Lawrence* was huge, since it meant gay Americans no longer had to fear being arrested merely for their private intimate behavior. But even better was the fact that, although he was careful to say the case was not about gay marriage, Justice Kennedy seemed to suggest, however obliquely, that marriage equality might one day become a reality. He wrote that antisodomy laws "seek to control a personal relationship that, *whether or not entitled to formal recognition in the law*, is within the liberty of persons to choose without being punished as criminals." Suddenly, the Supreme Court was at least recognizing the possibility that gay relationships might one day be entitled to formal recognition.

Justice Kennedy's wording was enough to send Justice Antonin Scalia into a full-scale counterattack. In his dissent in *Lawrence*, Justice Scalia used highly politicized language to comment:

> Today's opinion is the product of a Court, which is the product of a law-profession culture, that has largely signed on to the so-called homosexual agenda, by which I mean the agenda promoted by some homosexual activists. . . .
>
> Many Americans do not want persons who openly engage in homosexual conduct as partners in their business, as scoutmasters for their children, as teachers in their children's schools, or as boarders in their home. They view this as protecting themselves and their families from a lifestyle that they believe to be immoral and destructive.

Justice Scalia then went on to draw a direct parallel between the Court's reasoning in *Lawrence* and marriage equality:

> Today's opinion dismantles the structure of constitutional law that has permitted a distinction to be made between heterosexual and homosexual unions, insofar as formal recognition in marriage is concerned. If moral disapproval of homosexual conduct is "no legitimate state interest" for purposes of proscribing that conduct, . . . what justification could there possibly be for denying the benefits of marriage to homosexual couples exercising "[t]he liberty protected by the Constitution," . . . ? Surely not the encouragement of

procreation, since the sterile and the elderly are allowed to marry. This case "does not involve" the issue of homosexual marriage only if one entertains the belief that principle and logic have nothing to do with the decisions of this Court.

In 2003, Justice Scalia believed that Justice Kennedy had thrown open the door for marriage equality. As it turned out, his prediction was 100 percent accurate.

BACK IN 1992, while I was clerking in Boston, Judge Wolf thought I should meet a good friend of his, a woman named Margaret Marshall, and kindly arranged a meeting. Margie, as she's called, was a white South African who, while in college in the 1960s, had led a powerful antiapartheid movement called the National Union of South African Students. She had bravely used her position to amplify the voices of antiapartheid South Africans at a time when doing so was considered a radical and dangerous act. As a result, after coming to the United States for graduate studies, she decided not to return to South Africa, fearful that her political activism might lead to persecution at home.

Marshall had attended Yale Law School, then spent some time in private practice, eventually at the Boston firm of Choate Hall & Stewart, the position she held when we had lunch. As she was advising me about my career, I was impressed and inspired not only by her activism but by how she managed to combine that commitment with her private practice. A few years later, Margie Marshall was appointed an associate justice of the Massachusetts Supreme Judicial Court, only the second woman ever appointed to that position. Then, in 1999, she became the first woman to be appointed chief justice. And that is where she was serving when Mary Bonauto brought the *Goodridge* case.

In November 2003, the court voted 4–3 in favor of the *Goodridge* plaintiffs, making Massachusetts the first state to legalize marriage equality. Chief Justice Marshall wrote the majority opinion, and when I read it, tears came to my eyes. Even though I knew that she had stood up for the rights of minorities throughout her life, I was still amazed at the courage Chief Justice Marshall showed in that opinion. She took on every trope of the antigay right, dismantling their arguments with each stroke of her pen:

> [T]he plaintiffs seek only to be married, not to undermine the institution of civil marriage. They do not want marriage abolished. They do not attack the binary nature of marriage, the consanguinity provisions, or any of the other gate-keeping provisions of the marriage licensing law. Recognizing the right of an individual to marry a person of the same sex will not diminish the validity or dignity of opposite-sex marriage, any more than recognizing the right of an individual to marry a person of a different race devalues the marriage of a person who marries someone of her own race.

Chief Justice Marshall did not mince words about the reasons behind denying gay people the right to marriage, referring at one point to the "destructive stereotype that same-sex relationships are inherently unstable and inferior to opposite-sex relationships and are not worthy of respect." She wrote later in the opinion, "The marriage ban works a deep and scarring hardship on a very real segment of the community for no rational reason," explaining that it "suggests that the marriage restriction is rooted in persistent prejudices against persons who are (or who are believed to be) homosexual." And, just as Justice Scalia had predicted, she also quoted from the Supreme Court's recent decision in *Lawrence*.

The *Goodridge* decision panicked a lot of political conservatives, including President George W. Bush. In his State of the Union address, delivered two months after the decision, he criticized "activist judges," who were "redefining marriage by court order, without regard for the will of the people and their elected representatives." President Bush then went a step further, implying that he might want there to be a constitutional amendment to stop gay people from marrying: "If judges insist on forcing their arbitrary will upon the people, the only alternative left to the people would be the constitutional process. Our nation must defend the sanctity of marriage."

Conservatives in the chamber jumped to their feet, applauding wildly. One person who was not clapping, however, was Gavin Newsom. The recently elected thirty-six-year-old mayor of San Francisco, Newsom was at the State of the Union address as the guest of California Representative Nancy Pelosi, and as he listened to the president, he was getting annoyed. If gay people wanted to get married, why not let them get married? In fact, he thought, why not let them get married *now*? So, a few weeks after President Bush's address, Mayor Newsom ordered the San Francisco County Clerk to start issuing marriage licenses to same-sex couples, who then proceeded to descend in droves upon San Francisco's enormous Beaux-Arts City Hall building, the same place where the brave and groundbreaking gay rights hero Harvey Milk had been shot to death a quarter century earlier. Four thousand couples received marriage licenses before the California Supreme Court put the judicial kibosh on Mayor Newsom's experiment a month later.

When I heard what Gavin Newsom was doing, I thought it was incredible. In fact, I thought, *That's so California! No one here in New York would ever do something like that.* Perhaps that is true of New York City officials. But two weeks after Mayor Newsom's announcement, the twenty-six-year-old mayor of the Village of New Paltz announced that he, too, would allow gay couples to marry. Mayor Jason West performed twenty-five ceremonies before being arrested and charged with multiple misdemeanors of "solemnizing marriages without a license." Mayor West's efforts were also shut down by a court order, but after years of slowly ramping up, the fight for gay marriage was now truly on.

A few weeks after officials shut down the New Paltz weddings, I received a call from an American Civil Liberties Union attorney named Matt Coles. Matt told me that the ACLU was planning to bring a lawsuit on behalf of couples who had signed up to get married in New Paltz but had not succeeded in doing so before the shutdown. He wanted to know if I would take on the case pro bono, not because I had any kind of reputation as a gay rights activist, but for far more pragmatic reasons. For one thing, Matt knew that bringing in a lawyer from Paul, Weiss, a firm known for its litigation prowess, meant gaining the resources of a big law firm, which would be a tremendous help to a nonprofit like the ACLU. But there was another reason as well.

Matt also knew that I had clerked for Chief Judge Kaye and that, as a result, I knew most of the other judges on the Court of Appeals at that time and was familiar with the way that the Court of Appeals operates. Being able to make a personal connection was crucial in a case like this, because marriage equality was still a foreign concept to most people. Matt felt that having a familiar person, who happened to be gay, standing up and making the argument to the judges might help to shift the equation in our favor.

The personal is political, as the saying goes. And that became abundantly true in my own life over the next two years as I prepared, filed, and argued the case for marriage equality in New York.

THE FIRST TIME I asked Rachel if she wanted to get married, she responded with "Don't be ridiculous."

We had been domestic partners for a couple of years at that point, and although I had never been the type to fantasize about walking down the aisle in a frilly white dress, I was surprised that I had recently begun to think about actually getting married. Rachel and I still could not marry anywhere in the United States because Massachusetts, the only state that permitted marriage for same-sex couples, then offered that right only to Massachusetts state residents. But we could get married in Canada, and in the first months of 2004, hundreds of gay American couples, including some friends of ours, made the trek north to do just that.

Yet even though we could finally get legally married, we still had conflicted feelings about it. For one thing, it was not entirely clear at first that the state of New York would recognize Canadian marriages between gay couples. But it was absolutely clear that the U.S. federal government would not, because of DOMA. At the time, Rachel thought, *What's the point?* As she explained:

> We would not have had the same rights as straight married couples so it did not feel like an act of equality—it felt like begging for acceptance as if we were trying to say we're normal. It felt like an act of conformity, not an act of affirmation. And I did not feel like doing that. I wanted to have equal rights as a married lesbian couple. Getting married at that point felt like a pretense because it had no real substance. We wouldn't get any additional rights, and no New York official would recognize our marriage as socially, legally, or even emotionally equivalent to the marriages of straight people.

I understood how Rachel felt. I too was frustrated by the lack of real recognition and rights for gay Americans. But at the same time, I found myself increasingly wanting to get married, and to get married to Rachel. On top of that was the fact that we had started talking about having a child. Both of us had known from the very beginning of our relationship that we wanted children, and with both of us edging toward forty, it was time to get moving if we were truly serious.

For a lesbian couple, having a baby is not a simple endeavor.

Pretty much every available avenue—from using a sperm donor (anonymous or otherwise) to adopting—involves multiple steps and lots of legal documents, so we knew it might be a while before any baby showed up. As we started making plans for our long-term future as a family, I asked Rachel again, "So, would you like to get married?" Once again, she said no. But she was not calling the idea ridiculous anymore, because something surprising had happened as our gay friends started getting married.

Rachel had been to a lot of straight weddings in her life, and even when she loved the bride and groom, she hated the weddings themselves, because they made her feel excluded. Once we started going to the weddings of our lesbian and gay friends, however, that changed. These weddings were full of wondrous joy. Everyone there, not just the brides or the grooms, was filled with gratitude, love, and awe. For the first time, Rachel felt not only included but actually engaged in these weddings. She began to understand that marriage was not simply a social construct or legal partnership with rights and benefits—something for a lifelong activist such as herself to fight for in Albany—but a personal promise that is shared with the community.

Rachel also came to realize that there had been another, deeper reason behind her disdain for marriage, that there was also an element of self-hatred involved. For years, the idea of getting married had embarrassed her. It was not only that it felt like scrabbling for second-class status; on some level, it also felt unseemly and almost cartoonish. She had carried inside her the assumption that she did not deserve the right to marry. But now, witnessing these other profoundly happy celebrations, something shifted. She began to see how the power of marriage was more than merely symbolic or legal—marriage meant something very fundamental about your commitment to another person, your integration of all of your family relationships, and most of all your very sense of self.

When Rachel realized that getting married was a legitimate—

even healthy—thing to do, she decided that it was time. One morning in the spring of 2005, she looked at me and said, "We're having a child together. Let's get married. I want us to publicly celebrate our commitment to each other. We don't have many rights, but whatever rights we do have, I want us to have them together as parents." That was good enough for me. A few weeks later, as if on cue, Rachel became pregnant.

Suddenly, Rachel and I were transformed from domestic partners to engaged parents-to-be. We had a wedding to plan, baby books to read, and a nursery to design. I was ecstatic. Actually, we had two weddings to plan: one small, legal ceremony in Toronto, to be followed by a large Jewish wedding at Rachel's parents' home in Rhode Island.

We flew to Toronto on Friday, September 9, 2005, and in the presence of Rachel's family and two close friends, we took our vows in the modest wood-paneled office of the city clerk. Following Lavine family tradition, we went out afterward for a wedding feast at a Chinese restaurant, just as Rachel's parents had done after their wedding, but that was the extent of the celebration; within twenty-four hours, we were back in New York. My parents did not make the trip, but I was not surprised or upset by that. I knew that they were planning to come to the Rhode Island ceremony the next week—which was already one more wedding of their daughter than I had ever expected them to attend.

Not only did they attend, but they also invited several dozen of their friends and family from Cleveland. Yes, fourteen years after she'd banged her head against the wall, my mother embraced my Big Gay Wedding and happily took part in it. At our Jewish ceremony, the traditional Sheva Berakhot, or Seven Blessings, were recited, and we invited various family members and friends to read them during the ceremony. My parents read one, standing up in front of 150 guests on that beautiful fall day, to support us in our marriage.

Our dear friend Rabbi Jan Uhrbach married us, which was itself a courageous act. Because she is a Conservative rabbi, Jan was technically not supposed to be officiating at weddings for same-sex couples at that time. (The Conservative movement did not change its position until later in 2006 after a close and contentious vote.) But Jan has always pursued the path she knows to be just, regardless of official disapprobation. She fought for openly gay and lesbian students to be admitted to the Jewish Theological Seminary, where she had studied and then taught, and argued for the Conservative movement to ordain openly LGBT rabbis.

Having Jan perform our marriage ceremony was profoundly meaningful to Rachel and me, and we were deeply moved by her words. In particular, we both have remembered this important truth: Jan told us that we would learn that in any marriage, there will be wonderful parts and there will be terrible parts. She reminded us that one of the reasons we have a wedding is not only to publicly demonstrate our love for each other but to make the community integral to the promises we made that day by supporting us during the terrible times. Finally, Jan reminded us about what makes marriage different: When you marry, you have closed the door to the idea of leaving the relationship. You say to each other, I will stand with you for the rest of my life—no matter what.

After our ceremony, Rachel and I—like Thea and Edie before us—felt the inexplicable difference between being married and not married. We had no idea how powerful it would be. It was not only the power of the public recognition of our love for each other, but also the feeling of dignity that the marriage ceremony had conferred upon our relationship. When Rachel and I married, I was in the thick of the New York marriage equality case, drafting our brief and thinking about the upcoming oral argument in Albany. Standing up in front of family and friends, holding the hands of three-months'-pregnant Rachel, I understood not only intellectually but also viscerally what I was really fighting for.

But despite the feelings of dignity our marriage bestowed upon us, there was still no guarantee that the rest of the world would recognize it. We found that out the hard way, just after our son was born.

ON APRIL 5, 2006, Rachel gave birth to our son Jacob at one of the most prestigious teaching hospitals in New York City. I was with her in the delivery room, watching as she underwent a successful cesarean section and our beautiful boy came into the world. I stood nearby while a nurse cleaned him up, counted his fingers and toes, and did the Apgar test to make sure he was healthy. The nurse then put the baby into my arms, and I carried him to Rachel so that she could see him for the first time. The whole experience was magical, and everyone in the delivery room could not have been nicer or more inclusive.

As Rachel and I held Jacob and cooed over him in her hospital room, we could not get over how beautiful he was. He had an unusual golden-peachy tone to his skin, which to our besotted eyes made him even more gorgeous. "Just look at him!" said Rachel. "He's the color of an apricot!" What we did not realize was that his warm and appealing skin tone was the result of infant jaundice, which can cause serious problems in a newborn. So, not long after his birth, Jacob was whisked to the neonatal intensive care unit (NICU) and put under bright blue-green lights for phototherapy treatment. Rachel was still bedridden, recovering from her C-section, so while Jacob was in treatment, I would go to the NICU multiple times a day to bring him to Rachel to nurse or to feed him myself with formula to help with the jaundice, wearing my hospital-coded bracelet to prove that I had the authority to do so.

Both Jacob and Rachel received excellent care, but after five days, we wanted to be out of the hospital and back home. Jacob's jaundice had finally dissipated, and while Rachel was not fully healed, we had had more than enough of hospital food, hospital beds, and stale hospital air. It was a Sunday morning, and as I went out to the car and fiddled again with the extra-padded baby seat that had taken me hours to install in my mother's old car, which we had affectionately named "Black Beauty," I could not wait to bring Jacob home.

Rachel was resting in bed, still wearing her hospital gown because putting on clothes would irritate her sutures. I told her that I would go get Jacob from the NICU and bring him back to her room so that she could get dressed with my help and then we could all leave together. I walked down the hall to get Jacob, but when I picked him up and wrapped him in a blanket, the nurse on duty said, "Excuse me. Where do you think you're going?"

"We're checking out," I said. "We're going home today."

"You cannot take that baby," she said sharply. "Only the mother can take him."

I stared at the nurse, my face flushing with anger. For the past five days, I had been coming in and out of this very NICU to feed and care for my son. I had a hospital bracelet on my arm that had allowed me to be present from the birth onward, no matter where Jacob was. We had signed papers both with our own ob/gyn's office and the hospital giving me full authority to care for and sign paperwork for our son. All the doctors and nurses—including this one—had seen me here, hardly sleeping or eating for the past five days as I fretted over his health. And now this nurse was treating me as if I were a stranger to my own son.

"Listen," I said. "My wife is still recovering from her C-section. She can barely walk, much less carry the baby to the car. Are you really going to make me get her out of her bed to do this?"

"Hospital policy," she said. "Only a parent can take a child out."

Her words felt like a slap in the face. Seething, I laid Jacob back down and stalked to Rachel's room. "Honey," I said. "You're going to have to go get Jacob."

"Why can't you do it?" she asked.

"Because the nurse won't let me take him," I said. "She says only his *mother* can take him."

Rachel pulled herself out of the bed and hobbled down the hallway in her hospital gown. My normally feisty wife was too weak and exhausted to do more than stand in the NICU, swaying back and forth as she signed the final paperwork, while the nurse gave us a fake smile. Afterward Rachel told me that she had also been too afraid to argue with the nurse. It was a Sunday morning, and if we fought with the nurse, she could retaliate by keeping our baby for another day and we would have very little recourse until Monday. It was the first time, Rachel said, that she had ever felt so vulnerable: now homophobia could hurt not just us but our defenseless child.

Rachel picked up Jacob and walked out of the nursery with him, then immediately handed him to me. (The day before, when they had brought Jacob's birth certificate to Rachel to sign, she had wanted to strike "Father" and list me in that space as co-mother. I had insisted that she leave it blank, and she did so unhappily. I was afraid that it might somehow be construed as tampering with an official document, delaying or even jeopardizing my adoption of Jacob.) The three of us staggered to the car, emotionally spent. Suddenly the world seemed a much scarier place.

Despite our legal marriage in Canada, I was not considered a "presumptive parent" because I was gay. But if I had been Rachel's husband, that nurse would have let me take Jacob home, no questions asked—especially after five days of caring for him in the NICU. I was fuming, but the experience at least offered me some clarity: we would never have true equality until we could legally marry in our home state and be treated like all other spouses and parents.

Incredibly enough, just six weeks later, I would have the opportunity to try to make that happen. I was scheduled to stand in front of New York's highest court on May 31, 2006, to present my argument for marriage equality. I always want to win every case, but especially after our debilitating experience at the hospital, I knew that I had to win this one.

4

BE BRAVE—DO
THE RIGHT THING

From the moment Matt Coles called me, I was obsessed with figuring out how to win the case for marriage equality in New York. At that point, the only state that had legalized marriage between lesbian and gay couples was Massachusetts, and the idea that other states might follow caused many Americans to break out in hives. As a result, our message to the judges would need to be: *Be brave. Do the right thing, even if it's hard.*

In other words, what we had to do was convince the judges that New York was different—that it should be a trailblazer among the fifty states, a leader of other states rather than a follower. This wasn't a crazy idea. New York, after all, has one of the largest populations of openly LGBT residents, behind only California and Texas. It also has a history of acting boldly in gay civil rights. In 1980, more than twenty years before the Supreme Court's *Lawrence* decision removed the criminal sanction from gay sexual relationships, the New York Court of Appeals, New York's highest court, had struck down its own antisodomy statute in a case called *People v. Onofre*. And New York was also ahead of the curve with respect to second-parent adoption by gay parents as well, thanks to the *Jacob* and *Dana* decision back in 1995.

So why shouldn't New York continue to lead the way in gay

civil rights? Sure, six out of ten Americans still believed gay marriage should be illegal, but New York was better than that. This
was the argument that I believed would give us our best chance in
the New York Court of Appeals, which ultimately would decide
the issue.

In the beginning, however, it was not clear that our case would
make it that far. As soon as New York shut down the New Paltz
marriage experiment, attorneys from all over the state rushed to
file lawsuits. At least five suits began making their way through
the court system, and as is typical in a big civil rights case, there
was fierce jockeying for position. Everyone wanted to be the
lawyer who brought marriage equality to New York State. The
ACLU and Lambda Legal, both of whom had been working on
the issue for years, each wanted their case to be the one chosen by
the Court of Appeals to decide the issue.

We filed our case, *Sylvia Samuels et al. v. New York State Department of Health*, on behalf of thirteen plaintiff couples. It was a
common practice in those days to have a "rainbow coalition" of
plaintiffs in gay rights cases. The theory was that by having many
different kinds of couples (gay men, lesbians, older people, parents, couples of different races) as plaintiffs, the judges would be
able to see the breadth of the affected population.

But as I soon found out, there is at least one significant problem
with this strategy. In a case with so many couples, inevitably some
of them break up. A few of our plaintiff couples separated over the
next two years, which did not help. We needed to bring in some
new plaintiffs who we knew that we could count on not to separate while the case was pending, so I decided to add New York
State Assemblyman Daniel O'Donnell—the brother of comedian
and talk show host Rosie O'Donnell—and his then boyfriend
(now husband) John Banta. The ACLU was worried that Danny
would receive the lion's share of the press attention, but I insisted.
As a private firm lawyer, I have more freedom; I don't have a

constituency I have to please, and I do not have to raise money. I focused on what I thought would best help to win the case.

Bringing in Danny O'Donnell was not the only time the ACLU and I clashed over strategy. While ACLU attorney James Esseks and I were mostly on the same page, Matt Coles and I had our differences.

From the start, we disagreed about how best to argue the case. Matt insisted that we open our brief with what is known as the substantive due process argument, based on the decision of the Supreme Court in the 1967 case *Loving v. Virginia*, a case defended by an interracial couple whose marriage was not recognized in their home state. For this argument to succeed, however, the court would have to conclude that the fundamental right to marry necessarily includes marriages between gay couples. I did not think we would succeed in convincing the court of this argument back then, since historically no one ever thought of marriage as an institution involving gay people. Instead, I believed the far better strategy would be to emphasize the equal protection argument, which posits that the Constitution does not allow the government to treat gay people any differently than straight people with respect to marriage. In my mind then and continuing today, this equal protection argument is, at its core, what LGBT rights cases are really all about—the simple proposition that gay Americans, like all Americans, have the constitutional right to equal protection under the law.

Disagreements will arise in any case with multiple lawyers. But when I told Matt I thought he was making a mistake with his strategy, things got heated. We were on a conference call with several other lawyers, and when Matt continued to insist that we open the brief with the due process argument, I pushed back.

"Listen, Matt," I said, "I'm telling you, I know how these judges think. I clerked on the New York Court of Appeals. This is really not the way to go." The main reason Matt had brought me on to this case, after all, was because of my experience clerking on the court. Why not try to use what I knew from that experience to improve our chances?

But Matt apparently had heard enough. He informed me that he was tired of hearing about my Court of Appeals experience and that I needed to just listen to him. I am sure the conversation went on, but I did not hear it because I had already hung up the phone. As a corporate litigator, having an adversary yell hardly fazed me, but I was not about to be publicly scolded by a colleague.

Andrew Ehrlich, one of the Paul, Weiss associates (now my law partner) working with us on the case, was also on the conference call. He told me that after I hung up, there was a moment of silence on the line, and then Matt said, "Is Robbie going to call back in?"

"I don't think so," Andrew replied.

We ultimately ended up opening the brief with due process, as Matt had insisted. I worked hard on that brief—even reading stacks of paperwork and taking numerous calls from the ACLU during my honeymoon with Rachel in Venice. I suppose there is some irony to fighting so hard for marriage equality that you risk spoiling your own honeymoon.

THE FIVE MARRIAGE equality cases made their way through New York's lower courts, and by the beginning of 2006, four of them—including ours—had lost at the intermediate appellate court level, while the fifth had been tossed out. Now it was on to the highest level, the Court of Appeals, but which case would the judges choose to hear? There was frantic lobbying behind the scenes, but ultimately the court decided to roll all four cases into one, giving it the name of Lambda's original case, *Hernandez v. Robles*. The lawyers on the various cases decided that four attorneys, including Lambda's Susan Sommer and me, would present oral arguments, which were scheduled for May 31, 2006, just six weeks after Jacob was born.

This was it: we were going to pull together to win marriage equality for all New Yorkers. I had taken part in some high-stakes cases for Paul, Weiss, so I was used to working under pressure, and for the most part I even enjoyed it. But this was different.

Unlike in 1995, when I was deeply closeted during my clerkship with Judge Kaye, I was by now a reasonably high-profile lesbian. There were few other openly gay partners at Paul, Weiss, and when I had first made partner, I had merely been peeking out of the closet. By the time Rachel and I married, I felt comfortable enough to invite more than a dozen colleagues from the firm and their spouses to our wedding. Rachel and I also worked actively for pro-LGBT political causes and candidates, often holding fund-raisers in our home. For the purposes of this case, I was not just a lawyer arguing for marriage equality; I was the lesbian lawyer arguing for the right to marry. And everyone knew it.

Of the seven judges on the Court of Appeals at that time, I knew four of them personally. I knew Judge Kaye well, of course, from my clerkship with her. Judges George Bundy Smith and Carmen Ciparick also had been on the court during my clerkship, so I knew them as well. There was one other judge whom I also knew very well, but for a very different reason.

Back when I was a summer associate at Paul, Weiss, I was sent down to Huntsville, Texas, to work on a pro bono death penalty case. We were representing a convicted murderer, a mentally disabled man named Johnny Paul Penry who had been convicted of raping and killing a young woman in 1979. Although Penry had been on death row since 1980, the Supreme Court had granted him a retrial, saying that the jury had not properly considered evidence of his mental retardation.

Robert Smith, the Paul, Weiss partner on the case, was a conservative, Federalist Society kind of guy, not your typical anti–death-penalty lawyer. (According to its website, the Federalist Society "is a group of conservatives and libertarians interested in the current state of the legal order . . . This entails reordering priorities within the legal system to place a premium on individual liberty, traditional values, and the rule of law.") I worked very closely with Bob, primarily helping him prepare for the cross-examination of prosecution witnesses, and he taught me a great deal. I became hooked on the process of preparing for trial, and I made a special request (one that was granted) for Paul, Weiss to allow me to stay the entire summer in Huntsville.

It was a long, emotional, intense summer, and by the end I had bonded with the whole Paul, Weiss team, including Bob Smith. Watching how vigorously this powerful corporate lawyer fought for his client, a man whom society would just as soon forget, was a great lesson for a young law school student. I never forgot the example that Bob had set. And now, sixteen years later, I was about to see him in a very different context. Bob was now a judge on the Court of Appeals, the fourth judge I knew.

I liked and respected Bob, but it was clear that our chances of getting his vote were slim. We only needed four votes to win, though, and I thought I knew how we could get them. I knew that we had Judges Kaye and Ciparick, and I believed that we could get the vote of Judge Albert Rosenblatt, too. As a result, we only needed one more vote. I thought our best hope would be to so convince Judge Rosenblatt that we were right, he would then try to persuade his colleague, Judge George Bundy Smith, to vote our way. Judge Smith, who is African American, had been a Freedom Rider in the sixties, so he obviously was a proponent of civil rights. But could we convince him to see marriage equality as a civil rights issue as well? I believed that Judge Rosenblatt was the key to making that happen, a point I kept in mind as I prepared.

But just a few weeks before the oral argument, Judge Rosenblatt announced a stunning decision: he was recusing himself from the case.

We received the word through a court order, and the minute I heard the news, I slumped forward and put my head in my hands. Without Judge Rosenblatt, our chances of winning were reduced to almost nothing. In theory, we could still end up with a 3–3 tie, at which point the case would be reargued and a seventh judge would be brought in to cast the deciding vote, but it seemed very unlikely that we could get any of the other three judges (two of whom were Upstate women appointed by Governor George Pataki) on board.

Judge Rosenblatt's recusal was extremely disappointing, not to mention somewhat baffling. Initially there was speculation, later confirmed by the local New York City gay paper, that the reason for Judge Rosenblatt's recusal was the fact that his daughter, an attorney in Los Angeles, had worked on amicus briefs in two other marriage equality cases brought by Lambda Legal. As far as I know, Judge Rosenblatt has never spoken publicly about why he recused himself from *Hernandez*. But his decision left us scrambling as we approached the date of the oral argument. Winning now appeared to be a long shot, and we had to be prepared for anything, including pointed questions about polygamy, incest, and bestiality, which at the time were the favorite go-to points of the anti–gay-marriage groups. This was going to be quite a ride.

THE ORAL ARGUMENT became contentious quickly.

Susan Sommer from Lambda went first for our side. Marriage, she told the court, is a "well-settled, long-recognized fundamental right":

> The decision whether and whom to marry is among life's most momentous decisions: to enter into one of life's most intimate, significant, and sustaining relationships with one other person that you love, a relationship that the state supports and sanctions in a myriad of tangible and intangible ways.

No one disagreed with that assertion, although Judge Robert Smith immediately interjected to ask whether that fundamental right to marriage was meant to include gay people. Susan parried that exchange deftly enough, but she soon found herself stuck in the mud on the polygamy issue.

SUSAN SOMMER: [N]othing in this case will decide one way or another whether a claim to polygamy is one that establishes a fundamental right and has to be . . .

JUDGE ROBERT SMITH: So . . . does that imply that a claim to polygamy would be open if we decide in this case?

SOMMER: No, it implies, actually, the contrary: that it would not change the status of a claim to polygamy . . .

JUDGE SMITH: What is that status, in your view, today?

SOMMER: Well, there is actually a nineteenth-century Supreme Court precedent that upheld [bans on] polygamy. But it's not an issue that has visited the courts . . .

Oy, I thought, as I sat at the plaintiffs' table. This was really not the direction we wanted to be going in. Dwelling on polygamy meant missing opportunities to make our own points; it meant we were playing defense, instead of offense. But Susan could not seem to get Judge Smith off the subject, so the polygamy discussion went on for several excruciating minutes before she wound her way back to fundamental rights. And then Judge Smith suddenly switched tacks, asking pointed questions about the role of procreation and children in marriage.

You make the point that no other state [besides marriage] gives lots and lots and lots of benefits to married people that it doesn't give to single people. Isn't the justification for that, in very large part, to preserve the proper—to preserve what the legislature could deem the right environment for the begetting and raising of children?

Judge Smith was tipping his hand as to how he would vote, and it definitely was not our way. We would somehow have to sway one of the other judges, and we would have to put up the argument of our lives to do it. Susan finished her time, and then it was my turn.

As quickly as I could, I got into my "New York is different" argument. I told the judges flatly that if they followed their own precedents in cases like the *Onofre* sodomy case, then they would have to conclude that gay couples had a constitutional right to marry in New York. Judge Smith jumped in again, bringing the discussion back to the question of children.

"Could a legislature rationally conclude that on the whole it's preferable for our children to have a mother and a father, rather than two mothers or two fathers?" he asked. I responded by explaining that the scientific evidence—as presented in briefs and statements from the American Pediatric Association, the American Psychiatric Association, and others—showed that there was absolutely no difference for the well-being of children if their parents were straight or their parents happened to be gay. Judge Smith pounced, asking, "[I]s it that there's absolutely no difference, or no difference has been proven?"

Almost as soon as he had raised his question, I realized we had a problem. I could only respond with what had been filed in amicus briefs—essentially, summary statements about what various studies had shown. But I now understood that this was not enough. We should have entered our own experts into evidence to build more of a factual record and make this point airtight. As an experienced trial lawyer, Judge Smith knew that we had not done our homework, and he wasted no time trying to pick a hole in our argument. I doubt we could have won his vote in any case, but I was keenly aware that our mistake might hurt us with the other judges.

Susan Sommer had been hit with the polygamy question, and

now it was my turn to face another prevailing antigay argument. Following up on the question of children, Judge Victoria Graffeo asked:

> There are children raised in other kinds of family constructs. You could have siblings, two sisters who are raising the children of one of the sisters and the legislature hasn't afforded those individuals all the same rights as a married couple . . . [w]as the legislature denying them due process or equal protection in denying the benefits of marriage as well?

In other words, she asked me the siblings question. This was in the grand tradition of what lawyers like to call slippery-slope arguments: if we permit gay marriage, what is there to stop brothers and sisters from demanding the right to marry? I did not want to get sidetracked, but I had to respond, so I said:

> [That's] a good question. Let me try to answer it. First of all, on due process . . . there would be no fundamental due process right there, because I don't think anyone can really believe that a relationship between two sisters raising children is anything like the relationship between the appellants, the same-sex couples here. So it's just fundamentally different.

But Judge Graffeo needed clarification. What made it different? The fact that there was a sexual component? Now I was starting to get exasperated. I did my best to maintain my composure, explaining:

> Exactly. The relationship of having someone in your life choose what's going to happen when you're on an operating room table . . . How you will be buried. How you want

to spend your finances. Whether you want to buy a house together. What choices you want to make about your children. Physical intimacy. All those things, I agree that sisters sometimes share [some of] those. But I think we can agree that for the most part the nature of that relationship is fundamentally different.

I could not believe that in 2006 we still had to answer questions like this. Opposite-sex marriage had always been legal, but so far it had not led to a rash of brothers wanting to marry their sisters and sisters their brothers. So why should marriage equality for gay people lead to two sisters or two brothers wanting to marry? The very premise was absurd.

Every chance I had, I just kept hammering away at the same points: New York is different. This court is different. New York should not follow the precedents of other states; it should lead. "This is a state that has a proud and distinctive tradition of interpreting its state constitution in matters of import to New Yorkers in ways that are different," I told the judges. *Be brave! Do the right thing!*

The New York Court of Appeals had already recognized, in the adoption cases, that same-sex couples were raising children. And in this case, the state had conceded that it would be good for those kids for their parents to be married. So then we got to what I like to call the "slutty heterosexuals" argument. This was the argument that straight couples needed to be allowed to marry because, unlike gay couples, there was the possibility that they could accidentally get pregnant and have children.

Clearly, as this Court has recognized in *Jacob* and *Dana* and as the New York legislature has recognized, same-sex couples throughout this state are having children. It's good for those couples to be married. The state concedes that. It would be good for those children for their parents to be married. The state concedes that. So . . . procreation, in and of itself, doesn't work [as an argument against same-sex marriage].

So then you get to accidental procreation . . . What that says is, because only heterosexuals can accidentally procreate, or procreate with "minimal planning"—although I have to tell you, I'm not sure I understand what that means.

I had to pause here while everyone in the courtroom cracked up. But the next point I made was dead serious:

Because only straight couples are in that situation, then it's okay for only straight couples or straight families to be afforded the protections of marriage. But that suffers from the same flaw. Because, if you have to look at who is not included . . . you are not helping any children anywhere in New York by excluding same-sex couples from marriage. And in fact, given the state of New York policy; given the fact that so many same-sex couples exist in this state that it would be good for them and good for their children, I think that this Court could only conclude that drawing the line to keep straight families in and same-sex families out is irrational.

I felt I was making a strong showing—but was I making headway with any of the three judges whose votes we needed? A few minutes later, this exchange with Judge George Bundy Smith made it seem like I might be gaining some ground.

JUDGE GEORGE BUNDY SMITH: Suppose we agree with you. What follows? We say, "Okay, we've got to give a marriage license. Gays can be married." What will be the result, the practical results of that?

ME: There's an excellent brief on that, Judge Smith, that I would
refer you to. It was filed by [Mary Bonauto of] the Gay and
Lesbian Advocates and Defenders in Massachusetts. And they
talk about what happened in Massachusetts after the *Goodridge*
decision.

JUDGE SMITH: I'd like to know what will happen here. What do
you contend will happen?

ME: What I would say is, exactly what's happened in Massachusetts, which is basically nothing. There is nothing that has
been seen as unusual about this. There's not people rioting in
the streets of the Commonwealth of Massachusetts. There's
not a breakdown of civil society in Massachusetts. And there
surely isn't a breakdown of marriage in the Commonwealth
of Massachusetts . . . Public opinion is overwhelmingly in
favor of what's happened there. So I would say the same thing.

My time ended on that note, but I would have one more chance
to make my case in the few minutes I had reserved for rebuttal.
I would be the last lawyer to speak, and I wanted to leave the
judges thinking about the strongest points of our argument.

But first, I would have to get past the distraction of Judge Robert Smith.

As much as I liked and respected Judge Smith, it had been very
tough facing him. He took every opportunity to try to poke holes
in my argument, but that was to be expected. What I did not
expect was his demeanor: he clearly knew how he was going to
vote, and he seemed to be enjoying playing the contrarian.

During my rebuttal, Chief Judge Kaye urged me to revisit the
procreation argument, which, as she noted, "has been so exten-
sively urged by your adversary." I took it up again:

Let me be clear on procreation. First of all, we're not running away from procreation, Your Honors. We believe that

there is, of course—that procreation has something to do with marriage. But the problem with the procreation argument is—

And it was here that Judge Robert Smith began snickering. The best thing I could have done was ignore it, but my years of knowing Bob first as a mentor, then as a colleague, and then as a law partner took over. "I see Bob"—*whoops!*—"Judge Smith, excuse me, laughing." At that moment, he was not a judge in a case I was desperate to win; he was just Bob, the Paul, Weiss partner with whom I had worked so closely. I then quickly pulled myself together.

It has a lot to do with marriage. We can see that too. But the point is, that in the analysis this court does under the rational basis test . . . it looks not only at the people who are included in the classification, but it looks at the people who are excluded by the classification. And to answer one of George Bundy Smith's questions, there are 46,000, more than 46,000 families in this state that are same-sex families with children.

And there is no dispute here that there is no rational interest being served in procreation, in stable families or in healthy children, happy children, in excluding those families from the benefits of marriage. . . . There's absolutely no connection.

When my time expired, I knew I had done the best that I could. Our chances were slim, but I still had hope that we might have turned one of the judges our way. Now all we could do was wait.

FIVE WEEKS AFTER the argument, on the morning of July 6, the court released its decision. When it came down, I was despon-

dent. We had lost, 4–2. And what made it even worse was reading Judge Robert Smith's majority opinion, which essentially said
that gay parents were not as good as straight parents. As a new gay
parent myself, reading a passage like this was deeply painful:

> [T]he Legislature could rationally believe that it is better,
> other things being equal, for children to grow up with both
> a mother and a father. Intuition and experience suggest that
> a child benefits from having before his or her eyes, every
> day, living models of what both a man and a woman are
> like. It is obvious that there are exceptions to this general
> rule—some children who never know their fathers, or their
> mothers, do far better than some who grow up with parents
> of both sexes—but the Legislature could find that the gen-
> eral rule will usually hold.

"Intuition and experience" tell us this? My intuition and experience told me that children do far better growing up in loving,
stable families, regardless of the parents' sexual orientation. I was
shocked that Judge Smith had actually included such a weak argument at the heart of his opinion, but his opinion soon became
even worse. Incredibly, he also used the slutty heterosexual argument as a basis for his decision:

> [T]he Legislature could rationally decide that, for the welfare
> of children, it is more important to promote stability, and to
> avoid instability, in opposite-sex than in same-sex relation-
> ships. Heterosexual intercourse has a natural tendency to
> lead to the birth of children; homosexual intercourse does
> not . . . The Legislature could also find that such relation-
> ships are all too often casual or temporary. It could find that
> an important function of marriage is to create more stability
> and permanence in the relationships that cause children to

be born. It thus could choose to offer an inducement—in the form of marriage and its attendant benefits—to opposite-sex couples who make a solemn, long-term commitment to each other.

In other words, because straight people might accidentally get pregnant, we had better offer them marriage as a way to promote stability. Gay people cannot have children by accident, so they and their planned-for, much-wanted children don't need the benefits and protections of marriage and are on their own. The whole argument was irrational and absurd. I was deeply disheartened that we had had our chance to make history and had lost, but I was especially disappointed that the reasoning behind our loss did not even acknowledge, much less grapple with, the arguments about New York being different that we had so carefully developed in our briefs and in court.

In her opinion, Judge Kaye made mincemeat out of these arguments, but it was only a dissent:

> Defendants primarily assert an interest in encouraging procreation within marriage. But while encouraging opposite-sex couples to marry before they have children is certainly a legitimate interest of the State, the *exclusion* of gay men and lesbians from marriage in no way furthers this interest. There are enough marriage licenses to go around for everyone.
>
> Of course, there are many ways in which the government could rationally promote procreation—for example, by giving tax breaks to couples who have children, subsidizing child care for those couples, or mandating generous family leave to parents. Any of these benefits—and many more—might convince people who would not otherwise have children to do so. But no one rationally decides to have children because gays and lesbians are excluded from marriage.

James Esseks, the ACLU lawyer, summed up one of the great ironies—and great disappointments—of the New York decision:

> A week or so before we got that terrible decision from Bob Smith in *Hernandez*, we had just won a decision from the Arkansas Supreme Court in which we had challenged, under the Arkansas state constitution, a statute that barred foster parenting by gay people or by any family that had a gay adult in it, if it was not the parent.
>
> The crux of the argument made by the state of Arkansas to defend its ban on foster parenting was that gay people were bad for kids. And the factual findings by the state trial court judge in Arkansas and the decision by the state Supreme Court made it clear that that was all ridiculous.
>
> So then, the core of Bob Smith's opinion a week later is that it's constitutional for the state of New York to exclude same-sex couples from marriage out of a theoretical possible potential concern by the legislature that gay people might be bad for kids. I thought, "How can it be that we can win this issue in Arkansas and we can't win it in New York? The world has turned topsy-turvy."

With the exception of Judge Kaye's eloquent dissent, everything about the *Hernandez* decision was disappointing. If I could not get someone like Judge Robert Smith to understand how incorrect and illogical his reasoning was, what hope did we have? Were gay couples always going to be denied the protections of law and the respect of the state?

It certainly felt that way. And an incident three weeks later only served to underscore the fact that, for too many people, gay parents were not viewed as legitimate parents.

A few weeks after our son Jacob was born, I had started the process of adopting him. I was grateful that the *Jacob* and *Dana* decision made it possible for me to adopt him in the first place—but because we were a lesbian couple, we had to go through a formal second-parent adoption, as if I were a stranger to my own son. (People sometimes ask us if our son Jacob was named after the adoption decision. Proud as I am of it, Jacob Philip is named after Rachel's and my grandfathers, in keeping with Jewish tradition.) This meant that we had to fill out reams of paperwork and compile stacks of documentation, including, among many others, letters from Harvard, Columbia Law School, Paul, Weiss, our friends, former classmates, our synagogue, even our doctors. We also had to schedule a visit from a social worker to check our home and make sure we were both suitable parents. Once again, just as at the hospital following Jacob's birth, we were going through indignities that no straight married couple would have to suffer. And to add insult to injury, although we could afford it, it wasn't cheap.

Rachel, not surprisingly, was outraged about this. She wanted to sue the state of New York, to formally protest having to jump through all these hoops just because we were gay. "Honey," I said, "I really prefer to file the lawsuits, not be the plaintiff in one of them." I certainly shared Rachel's frustration, but I just wanted to get through the adoption process as quickly as possible and without any snags. Having no legal tie to Jacob made me extremely anxious. I was petrified that something might happen to him, or to Rachel, and we would have some horrible legal complication on top of everything else. I just wanted to get it done. Even though Rachel's family loved me and automatically regarded me as equally Jacob's mother, not having any legal rights to my child terrified me.

The most irritating part, from our perspective, was the social worker visit. We had to schedule—and pay for—a social worker to come to our home, interview us, and write a report. This is the same kind of visit required for people who take in foster children, but our situation was completely different. We were not strangers

to Jacob; Rachel was his biological mother, and he had been living with us since he was born. Rachel just could not believe we
had to submit to this, and on the morning the social worker came
to our house, in late July 2006, she was fuming.

Rachel is a direct person—a truth-teller—especially when she
thinks an injustice is being done. She rarely hides her opinions,
preferring to engage with others, even if that means challenging
some unspoken social rules. So all I could think from the moment
that our doorbell rang was this was a situation full of potential
land mines. *Please let us just get through this as quickly as possible.*
The social worker seemed pleasant enough, but as she poked and
prodded about my childhood, my relationships with my parents
and brother, Rachel's previous girlfriends, her political activism,
my salary, and our finances, I could not wait for the hours-long
interrogation to end. Rachel and I answered the multitude of
extremely intrusive questions as best we could, and finally, merci-
fully, the social worker stood up to leave.

I was thrilled. Knowing how anxious I was, Rachel had been
circumspect and polite throughout, even when asked some particularly prying questions, and it seemed clear that we had passed
the test. We saw the woman out of our apartment, and I breathed
a sigh of pure relief. "Well, thank God that's over," said Rachel.
"That was unbelievable."

Believe it or not, two minutes later we heard a knock at our
door. I cautiously opened it, and there—incredibly—stood the
social worker again. "I'm sorry," she said, "I just remembered
something I forgot to ask. May I come back in?" I could sense
Rachel's wariness as we had already spent more than two hours
being interrogated about some of our most private experiences,
but what else could we say? We invited her back in, and she got
right to the point.

"I wanted to ask, what do you plan to say to Jacob about your
family?" she said.

Rachel and I looked at her blankly. "What do you mean?" Rachel asked.

"Well, being a family with two moms," she said, "I'm just wondering what you plan to say to him about that."

To her credit, Rachel kept her cool. She explained that we would tell Jacob that there are many different kinds of families, and that some kids have a mom and a dad, some kids have only one parent, some have two moms or two dads, some are raised by their grandparents, but what makes a family is that you love and take care of each other. We were both feeling pretty pleased with Rachel's answer, but the social worker frowned.

"Well, that's not exactly what I mean," the woman said. "What are you going to say to him when he's grieving the loss of the father?"

Rachel and I stared at the woman, flabbergasted. And she was not done yet.

"You know, when Jacob is eight and goes to the park, and he's with his friend Johnny, and Johnny's playing ball in the park with his father," she said, "what are you going to say to him about why he does not have a father to play ball with?" I just closed my eyes, and thought to myself, *She deserves what is coming next.*

"Well, by the time he's in that Manhattan park playing with his friend Johnny," Rachel began, her voice a sheet of ice, "Johnny's father will probably be on his third wife. And if Johnny's lucky, his dad may still be paying child support on a regular basis. So I don't think I'm going to be explaining anything to Jacob about that issue. Also, in case you were wondering, most of the abuse that happens to children occurs within the family by a male relative they know. I worked for an organization that provides shelter, counseling, and legal services for victims of domestic violence, sexual assault, and child abuse"—Rachel was on a roll now—"and I would be glad to provide you more information about that issue if you're interested."

For one excruciating moment, Rachel and the woman just stared at each other. Then the woman said weakly, "I did not mean to offend you."

"Too late," Rachel responded.

I then jumped in to say, "Okay, so I guess that's that, then? Thank you so much for coming by!" I ushered her back out the door, and by that point, I think she was as glad to leave as we were to see her go. She did end up giving us a positive report, and the adoption ultimately went through, so there were no lasting repercussions from the visit. But coming just three weeks after the heartbreak of losing the New York marriage case, I felt devastated all over again at having to face so much official ignorance and indifference.

I was not the only New Yorker struggling with the repercussions of our loss in *Hernandez*. Just four blocks away from my apartment, a couple of women in their seventies had been waiting nearly forty years to get married in New York. Now that I had lost the New York marriage case, it was clear they could not do so, and they needed to decide what to do next.

5

A VERY LONG ENGAGEMENT

Once we had lost the case for marriage equality in New York, Edie Windsor and Thea Spyer had a decision to make. They had been hoping to get married in their home state of New York since traveling was very difficult for Thea, whose three-decade battle with progressive multiple sclerosis had rendered her quadriplegic. (By then, Thea's motor skills had deteriorated to the point where she could move only her left hand, but that was enough for her to control her mechanized wheelchair and use her computer.) After the *Hernandez* decision, no one knew when, or even if, New York would have marriage equality, although the New York courts had started to recognize marriages between gay couples entered into out of state.

"Do you want to get married in Canada?" Edie asked Thea one afternoon in the summer of 2006.

"Not really," Thea answered (presumably thinking about how difficult it would be for her to travel). "But if you really want to do it, we can."

"No, that's okay," Edie said. She certainly did not want to have to *schlep* Thea all the way to Toronto with all of the necessary equipment—ramps, lifts, et cetera—that would be required.

That is where the matter stood until the following spring, after Thea had seen one of her doctors. Despite her physical disability, Thea was as sharp intellectually as she had always been. As a psychologist, she continued to see a full slate of therapy patients. She had Edie to boot, so her life was very happy and fulfilling despite the MS. But on this visit, the doctor had terrible news for both of them: Thea's heart had weakened considerably. Without invasive open-heart surgery to replace a valve (which Thea was understandably not willing to undergo), she likely would not live for more than another year.

The very next morning after receiving this sobering diagnosis, Thea woke up, turned to Edie, and asked, "Do you still want to get married?"

"Yes," Edie answered. "I do."

"Me too," said Thea.

So in late May 2007, Edie and Thea flew to Toronto with four best women and two best men, along with a box of tools to disassemble and reassemble Thea's electric wheelchair. Thea and Edie were married in a small ceremony at a hotel connected to the Toronto airport, so that Thea's wheelchair could be rolled straight into the hotel. More than forty years after they first met, Thea and Edie were, at long last, a legally married couple. What had once seemed like a fantastic dream, something that they could only acknowledge privately between the two of them, was now a matter of legal and public record. Despite Thea's somber medical prognosis, it was an incredibly life-affirming moment for both of them. This was a couple who had really, really, really wanted to get married.

ONE FRIDAY NIGHT in 1963, Edie had first made her way to a restaurant in Greenwich Village comanaged by Elaine Kaufman (who later went on to establish Elaine's on the Upper East Side). A gorgeous, brilliant, and vivacious computer programmer for IBM, Edie had just returned to New York after spending two semesters on a postgraduate math fellowship at Harvard.

Edie had moved into a rent-controlled apartment on the Upper

West Side, far from the bohemian Village, the kind of neighborhood where, as she put it, "I was the only woman in the building who wore blue jeans on weekends." She was thirty-four, and
although she'd dated a few women during her first decade living
in New York, she had not yet found lasting love.

But one night she called an old friend who was also a lesbian.
As Edie told her friend how lonely she was, she burst out with
a desperate plea. "Oh, God," she said, "if you know where the
lesbians go, please take me there." The lesbian bar (the Bagatelle) that Edie used to frequent before her Harvard fellowship
had closed, and she no longer knew where to go in New York
City to meet other lesbians. Her friend told her that the Portofino
restaurant in the Village was the place to be on Friday nights, so
they made plans to go there together.

The next Friday night, Edie and her friend were sitting at a
table at Portofino when a friend brought a woman named Thea
Spyer to their table. Thea was striking, with coal-black hair that
fell to her shoulders, piercing eyes, a self-assured manner, and
powerful magnetism and charisma. The daughter of a prominent
Dutch Jewish family that had done well in the pickle business,
Thea carried herself with the poise and self-confidence of an aris-
tocrat. Edie was mesmerized—by her beauty, her intellect, and
her bearing.

After dinner, the four women made their way to a party
together, and then eventually to Thea's place. Thea put on some
records, and she and Edie started to dance . . . and dance . . . and
dance . . . Edie had always loved dancing, but she could never find
a lesbian dance partner who really knew how to lead. But Thea
did so effortlessly, and the two of them spun around the small living room like they'd been doing it for years. Their bodies, Thea
would later say, "just fit." Edie kicked off her shoes and danced
until she had worn a hole in one of her stockings. (Whenever
I think about this scene, which was described in detail in our

original complaint in the district court, I can't help thinking of the famous dance scene in the film *The King and I*, with Thea, of course, as Yul Brynner and Edie as Deborah Kerr.)

From that night on, Edie was very interested in Thea. But Thea was taken, living first with one woman and then with another. Every once in a while, Edie and Thea would find themselves together at the same party, and as always they would dance together until Edie's date and Thea's live-in lover grew irritated. But no matter how much fun they had or how well they fit together, at the end of each night, Edie would end up going home alone.

This went on for two excruciating years. Giving up hope, Edie started going to a therapy group, where she sought help accepting the fact that she would never be able to have a successful relationship with another woman. By then, Edie had almost given up on the idea, and over the previous few months, she had been trying to convince herself to just find a nice man with whom to settle down, preferably a man with children who needed a mother. "I did not want to live a life without love," she would later say, and that was what she feared she was facing. She had almost, but not quite, given up hope. But in the spring of 1965, a friend told Edie that Thea was currently single and that she was going to the Hamptons for Memorial Day weekend. This was Edie's chance.

Thea was planning to drop off her friend Jane at the Hamptons home of a lesbian couple Edie knew, so Edie picked up the phone and called the couple. "I'm so sorry to be so presumptuous," she said, "but would you mind terribly if I came out to visit you this weekend?" To Edie's great relief, her friends said they'd be delighted to have her. When Edie arrived at their house that Friday, a whole group of women were getting ready to go out for dinner. Afraid she would miss Thea, she told the others, "You go ahead. I'm not hungry." Edie was afraid that if she left, even briefly, she'd miss the chance to see Thea. So Edie waited. And waited. A few hours later, the group stopped back at the house before continuing on to a bar for dancing. Once again, Edie begged off. She hated to miss the dancing, but she absolutely had to be at the house when Thea arrived, because that might be her only chance to see her. At four a.m., the group stumbled back to the house. And then somebody casually mentioned to Edie that Thea had had to work late and was not arriving until the next morning.

The next day, the waiting continued. The women staying in the house set out for a picnic on the beach, and once again Edie stayed behind. This was now getting to be ridiculous. Edie was waiting interminably for a woman who might not show up, and who might not have any interest in Edie even if she did. The slow, hot summer day dragged on and on until Edie finally heard a car pull into the driveway. A moment later, Thea and Jane walked in.

The women greeted each other, and when Edie looked at Thea, wearing a pair of white pants and a white shirt with a rope belt, she could scarcely breathe. Edie, Thea, and Jane went into the kitchen for coffee, and Edie stood slightly behind Thea at the counter, close but not daring to touch her. Here, in Edie's own words, is what happened next:

We were each having a cup of coffee, and—how to describe it? It felt like years. It could have been minutes. I almost touched her. I mean, I tell you, I almost touched her and I felt like an idiot. And then finally, her hand was on the counter. I went to put my hand on top of hers, and then withdrew it.

And Thea's friend Jane is saying, "Oh, wow. It's getting late. I better go upstairs and change." And she is very funny, so part of this is her being funny. She knows that there is something going on.

There's a phonograph on the floor in the corner of the living room, and finally Jane went upstairs, yelling, "I'll be right down!" Thea went over to put something on the phonograph, which involved kneeling down. And when she got up, I grabbed her. And then we took her car and went to East Hampton and we made love the whole afternoon.

After that day, Edie and Thea went out on occasional dates over the next two years, but then Thea wouldn't call Edie for weeks at a time. Or they would make a plan to have dinner, and Thea would cancel at the last minute. Thea was, as Edie would later say, "a pain in the ass." Edie had certainly managed to get Thea's attention, but what did she have to do to keep it?

Little by little, however, Edie's charm, their obvious chemistry, and the love they clearly felt for each other began to wear Thea down. One day, as they lay together on a beach in the Hamptons, Thea asked, "Edie, what do you want from me?"

"Not much," Edie said. "I would like to date for a year. And if that goes the way it is now, I think I would like to be engaged, say for a year. And if it still feels this goofy joyous, I would like us to spend the rest of our lives together."

Almost against her will, Thea found herself agreeing. Thea had had a series of live-in girlfriends in the past, and she had never imagined that she would settle down again with another woman. Yet as they spent more and more time together, Thea found that she couldn't deny the powerful connection between them.

In 1967, Thea rented a house for the summer in the Hamptons where they would spend the weekends together. Edie bought Thea a motorcycle and had it custom-painted white. She then proudly posed for photographs on it, wearing a white bikini to match. The two women were inseparable, sunning on the beach, eating out with friends, dancing until late into the night. But although Edie knew that she only wanted to be with Thea, she always told her, "No commitment. The day you think someone else looks better, you go." By the end of that summer, however, Thea too knew there was no one else with whom she wanted to be.

On their way out to the Hamptons one Friday afternoon late that summer, Thea stopped the car, pulled over by the side of the road, and got out. She went down on one knee and took Edie's hand in hers. "Will you—" she began, but before she could finish the sentence, Edie jumped in to say, "Yes! Yes!"

"Let me finish!" Thea cried, annoyed that Edie had interrupted her carefully planned proposal. She pulled out a circular diamond pin and presented it to Edie. It was not legal at that time for two women to marry anywhere in the world, but that did not make Thea's proposal any less real or powerful. Thea pinned the diamond brooch to Edie's blouse, and thus began what became a very long engagement.

Thea had chosen a pin instead of a ring for a very specific reason. She had previously invited Edie to speculate about what would happen if Edie showed up at the office one day wearing a diamond engagement ring. Edie explained that that was clearly impossible since everyone at IBM would then ask, "Who's the lucky guy and when do we get to meet him?" and those were not questions that Edie could or would answer. Edie adored her colleagues at work, but she had not dared to tell any of them that she was a lesbian. But she could wear a diamond pin whenever she liked, and no one would ever ask to meet her fiancé.

I have told this story of Edie and Thea's engagement dozens of times by now, yet it never ceases to amaze me. The year 1967, when it happened, was two years *before* the Stonewall riots in Greenwich Village that led to the modern gay rights movement. The idea that two women could have had the courage, the self-esteem, not to mention the foresight to become engaged to each other then is nothing short of miraculous.

In the 1950s and 1960s the only books that a gay person could read that actually talked about lesbians (as opposed to obliquely referencing them) were pulp fiction. The following passage from such a novel, *Three Women*, is a reminder of what those times were like:

> She had realized then for the first time that her love for Byrne made her different. But everyone was entitled to love . . . Yet she knew now that they must always hide their feelings, no matter how wonderful their love seemed. The world's judging eyes condemned them, forced them to sneak and lie. Something in Paula screamed against that pain and injustice, but she did not forget that loving Byrne was as natural and right for her as marriage and children were for others.

"As natural and right for her as marriage and children were for others?" Edie and Thea not only believed that their love was natural and right, but that they were even entitled to get married. That's amazing enough when it happens between any couple—gay or straight—today, but it is almost unbelievable that it happened between two women in 1967. (It is worth noting, in the interest of accuracy and true to the pulp genre, that one of the women in *Three Women* was murdered, the second was her killer, and the third ended up getting married to a man.)

BY THE TIME of their engagement, Edie had been working at IBM for nearly a decade. She had first moved to New York City in the mid 1950s "in order to be gay," as she would later put it. Her first apartment was a tiny walk-up with a shared bathroom on West 11th Street, a few blocks from Washington Square Park. It was not glamorous, but it was in the Village where she had wanted to be.

The biggest problem that Edie had at that time was actually not that she was gay since she, like most gay people in the 1950s, lived most of her life in the closet. Her biggest problem was that she would have to earn her own living. As a middle-class Jewish woman growing up in Philadelphia, Edie, like so many others, had assumed that her husband would end up supporting her financially. While Edie had a bachelor's degree in psychology from Temple University, that was not much help for a twenty-three-year-old woman trying to make it on her own in Manhattan. As she later explained to Chris Geidner of BuzzFeed: "I wanted to be like everybody else. You marry a man who supports you—it never occurred to me I'd have to earn a living."

So Edie taught herself dictation and typing in order to find a job as a secretary. Even though she landed a job as the "confidential secretary" to the CEO of the Associated Press, it paid little better than a regular secretary's salary, and she soon realized that there was no realistic possibility of promotion. She switched to bookkeeping for a while, working for a necktie manufacturing company, but that was no more promising. Finally, Edie realized that she needed a real profession. She had always been good at math, so in 1955, she decided to apply to New York University's graduate program in applied mathematics.

Unable to afford the tuition, Edie applied for a secretarial job, knowing that the university covered tuition for its employees. Originally, the university was reluctant to hire her because Edie was so overqualified for the job, but eventually they placed her in a secretarial job at NYU's Math Institute that was partially subsidized by the Atomic Energy Commission (AEC) so they could pay her more. She worked from eight to four each weekday, then took math classes in the late afternoons and evenings. In her spare time, with the money she saved from the free tuition, she took piano lessons and tap dancing classes, and on weekends, she went to the Bagatelle to sip coffee and read magazines. It was a busy and exciting life, and although she had not yet found lasting love among the lesbians of Greenwich Village, she did find another kind of love—for computers.

From the moment that Edie started studying computer programming, she knew that she had found her calling. When she helped out a few fellow students by typing their research papers, they reciprocated by teaching her how to operate the eight-ton UNIVAC computer that took up almost the entire floor of the Math Institute building on the NYU campus. "The first night I was working on the machine, I was terrified," Edie recalled. She learned how to load tapes and input data on the UNIVAC, which was used by the AEC.

Edie's obvious computer skills and her experience led to a full-time job at IBM in 1958. At IBM, Edie was a talented programmer, eventually earning their highest technical rank. She loved her colleagues at IBM but still could not bring herself to reveal to any of them that she was gay. "I never thought I was inferior," she has explained, "but I was worried that they might think that I was inferior. So I lied all the time." Edie worked closely with one male colleague who was also gay, and although each knew the truth about the other, neither of them ever said anything, even though they worked together for ten years. That was just how life was at that time when most gay people had no choice but to live their lives in the closet. The stakes were just too high.

During the years when Edie was single, she often went out socially with her IBM friends. "It was an amazing group, just amazing, and the weirdness of it is that I lied to every wonderful person whom I really loved," she explained. "I mean, we ate lunch together, we drank together after work, we partied together." She went out with the group on weekends, too—until she got together with Thea. Her colleagues loved to go to wine tastings on the weekends, but Edie could not bring Thea as her date, and she certainly was not going to leave her at home, so she just stopped going. When her colleagues asked why, she made up excuses. And when others noted that Edie seemed to get a lot of calls at work from Thea, she explained that that was because she was dating Thea's brother, Willy—actually the name of a wooden doll from Thea's Dutch childhood that the couple kept in a closet in their apartment.

But as her relationship with Thea grew more serious, Edie hated having to keep it secret. She was still too scared to tell her IBM colleagues, but there was another group of computer programmers she had come to know well—people she did not work with every day but saw twice a year at a biannual conference. Each time the conference rolled around, she sat silently as her friends regaled each other with stories of their children, their spouses, and their family lives. "I knew about everybody's wife, and how she was, and I knew whose kid was no longer on a three-wheeler but was on a two-wheeler, everything," Edie remembers. But she never revealed anything about herself. Until one day, she did.

The night before the conference started, she went out for drinks with a group of fellow programmers. "Guys, the most important thing in my life is happening," she blurted out. And then she told them about Thea. To her surprise and relief, everyone was supportive. One male friend told Edie the next morning that he couldn't help fantasizing about Edie with another woman. "Oh, honey," Edie said, laughing it off. She had spent years feeling petrified that her friends would ostracize her—this, she could handle.

Despite having to remain closeted to most of the world, Edie and Thea had a thriving social life in Manhattan and in the Hamptons, where Edie bought a small cottage on the wrong side of the tracks for Thea's birthday in 1968. The couple threw rollicking dinner parties, with Thea, a gifted cook, preparing homard à l'Américaine from Julia Child's *Mastering the Art of French Cooking* for dozens of guests. They went to parties and dances, twirling around dance floors all over New York doing the merengue, the lindy hop, the hully gully. Later, they enjoyed making up lyrics to the latest unintelligible seventies disco hits.

In 1974, after sixteen years at IBM, Edie decided to retire. The company was closing its Manhattan office, and the only remaining positions available in New York City were in sales, which did not interest her. Now in her mid-forties, Edie was burned out from the job and wanted to travel more for pleasure. As a private therapist, Thea could set her own schedule, and if Edie quit, the couple would be able to take trips wherever and whenever they wanted. "I did not see the point of going on," said Edie. "I was exhausted from sixteen years of really working my ass off." It was time for her and Thea to enjoy the fruits of their labors—which they did for three joyous years, touring Europe and reveling in their hard-earned, newfound freedom.

Then, one day in 1977, as they were preparing for a trip to Japan, they realized that Thea had started to drag one foot when she walked. That began a whole new chapter in their lives.

AT FIRST, IT was just a small issue, the kind of thing that happens to hundreds of people every day. Edie made a joke of it, noting that Thea must need a pair of new shoes. Neither woman thought much about it until later, when Thea began stumbling more often. Then Thea couldn't swing a golf club correctly anymore; her foot seemed stuck. Concerned, she made an appointment with a doctor to find out what was wrong.

After examining Thea and giving her a spinal tap, the doctors told her they weren't sure what the problem was. At the time, multiple sclerosis was not as well understood as it is now. But as Thea's condition continued to worsen over the years, they realized that it was something far more debilitating: Thea had progressive multiple sclerosis, which meant that over time she would gradually become quadriplegic, losing motor control over her limbs.

Edie leapt into action, doing research about MS, going to lectures, and even taking a three-month nursing course. Both she and Thea were determined that their lives would change as little as possible, despite the disease. They put up a sign on their refrigerator that said "Don't Postpone Joy" and they meant it.

Thea began using a cane, but within a couple of years, as her legs continued to weaken, she switched to Canadian crutches. What Thea dreaded, though, was the inevitable move to a wheelchair. Then in her late forties, Thea could not get accepted to clinical trials in the United States. The couple hoped that they might be able to get Thea a particular drug that was being tested in the United States but administered in Israel; it had shown promise in treating MS patients at Hadassah Hospital in Jerusalem.

As her motor control continued to deteriorate, Thea and Edie booked their tickets and flew to Tel Aviv in 1980, planning to stay a month. Yet as soon as they arrived, they learned that this new drug was no longer being administered in Israel because patients had experienced serious complications. Edie and Thea were tremendously disappointed, of course, but true to form, they decided to make the most of the situation. They had a month in Israel ahead of them, so they made arrangements to go sightseeing. Although both Edie and Thea were Jewish, they had never had much interest in Judaism until this visit. But from the moment they got off the El Al plane, they both felt a deep connection to Israel and an increased interest in their heritage. They soon realized that there was so much to see in a country that was then still very young, yet also very ancient, and they took full advantage of it.

One day in Jerusalem, while Edie was recovering from a bout of flu in their room at the King David Hotel, Thea made her way down a long flight of steps in the Old City with a taxi driver. When she got to the bottom, Thea realized that there was no way she could get back up the steps. The taxi driver turned to her and said, "Wait—I will go get the army." He returned shortly with three young female soldiers from the Israeli army who had been walking nearby. The women cheerfully strode over, picked Thea up in their interlocked arms like Queen Esther, and started carrying her up the flight of steps. "Stop!" Thea suddenly commanded like an Israeli general. "Please give the driver my camera to take a picture, because nobody will believe this!" That photograph, of a beaming Thea in the arms of those soldiers, still hangs on the wall in Edie's bedroom.

Not long after the Israel trip, Thea was forced to acknowledge that she needed to use a wheelchair. Edie walked into a surgical supply store and bought what she now calls a "goofy blue wheelchair." She had never bought one before, so she did not realize that they could—and should—be tailored to the user's individual needs. "I had no idea that you do all kinds of dimensioning," she explained. "It's like buying a special car." There was a steep learning curve in dealing with Thea's MS as its toll on her body increased.

Over the next twenty-five years, as Thea lost the use of almost all of her limbs, Edie was right by her side. She installed a system of lifts to raise and lower Thea in and out of bed. She swam with Thea in the pool in their Hamptons backyard, working with Thea to keep her joints and muscles as limber as possible. The couple modified their Manhattan apartment, removing a closet to create more space in the hall, widening the doorways, even installing angled mirrors in the kitchen so that Thea could see what was bubbling on the stove. They bought a customized van with a ramp and automatic lockdowns for Thea's wheelchair. Edie often told me that "the MS happened to both of us":

We always had an aide from 8 a.m. to 8 p.m., and then it was my shift. And the doctors kept saying to me, "You can't go on doing this. You need 24-hour help." And I would say, "That's my time with her." And I would throw my arms around her. Eight p.m. on was ours.

Through it all, Thea continued to see patients as a practicing psychologist—including me, for those two sessions in 1991. Although Thea had been using a wheelchair for years by then, in therapy sessions, she projected nothing but strength. She was always impeccably dressed, never a hair out of place, and instead of sitting in her wheelchair, she would transfer herself into an office chair before patients arrived. You would never look at Thea and think she was disabled, because whatever physical limitations she had were more than made up for by the power of her presence.

A friend of mine who saw Thea as a patient for years describes going to her sessions:

> Thea was always perfectly pulled together. She was very cocky. Very definite, no hesitation. And she was usually right about everything. She never stopped being Thea, no matter how diminished her body was.

For me, Thea was a comforting presence, even from afar. Each summer when the New York Gay Pride Parade rolled through town at the end of June, I would walk down lower Fifth Avenue, watching the floats and marchers, and I would inevitably find myself looking for Thea. Occasionally, I would see her on the sidewalk outside their apartment building, sitting in her wheelchair. It somehow gave me a sense of assurance just to see her there, even though we never spoke again after those two sessions in the summer of 1991. I had never met Edie, had no idea what she looked like, and only knew her (from Thea's vivid description) to be a genius mathematician, so I wouldn't have been able to look for her at the parade in any event.

Edie and Thea spent most of their summers in the Hamptons, where Thea could exercise daily in their swimming pool. Always devoted to her patients, Thea offered them a creative way to get their therapy sessions in, even when she was out of the city. As my friend who was Thea's patient explains:

> She started what she called "iced coffee sessions" when she was in the Hamptons. You'd drive all the way there, have a session with her, then have an hour off with iced coffee, thinking about what you said. Then you'd have another session. She developed this because of her illness—she couldn't abandon her patients for that long.

Edie and Thea kept doing everything they had always done—traveling, going out to dinner, having parties with friends. But the one thing they could no longer do, to their great regret, was dance. Much later, Thea would say that this was the one loss that could make her cry. Dancing had been such a huge part of their courtship, and one of their great joys as a couple—which is why Edie finally decided they were going to keep dancing, no matter how they did it. One night at a party, she perched herself on the armrest of Thea's wheelchair, and the two of them zipped around the dance floor, spinning and zooming and laughing like a couple of teenagers.

No matter how dire Thea's physical situation became, neither woman dared to show either sadness or weakness in the face of it. They were afraid to, afraid that if one of them fell apart, they both would fall apart. In fact, as Edie tells it, in all the years they were together, they never cried in front of each other, except for once:

> We did not talk about it. Neither of us ever cried in front of the other. It was always separate. I mean, I knew she cried. I knew she cried when I was sick, and she knew I cried, but never in front of each other. We did not want to risk falling apart. I can remember walking along the street, you know,

crying, and saying to myself, "Look what they done to my song, Ma."

We did cry in front of each other once, but not on the subject of MS, on the subject of hiding, of being in the closet.

We were having some kind of terrific success at something—Thea had been honored and was in the papers, and I said, "Can you imagine what we could have been if we hadn't spent half our effort just hiding who we were?"

At first, Thea said, "Oh, I don't think so at all." But then we talked about it, and by the time we were done with this conversation, we were both crying our heads off. This was the first time that we had ever cried in front of each other.

IN 1993, WHEN New York City began offering domestic partnership to same-sex couples, Edie was ecstatic. It was not marriage, but at long last the couple would finally have some kind of legal recognition for their relationship. "I want us to be one of the first couples to register," Edie told Thea.

"Well, it's going to have to wait," Thea told her. "Because I have appointments with patients all day long."

Edie rarely put her foot down with Thea, but this time she most certainly did. "I have waited almost twenty-seven and three quarter years for this day," she told Thea, "and I am not waiting a single day longer." (It's fair to note that Rachel and I experienced similar tensions on our way to obtaining our own domestic partnership, and for arguably the exact same reason. It was not marriage, so what was the big deal?) Upon seeing the light, Thea cleared her schedule for the day, bought Edie a bouquet of flowers, and they went down to City Hall to register. They were the eightieth same-sex couple to register in New York City.

But as happy as they were to be officially recognized as a couple, domestic partnership still was not marriage. Neither Edie nor

Thea ever gave up their 1967 dream of getting legally married one day, ideally in their home state. But after our loss in the New York marriage case, when it was clear that New York would not be a realistic option for the foreseeable future, they made plans to fly to Toronto. Fortunately for Edie, for me, and for gay couples across America, her friend Brendan Fay had made arrangements with some friends of his who were filmmakers for the ceremony to be filmed. It seemed like a small detail, but would end up making an enormous difference.

6

THE REST WAS
JUST DANCING

The footage is a little shaky, the sound quality isn't great, but there they are: Thea, dressed in a black suit and white turtleneck, a corsage of two red roses pinned to her lapel, and Edie, perched on the armrest of Thea's wheelchair, wearing a cream-colored suit and a string of pearls. It is May 22, 2007, and after more than forty years together, seventy-seven-year-old Edie Windsor and seventy-five-year-old Thea Spyer are finally getting married.

After hearing Thea's grim prognosis, the couple had turned to their friend Brendan Fay for help in arranging their wedding. Brendan, who is a very kind man with a lovely, lilting Irish accent, had started the Civil Marriage Trail Project in 2003, a program to help gay and lesbian Americans make the trip to Canada to marry. By 2007, he had helped dozens of couples already, obtaining wedding licenses, arranging officiants, assisting with any and all details so that the couples could be legally wed.

Everyone knew that this would be a difficult trip for Thea physically. There were so many obstacles: getting through security; transferring Thea out of her wheelchair and into an airplane seat; finding ground transportation that could accommodate her wheelchair. Six friends eagerly volunteered to accompany them to

Toronto. And Brendan Fay arranged for Justice Harvey Brownstone, Canada's first openly gay judge, to officiate.

The ceremony took place at the Sheraton Gateway, a business hotel in Terminal 3 of the Toronto airport. In order to make the setting more appropriate, Edie made exhaustive arrangements to have the conference room decorated because Thea had wanted it that way, ensuring that there were flowers, palm trees, champagne flutes, and a cake, not to mention rose petals sprinkled on the floor. Edie had brought a photo of her and Thea at their fifteenth anniversary, which she propped on the icing in lieu of the traditional bride and groom cake topper.

With their friends seated nearby and the filmmakers capturing everything on video, Edie leaned close to Thea as she sat on the armrest of Thea's wheelchair, and Justice Brownstone began:

> Dear friends and family of Edie and Thea, we are gathered together today to witness a very happy and long-awaited event. Edie and Thea, you are here to obtain legal and societal recognition of your decision to accept each other totally and permanently.
>
> Over the past 41 years, you have been dancing. You have come to know and love each other, you have found joy and meaning together, and you have chosen to live your lives together. Now you seek to unite in marriage, and to this moment you have brought the fullness of your hearts, the dreams that bind you together, and that particular personality and spirit which is uniquely your own.

Edie and Thea had long dreamed of the moment that came next: the chance to say to each other, "With this ring, I thee wed . . . from this day forward as in all days past." Because of the MS, Thea could not move her hands, so one of their friends had to help when the couple exchanged rings, but Thea's voice was firm when she said, with tears streaming down her face, "I, Thea Spyer, choose you, Edie Windsor, to be my lawful wedded spouse." Edie spoke her vows in a quiet voice, slipping the ring onto Thea's finger, and then it was time for Justice Brownstone to speak the words they both had been waiting decades to hear.

Now, therefore, I, Harvey Brownstone, Judge of the Ontario Court of Justice, by virtue of the power invested in me under the Marriage Act of Ontario, do hereby pronounce you, Edith Windsor and Thea Spyer, to be legally married spouses and partners for life.

The look on Thea's face at this moment in the film is both beautiful and heartrending. I have watched it dozens of times by now, but it never fails to make me cry. As Justice Brownstone begins speaking the words "I hereby pronounce you," Thea dissolves into tears, her face flooded with emotion and relief. Edie embraces her, then dabs at Thea's eyes with a tissue. It is a moment that encapsulates so much about their relationship, from the ease and love with which Edie moves to care for Thea, to Thea's look of gratitude and understanding, to the deep and abiding love they so obviously share.

Later, after champagne and the toasts of their friends, Edie says incredulously, "I mean, we're *married*." Then she laughs. "I don't know about all that other stuff for the last forty-two years. The rest was just dancing."

FIVE DAYS LATER, on May 27, 2007, the *New York Times* ran their wedding announcement, complete with a photograph of Edie and Thea. After a lifetime spent in various stages of hiding who they were, the couple was now, officially and totally, out of the closet. The response to their official "coming out" stunned them.

They received hundreds of letters from all over the country

from people they had known in all facets of their lives—from playmates with whom they had grown up to schoolmates to work colleagues. What surprised Edie the most, though, was hearing from dozens of her former colleagues at IBM, the same colleagues she had been so afraid to come out to for all those years. "Almost every single person on my floor wrote to me, thrilled and excited," she said. Some of them asked her why she had lied to them for so many years, and all she could say was, "I had to because I was queer." Edie never could have imagined, in the years when she worked at IBM, that there would come a time when she and Thea could openly, proudly, and joyfully announce their marriage on the wedding page of the *New York Times* of all places.

Here's how Edie described the difference:

> Being married is so different that it's impossible to describe. I ask every single person who has been with someone for any length of time and then gets married, "Was it different the next day?" And every single person says, "Oh my God, yes." There is something profound—it's something that the whole world knows what it means.

For Thea, getting married also meant something else. "I feel like I can die now," she told Edie. "Everything is complete."

Before Edie and Thea left for Toronto, Brendan Fay had asked the filmmakers Greta Olafsdottir and Susan Muska to interview Thea and Edie for him. After the interview, the filmmakers called Edie and Thea with a proposal: they wanted to make a full-length feature documentary about the couple. Could they look for photos from the four decades of their relationship? Edie and Thea agreed. Over the course of the next two years, the filmmakers came and shot footage of the couple looking through old photographs together, doing Thea's exercises in the pool at their Hamptons home, spinning around a dance floor in Thea's wheelchair,

and talking, sometimes tenderly, sometimes humorously or passionately, about what it meant to be a lesbian couple whose love
had survived nearly half a century.

At first Edie, in an effort to protect Thea's dignity, made sure
that there were no shots of Thea appearing truly disabled. She
preferred Thea to be filmed sitting upright in her chair, dressed
for the day, in relative control of her circumstances. But several
weeks before the end of the shooting, Thea had a change of heart.
"You know, I've been thinking about this," she said. "People
need to see that shit happens in life. You can still live and love."
The finished film includes scenes of Edie lowering Thea into the
pool with a big mechanized swing and putting her into bed with
their elaborate pulley system. There is also a particularly touch-
ing scene of Edie pulling Thea's oxygen mask over her nose and
mouth, adjusting it, and kissing her forehead as she says good
night. Thea's decision to reveal the full extent of her disability
was incredibly courageous. To me, as a former patient of hers, it
shows exactly the kind of person, and therapist, Thea was. And,
of course, Thea was right. These scenes have had great meaning
to audiences of the film.

During the last year of her life, Thea was suffering from aortic
stenosis, which was getting worse, and at that time it could only
be treated by open-heart surgery. Thea told Edie she did not want
to have the procedure. "I won't recover," she said. "Please, I don't
want to do it." But there were no other options. As Edie recalls:

That summer, she began to have more angina. She couldn't
take nitroglycerine, so we had morphine. And we were in
Southampton and she had a slightly worse episode, and she
said, "Call the doctor and tell her I don't want to go to the
hospital, but is there anything else they can give me?"

And the doctor said no, that the only thing we could do
was bring her into the hospital in New York City. I said,

"She doesn't want to come to the hospital. She wants to spend the summer in Southampton with friends." And then Thea got on the phone with the doctor and verified that this was how she felt.

When we hung up—in the film, you can see this—she's sitting by the side of the pool, wrapped in a towel, and she said, "I had my summer, and I'm having it now." From there on in, her symptoms were worse, but she was still— there's a picture of us dancing that summer, and she was here at home.

One afternoon, Thea asked Edie, "Am I dying?"

"Probably so," Edie told her. "We're both two old ladies and we're both dying. But extremely slowly."

"Okay," Thea said. "That's all I need to know."

And so their life went on, day by day, through the end of that summer.

As the leaves started to turn to the brilliant colors of a New York fall, Edie and Thea went back to Manhattan. Thea continued to see her patients throughout the winter, even as her heart condition grew worse. Every morning when she woke up, she had terrible pain from angina, which would usually last for about ten minutes. Then, one February morning, the pain did not stop.

"Edie," Thea said, "I'm having trouble breathing." Thea had hospice care at that point, so Edie started to call the hospice. But the card with emergency phone numbers, which was usually posted on the wall, was not there for some reason. Edie shouted, "Where is the hospice phone number?" But before their medical aide could answer, "I know it," Thea said. She had always been able to remember numbers, often telling Edie that her head was so full of everybody's phone numbers that it was a wonder her brain could absorb anything else. She dictated the digits to Edie, who hurried to punch them into the phone. Thea's hospice nurse rushed over, arriving within minutes, but by the time he got there, Thea was gone. On February 5, 2009, at the age of seventy-seven, Thea Spyer died peacefully at her home from aortic stenosis.

Edie made three calls right after Thea died. One was to a friend of theirs, who started a phone tree to let their other friends know. People started showing up at the apartment, and before long the living room was full of friends, everyone reminiscing about Thea. The other two calls, however, were to patients of Thea's; she had two appointments scheduled for that afternoon, so Edie had to call to let them know that Thea had died.

At around five p.m., at Edie's request, everybody cleared out. "I really want to be alone," she told them. For nearly forty-four years, she had been kissing Thea good night. Now she was facing her first night alone without her. She had long known this day would come. She did not fall apart. But Edie was not a young woman either, and the toll of Thea's death would become apparent very soon.

ONE MONTH AFTER Thea died, Edie had a heart attack.

It started mildly, as a bout of stress cardiomyopathy, or broken heart syndrome, a common occurrence in people who have lost longtime spouses. But later her condition worsened considerably, and as a result of complications in the hospital, Edie had "a full-on, total heart stoppage, where there was no connection between the atrium and the ventricle." Edie has described her thoughts and feelings after Thea's death while she was lying there in her hospital bed:

> My state of mind, once I understood what had happened to me, I thought, *I don't have that long to live and I'm going to be pretty sick.* I told my cardiologist, "Send me home. I don't care if you're sending me home to die. It's okay, because I had a

great life, and I can't imagine a life now." And that was true. I was not being sad or dramatic. That was just how I felt.

Edie really did not see the point of going on by herself. Friends came to visit her at the hospital, including Susan, one of the film-makers. Then, on the day Edie was scheduled to go home, Susan came running into her hospital room waving a letter. It was from the San Francisco International LGBT Film Festival, asking if they could be ready by June, just three months away. Would the film be finished? Susan asked, "Can we be ready, Edie?"

"Up and at 'em," Edie told Susan. "Let's do it."

One day, she told Greta and Susan that she needed to see the whole documentary before the screening in San Francisco. The filmmakers balked, insisting that they wanted her to see it for the first time in a movie theater, but Edie was adamant and would not be swayed. "If you had seen me collapse after seeing just the film of us taking our vows, you wouldn't be saying this," she told them. "You do not want me to collapse publicly. I have to see the film first."

Greta and Susan arranged for a private screening, and as Edie watched the sixty-seven minutes of the film, she cried most of the way through, but she loved it anyway. "The film has a number of things that are miraculous for me," she says now. "One is, I can put it on, and there's Thea saying, 'Edie has never changed. She looks exactly like she looked then.' I can't tell you what that makes me feel like today. And the other is Thea saying, 'I had my summer, and I'm having it still.' I could cry right now thinking of that."

Edie & Thea had its world premiere in San Francisco on the day after Edie's eightieth birthday. At the big showing in the Castro, the audience gave Edie a six-minute standing ovation at the end, reporters began calling for interviews, and just like that, Edie was transformed: before the film, she was a sick, grieving spouse with little reason to live; now, suddenly, she and Thea were a source of inspiration to LGBT people everywhere. As the documentary started getting booked for more film festivals and Edie received more requests to speak, she felt all her old energy coming back. And she felt something else—anguish.

Despite the fact that Edie and Thea were legally married, the U.S. government did not see it that way, thanks to section 3 of the Defense of Marriage Act. Had Thea been a man, Edie would not have had to pay estate taxes on anything she had inherited upon Thea's death. But in the eyes of the government, the two women were legal strangers. Adding insult to injury, Edie was hit by a federal estate tax bill of more than $363,000 and a state estate tax bill of more than $275,000. At first, awash in her grief, she had not thought much about it. Now she wanted to fight back.

Over the years, Edie had been careful and methodical in their financial planning. Naturally gifted in math, Edie was able to create sophisticated strategies for investing, even teaching herself the Black-Scholes pricing model for options, typically used only by Wall Street derivatives traders or professional investors. And because she was Edie, she added a touch of whimsy to their financial planning, writing a short book for Thea called (in Dutch) *What Willy Should Know About His Money.*

Yes, this was the same Willy who, depending upon whom you asked, was Thea's brother, Edie's fiancé, or Thea's childhood doll. Edie wrote the book when Thea received the balance of her father's trust from her family and the couple needed to invest it wisely, minimizing tax implications. They set up a system where, from time to time, Thea would give Edie a sizable cash gift, calculated to distribute their finances more evenly while sidestepping tax burdens.

As brilliant as Edie was, she unfortunately had received some bad advice regarding those gifts. As with the estate tax, a husband can always gift funds to his wife without there being any tax liability at all. But because of DOMA, the amounts that Thea had given to Edie over the years were fully taxable, and combined with the current value of their apartment due to the dramatic appreciation in Manhattan real estate, this ended up pushing Thea's estate over the legal limit, which in turn triggered the enormous tax liability that Edie now faced upon Thea's death. Edie was able to pay the six-figure estate tax bills, but only by liquidating investments, mostly municipal bonds that had been earning a high rate of return. As Edie explained, paying that estate tax bill "meant selling a lot of stuff to do it. . . . I live on a fixed income and it wasn't easy."

Edie was angry at having to pay out that money, but more than that, she was, in her own words, "indignant" that the government refused to recognize the relationship that had meant so much to her, and that Thea, ill, weak, and fragile as she was, had gone to such great lengths to formalize legally. "I felt sick that we were being treated the way we were," she said later. So she decided to sue the government in the hope of getting her money back.

Now she needed a lawyer.

THERE WAS AN obvious place for Edie to turn: Lambda Legal, the nonprofit that had been fighting for the legal rights of lesbians and gay men since the early 1970s. Edie and Thea had been donating money to Lambda for years, so she expected to be received warmly. She picked up the phone one day not long after the documentary's premiere and dialed the organization's number.

The first time she called, nobody answered. Edie recalled, "I left a message saying, 'I have a documented marriage, and I'm looking for someone to support my case.'" By "documented marriage," Edie meant the documentary film, not her marriage certificate from Toronto. In Edie's mind, it was the film that proved that she and Thea had a long, committed relationship, which she felt was necessary for filing a lawsuit. This, in itself, was evidence of how far gay people still had to go—what straight couple would feel that they needed a documentary film to prove that they were married? But if it hadn't been for the film, Edie would say later, she never would have had the courage to sue the government in the first place.

Edie was eager to tell the Lambda attorneys about the documentary, but she could not get anyone to call her back. Frustrated by the lack of response, she asked a friend who had once volunteered at Lambda to contact them on her behalf. He did, and finally she got a response. "They had a junior guy who was an attorney," she recalls, "and he said to me, 'I'm sorry, Edie. It's the wrong time for the movement.'"

Edie was crushed. She did not care about timing, she just wanted to get the money back that was rightfully hers. But as with any legal challenge in the LGBT rights movement, timing is everything. In March 2009, just a couple of months before Edie called Lambda, Mary Bonauto and GLAD had filed a lawsuit in Massachusetts challenging DOMA on behalf of eight couples and three widowers. Mary's strategy of attacking DOMA so soon was not exactly greeted with enthusiasm by others in the LGBT movement. Both Lambda and the ACLU took the position that Mary was moving too fast and could create bad legal precedents that would be damaging going forward.

Unfortunately for Edie, that was probably not the only reason Lambda was reluctant to take her case. She was just one person, as opposed to the usual diverse coalition of plaintiffs, so that worked against her as well. And her case was about hundreds of thousands of dollars in estate taxes—money that she had actually been able to pay. Wasn't Edie just a bit too wealthy and privileged to be the face of gay rights in the fight against DOMA?

Now Edie was stuck. Lambda had turned her down. GLAD had its own case and was not an option in any event since they focused on cases in New England. Edie knew better than to try to reach someone at the Human Rights Campaign (HRC) for help, because of an exchange she had had with them a couple of years earlier, while Thea was still alive. The couple had gone to a town meeting where HRC executives were discussing LGBT movement priorities. When one of them dismissed marriage as an issue that should be put off for "years down the pike," Edie stood up and declared, "I'm seventy-seven years old, and I can't wait!" Her outrage had been so casually dismissed that Edie assumed her case against DOMA still would not coincide with HRC's timetable, so she did not bother to make the call.

However, one afternoon not long after Lambda had turned her down, Edie spoke to Brendan Fay, the activist who had helped her and Thea get married in Toronto. Ever energetic and creative, Brendan got in touch with his longtime friend Eddie DeBonis. Eddie worked as a headhunter for law firms, and Brendan explained Edie's situation to him. Could Eddie help find a lawyer to take her case? Eddie told Brendan he'd make calls to a few attorneys and call him back. I knew Eddie through Rachel—he had been active for years in local LGBT politics. When Eddie was married, he and his spouse invited us to attend their wedding, and we in turn invited them to our ceremony in Rhode Island. As a result, Eddie knew all about my work on the New York marriage case, and the first call he made was to me. "Would you talk with her?" he asked.

"Absolutely," I said.

I knew right away who Edith Windsor was, the very same woman Thea had told me about at length in our therapy sessions all those years ago, when both I and the world around me were very different. As I walked the four blocks to Edie's apartment the next morning, on April 30, 2009, I could not wait to meet this octogenarian math genius whom I had heard about from Thea.

Once I got over the shock of being back in the room where I had had those therapy sessions with Thea, it took me about thirty seconds to decide that I would take Edie's case. She was charming, articulate, intelligent, and had an absolutely straightforward complaint: if Thea had been "Theo," Edie would never have had to pay a penny of estate tax. Unlike the LGBT rights organizations that had turned Edie down, I had no constituencies to please or funds to raise; all I had to worry about was the case and the client. To me, this case and this client were perfect.

At Paul, Weiss, lawyers can pretty much take on any case pro bono (literally "for the good," but usually implying without a fee). Our firm has a long and proud history of public service and it encourages all of its attorneys to participate in pro bono cases, which it has always treated with the same care, attention, and resources as any other case. A few years earlier, as a young associate still in the closet, I might have feared that Edie's case would be too controversial, but by 2009 I did not think twice about it. By now, five states (including almost all of New York's neighbors) already had legalized marriage equality. In fact, it didn't even occur to me to ask my law firm for approval since I knew it would be okay.

A word or two about this for the nonlawyers who may be reading this book: looking back on this today, the fact that I was so confident about our firm's long-standing culture and traditions that I didn't call anyone to ask about taking on such an important pro bono case is pretty amazing. (I did call Brad Karp, the chair of Paul, Weiss, a couple of weeks later to tell him about Edie; he was thrilled to hear about it.) I knew that I could take this case. I just had to convince Edie that I was the right person to do it.

There was a large Apple computer sitting on Thea's desk in the corner of the living room where I had met with her as a patient in 1991. I asked Edie if I could show her something, and then I brought up on the large screen the video of my 2006 oral argument in the New York marriage case. "We lost," I told her, "but I think you can see from this that I'm qualified to take your case." I knew that, despite the loss, my oral argument was the best I could have made; in fact, several law school professors had told me that they used it in class to teach oral advocacy.

Edie watched a few minutes. "Yes," she said, "you are definitely smart enough. I loved the way you argued." She paused as a worried look crossed her face. "But how much is this going to cost me?"

"Nothing," I said, making a circular zero with my thumb and forefinger. "You can't afford our fees. We'll do it pro bono."

She was so relieved that I think she might have gasped. "That was mind-blowing," she'd observe later. "After all the refusals, this top-rated law firm will take my case pro bono? I was high, very high."

Edie had her lawyer. And now it was time for both of us to get to work.

7

IT'S ALL ABOUT EDIE, STUPID

One of the first things Edie shared with me was that her doctors had told her that because of her heart condition, she had only a few more years left to live. By the spring of 2009, when we first met, she had already had several heart attacks, including her second near-fatal episode after Thea's death a few months earlier. So right from the very beginning, my goal was to speed up the litigation process as much as we possibly could. I wanted Edie to live long enough to win her case, get her money back from the IRS, and be able to enjoy and celebrate her victory.

However, if the major gay rights organizations had had their way, we never would have filed Edie's lawsuit in the first place. On May 23, 2009, three weeks after I met Edie, the powerhouse legal team of David Boies and Theodore Olson filed a federal lawsuit in California seeking to overturn Proposition 8, the ballot proposition and state constitutional amendment that outlawed marriage between people of the same sex in that state. Passed by voters in the November 2008 election, Prop 8 was obviously a terrible setback. If we could not win a referendum on marriage equality in California, what hope did we have of winning in less progressive states? Yet although Prop 8's passage was an appalling disappointment, this new lawsuit felt to many like a silver lining. Having Ted Olson—a staunch Republican, former solicitor general, and lawyer for George W. Bush in the disputed 2000 presidential election—take on the cause of marriage equality appeared to be a huge step forward for the cause.

Once the Prop 8 suit was filed, however, the major gay rights organizations were not at all happy about it and tried to stop anyone else from trying anything similar. On May 27, 2009, a seven-page press release went out, cosigned by GLAD, Lambda, HRC, the ACLU, and others, urging people to "make change, not lawsuits." The press release offered this as the "bottom line": "If you're ready and it's right for you, get married. But don't go suing right away. Most lawsuits will likely set us all back. There are other ways to fight that are more likely to win."

At one of our early meetings, I showed Edie this press release. "If we file your case," I told her, "we'll probably get a lot of backlash like this." She had to be prepared for criticism, not only from antigay forces but from those on our side, too. Even the Prop 8 team was facing criticism from those who were afraid they were bringing their fight to the courts too soon. What if Olson and Boies fought their case all the way to the United States Supreme Court and lost? A loss could set the marriage equality movement and LGBT rights back many years. Some people even speculated (absurdly, in my view) that Olson, a lifelong conservative Republican, had joined the team for exactly that purpose—as a kind of Machiavellian move to thwart the advancement of gay rights.

As a result, I decided it was best for now to keep our work with Edie tightly under wraps. It would be months before we could file a lawsuit anyway, since we had to go through the time-consuming process of requesting a refund of Edie's tax payments from the IRS, getting it denied, filing an appeal, and waiting for that appeal to be processed and denied again. We had reams of paperwork to take care of and an entire strategy to figure out. So I quietly began assembling a team at Paul, Weiss to work on Edie's case.

Very early on, I called a colleague who had worked on the 2006 New York marriage case with me, Andrew Ehrlich. Soon after, tax attorney Colin Kelly and trust and estates attorney Rachel Harris joined the case, too. Later, I also invited Jaren Janghorbani, an associate (now partner) who had clerked for Justice Stephen Breyer at the Supreme Court, because even at this early juncture, I knew there was at least some chance that Edie's case could go that far. I did not know Jaren personally, but when I called her, she quickly signed on. Right from the start, people were taken with Edie's story and excited to help; Edie's situation seemed to resonate with everyone—gay and straight, young and old, male and female.

I also invited Julie Fink, a sharp young attorney who had just returned to the firm after finishing a yearlong clerkship. I knew that Julie would be a great addition to our team, but what I did not know was that she had recently become involved with a woman, making this case far more resonant for her than I realized.

In fact, not only did I give Julie a chance to work on her first gay-rights case, I also inadvertently outed her to much of the firm in the process. Here's how Julie remembers it:

> While I was clerking, I started dating women. Some people knew, some people did not. When I came back to Paul, Weiss, I remember getting a form from the Human Resources department that asked about diversity. One of the questions was, "Are you openly gay?" I hadn't really told anybody yet, so I wrote "no."
>
> This was in the very beginning of Edie's case, when we had a really small team. The New York legislature had just started talking about gay marriage again, and Robbie would email all of the gay lawyers, the LGBT group at the firm, with updates on what was happening. And because I had marked "no" on that form, I was not included on the list of

openly gay attorneys. So, all those emails would go to "grp-lgbt@paulweiss.com" . . . with a "cc" to "jfink@paulweiss.com."

I finally called the HR person and said, "This is obviously ridiculous. Just put me on the list—it will save Robbie a keystroke, and I'll actually be less out than I am right now."

WITH OUR CORE group in place, we began working on strategy. From the outset, I insisted that we keep the focus on one thing and one thing only: getting Edie's tax payments back. This was a lawsuit in federal court under the U.S. Constitution, not a political campaign to win marriage equality nationwide; it was a case about one elderly widow who had suffered a terrible indignity, and our effort to right that wrong.

As I would with any client, I explained the process in detail to Edie. We would file her case at the U.S. District Court for the Southern District of New York, which would randomly assign one of its judges to the case. Once that judge reached a decision, the losing side would almost certainly appeal, since Edie's case involved determining the constitutionality of a federal statute.

That appeal would then be heard by the U.S. Court of Appeals for the Second Circuit, which covers New York, Connecticut, and Vermont. The Second Circuit would appoint a panel of three judges to make a decision. Once that decision was reached, and appeals filed, the next step would be the Supreme Court, although we had no real expectation that we would ever make it that far. Other lawyers had already filed DOMA challenges, so the chances were slim that the Supreme Court would ultimately choose to hear our case.

In the fight for civil rights, cases can be generated at least two ways. An individual can file a lawsuit, on his or her own initiative, which happens to address a particular civil rights issue. Alternatively, an organization can decide that it wants to challenge a particular law, then look for plaintiffs who have suffered injury and therefore fit the mold for that case. Many judges dislike the latter type of cases, feeling that they are in some sense artificial since they have been constructed by the civil rights lawyers themselves. Second Circuit Chief Judge Dennis Jacobs, who could conceivably end up hearing Edie's case once we made it to that level, had made his feelings on this issue plain in a speech he gave at the Federalist Society:

> My point, in a nutshell, is that much of what we call legal work for the public interest is essentially self-serving: Lawyers use public interest litigation to promote their own agendas, social and political—and (on a wider plane) to promote the power and the role of the legal profession itself . . . [I]t has been reported that some firms in New York City pay money to public-interest groups for the opportunity of litigating the cases that public-interest groups conceive on behalf of the clients they recruit.
>
> There are citizens in every profession, craft and walk of life who are active in promoting their own political views and agendas. When they do this, it is understood that they are advancing their own views and interests. But when lawyers do it, through litigation, it is said to be work for the public interest. . . . Well, sometimes yes, and sometimes no.

So rule number one was: this case was about Edie Windsor and her tax payment—nothing more and nothing less. We would represent her as we would represent any Paul, Weiss client, with a strict focus on the particulars of her case rather than any broader political or ideological concerns. To be honest, this was not a hard decision for me to make since such a client-focused approach was the only one I had been taught and grown up with at Paul, Weiss. There was another obvious advantage to this approach as well. In addition to the risk that a couple or couples might split up, another problem with past gay rights cases with multiple couples as plaintiffs is that, all too often, the facts tended to fade into the background. Thus, rather than looking like a case about real people and their lives, these cases tended to look, unfortunately, more like a debate between pundits on FOX News and MSNBC. By focusing on Edie and only on Edie, we made sure that everyone saw our case as about the essential human dignity of one grieving widow.

Rule number two was: no talking about sex.

In many ways, Edie was the perfect plaintiff. She had been part of a stable, long-term couple, and because Thea was no longer alive, there was no chance they might break up during the case. Edie was articulate, polite, and conservative in appearance, with her pearls, perfectly bobbed hair, and manicured nails. Even though she was a lesbian, as an older woman, she was less threatening to social conservatives than, for example, a young, sexually active gay man. Edie is a beautiful woman, but upon seeing her for the first time, your mind would not necessarily turn to sex. And I wanted to keep it that way.

I had seen Edie speak in public a couple of times after showings of Greta and Susan's documentary, and she was not shy about describing the two maxims that she and Thea lived by: "Don't postpone joy" and "Keep it hot." As innocuous as that latter phrase might seem, I wanted the judges (and potentially Supreme Court justices) to see Edie and Thea's relationship for its qualities of commitment and love, not for anything having remotely to do with their sex life. It just seemed safer that way.

Edie had a rule for me, too. Rule number three was: nowhere in the filings, or in the arguments, or even in conversation, was I ever to refer to Thea as her wife. In their relationship, Thea was the proud butch and Edie was the femme, a dynamic that was quite common in lesbian relationships during the sixties, when they had first become involved. Edie felt strongly that referring to Thea as her wife would be an insult to Thea's memory, so she forbade us from using the term altogether. As far as we were concerned, Thea was, and would always be, Edie's spouse.

With those three rules in mind, we forged ahead and started drafting Edie's complaint. For months, we had managed to keep news of her impending lawsuit from getting out. As it came closer to the time when we would file, however, I grew increasingly nervous about the reaction that the major gay rights organizations would have. We had several meetings with Edie where I would ask, "Are you sure you can handle this? Things could get ugly." She insisted that she could, but I really feared that she would get savaged by both conservatives and progressive groups alike. By now, I was not only extremely fond of Edie, I felt protective of her, too—a dynamic that would only increase over time. Was there any way we could head off possible attacks?

That is when I came up with a plan. Why not bring in one of the very organizations whose reaction I feared? If we had one of the major LGBT groups on our side, it would go a long way toward defusing any criticism from the others. But who could we ask?

The answer occurred to me in a flash: the ACLU. Six years earlier, the ACLU had invited me to become co-counsel in the New York marriage case, so why not return the favor now? The ACLU was obviously a major civil rights organization with significant expertise in this area. I had already worked with James Esseks, now the director of their LGBT and AIDS project, on the New York case. It seemed like the perfect fit, so in September 2010, I called James.

As it turned out, the ACLU was looking for a DOMA case. Despite the May 2009 press release asking people not to start filing lawsuits indiscriminately, two months earlier, on March 3, 2009, GLAD had already filed a challenge to DOMA, *Gill v. Office of Personnel Management*, in Massachusetts. The administrative proceeding that ultimately became the case of *Golinski v. Office of Personnel Management*, on behalf of a lesbian attorney who worked for the federal court system seeking medical insurance for her spouse, had also been filed in California, which Lambda later joined. As a result, the ACLU had decided that it too wanted to take part in a DOMA challenge. When I called James, he was immediately interested. He recalls:

> I read the stuff, and I thought, "Wow. This is a great story"— and not just a great story to tell a judge, but a great story to tell America. Because this is the kind of story that people can identify with, and it will not make them scared and upset. It will get them comfortable with thinking, "You know, I wish my marriage could last 44 years, and how wonderful that she took care of her spouse as she gradually became a quadriplegic over the course of 30 years."

The beauty of Edie Windsor's case was that her personal story was so compelling and moving that people could immediately see the absurdity of how she was being treated. Besides, if you think about it, Edie—an out-and-proud lesbian with parents who had emigrated to Philadelphia as children, a female computer programmer in her eighties who had worked her way through graduate school and who had had a four-decade relationship with a Dutch psychologist whose family had survived the Holocaust— was practically a rainbow coalition all by herself.

Unfortunately, the small cottage in the Hamptons that Edie had bought for Thea for her birthday in 1968 and their Fifth Avenue apartment where I saw Thea as a patient would lead to our first disagreement with the ACLU, soon after they signed on.

"WE WERE WORRIED," James Esseks says now, "about 'How is this going to play?'" He did not add "in Peoria," but he might as well have. "If it plays as privileged rich lady—*boo hoo hoo*—has to pay some taxes, that is not a story that's going to move people."

Even Edie herself had expressed similar concerns early on. "I'm not sure we should use the amount," she told me, "because people will say, 'She's too rich—who gives a damn about that woman and her money?'"

The ACLU urged us not to focus on the amount of Edie's estate tax payment—even to leave it out of the press releases altogether. Yet the injury of the tax payment was the whole point of the case. We were not suing for some theoretical or abstract reason, we were suing to get Edie's money back. It made no sense to pretend that was not true. And although I understood the ACLU's concerns, from the start I did not believe the amount of money involved would really be an issue, so I pushed back.

For one thing, I argued, Edie might have been rich by the standards of middle America, but she certainly was not by Manhattan standards. She and Thea were not exactly Wall Street titans—they lived in a modest two-bedroom apartment that they had first rented and then purchased in 1986, and they had invested Thea's inheritance from her family wisely over the years. More importantly, Edie did not live differently in relation to many of the judges and the justices who might hear her case, and frankly, those were the only people we needed to persuade. I did not buy the notion that any plaintiff challenging DOMA had to appeal to everybody across America—that was just mushy "group think" that had nothing to do with the actual specifics of winning the case.

There was another simple reason why focusing on the money was the right strategy. We had a little joke in the office: *What do conservative right-wingers dislike even more than gay marriage? Taxes.* Edie could have been gay, straight, purple, or from Mars; the fact that she had to shell out $363,000 in estate taxes was sure to raise the hackles of conservatives, who hate taxes in general and the estate tax in particular. In fact, most Americans hate taxes and hate paying unjust taxes even more so. As I seem to recall, our founders had a war about this with the British a couple of centuries ago. Who in their right mind would think this beautiful little old lady, grieving the death of her spouse, should have to pay this huge tax bill simply because she's a lesbian? Fair is fair, no matter the amount of money in question.

Yet James was absolutely right about one thing: we would have to make sure the judges understood Edie's full story. We had to write the complaint in a way that would give the full context to the injury that she had suffered.

Fortunately, this was exactly what I had been trained to do at Paul, Weiss over the years. At many firms, attorneys write complaints in a spare, factual style known as notice pleading. *Plaintiff was standing outside such-and-such restaurant. It was raining. Plaintiff slipped and fell. We are asking for . . .* The goal is to say as little as possible, to simply give the other side notice of what your cause of action is.

Paul, Weiss complaints tend to be more narrative, which I prefer. I believe that the way to win cases is by truly persuading, and often the best way to do that is by effectively telling our client's story. As the associates and I started drafting the complaint, we worked closely with Edie, checking and double-checking facts. I learned the basics from the *Edie & Thea* documentary, then spent hours talking to Edie trying to get additional details. At that point, however, Edie was not used to telling stories from the early decades of her relationship, and she had a hard time thinking in terms of what might help us in our complaint. I tried every angle I could think of to get relevant information out of her, but as I would find out later, she left out some key pieces of her story.

By the fall of 2010, the complaint was ready to go. We started with Edie's story from the very first page:

The plaintiff in this action, Edith Schlain Windsor ("Edie"), met her late spouse, Thea Clara Spyer ("Thea"), nearly a half-century ago at a restaurant in New York City. Edie and Thea went on to spend the rest of Thea's life living together in a loving and committed relationship in New York.

After a wedding engagement that lasted more than forty years, and a life together that would be the envy of any couple, Thea and Edie were finally legally married in Toronto, Canada in 2007. Having spent virtually their entire lives caring for each other in sickness—including Thea's long, brave battle with multiple sclerosis—and in health, Thea and Edie were able to spend the last two years of Thea's life together as married.

We explained that, even though New York legally recognized same-sex marriages performed in Canada, Edie was still required to pay more than $300,000 in federal estate tax because of DOMA. And because of that:

Edie, now 81 years old, faces the rest of her life without Thea, with shrunken retirement savings, and with the added insult of the federal government refusing to recognize the validity of her marriage, not to mention her forty-four-year committed relationship.

That "added insult" was more painful for Edie than any financial loss she suffered. She told me, "I'm so indignant for Thea. I just want to say to them, 'Honor my spouse. Don't turn our relationship into nothing.'" How could the government pretend these two were nothing more than strangers to each other? Surely if people understood who Thea and Edie were, and how much they had been through together, they would see that these women deserved to be treated as a married couple.

In order to make sure the district court judge saw Edie and Thea as three-dimensional people, we dug deep into Thea's and Edie's lives, starting with their childhoods. Thea's was particularly wrenching, a history as rich and dramatic as any play or novel. She had lost her mother as an infant, and as Jews in Holland, her family had witnessed first-hand the devastation wrought by Nazi Germany. She fled Amsterdam with her stepmother as a young girl at the outbreak of the Second World War, going first to London, where her father, a Dutch soldier, later joined them just as the Nazi troops were about to invade, and then to the United States. As a teenager, she enrolled at Sarah Lawrence College, only to be expelled when a campus security guard saw Thea kissing another woman. She continued her schooling elsewhere, ultimately receiving a PhD in clinical psychology.

We went on to tell the story of Edie and Thea's meeting at Portofino, the Memorial Day weekend in the Hamptons when they got together, their engagement years before Stonewall, Thea's MS and years of quadriplegia, their domestic partnership, and finally their wedding in Toronto. In fact, we spent the first thirteen pages of the complaint simply telling Edie and Thea's story, before finally getting to the estate tax on page fourteen and the Defense of Marriage Act on page fifteen.

I hoped that the judge—we did not know who it would be until the District Court assigned one to the case—would see, through reading this story, how irrational DOMA truly was. Toward the end of the complaint, I wrote:

> Congress claimed that DOMA advances the government's interest in defending and nurturing the institution of traditional heterosexual marriage . . . By failing to recognize Thea and Edie's marriage, the federal government does nothing to "nurture" the institution of marriage; rather, it minimizes and denigrates a loving, committed relationship

that should serve as a model for all couples, whether homosexual or heterosexual.

As we were putting the finishing touches on the complaint, I
felt good about our approach. While I was anxious to get it filed,
there was one more hurdle to clear, and it would not be cleared
so easily.

WHEN I INVITED James and the ACLU to join Edie's case, he knew
something I did not: he knew that Mary Bonauto and GLAD,
having already filed *Gill* in Massachusetts, were preparing to file
a second DOMA challenge in Connecticut with another group of
plaintiffs as couples. Because Connecticut and New York are both
served by the Second Circuit Court of Appeals, this meant that
once our two cases moved past district court, we would in some
sense be in direct competition as to which case would get decided
first. And because Mary had long been the undisputed legal face
of the marriage equality fight, she probably would not appreciate
having to compete with another DOMA case.

James was anxious not to step on Mary's toes—in fact, he felt so
torn that for a while, he couldn't decide whether to join our case
at all. He kept asking me for more time to decide, which I reluctantly gave, but I would tell him, "James, the complaint is ready.
We need to file *now*, because Edie's not getting any younger." I
finally told him we would love to have the ACLU as co-counsel,
but that we were going to file either way. He went back and forth,
and when he finally signed on, he insisted that we negotiate with
Mary Bonauto about the timing of our filing.

I had not met Mary at this point in time. While I had admired
her tremendously for the work she had done and considered her
a true hero of the LGBT rights movement, I definitely did not
want to negotiate our filing date with her. I felt sure that she
would argue that it was not good for the movement to have more

than one DOMA challenge in the Second Circuit, and I knew she might even ask us not to file at all so that her case could move smoothly through the court system.

But all I could think was, *Edie deserves to get her money back.* I could not, in good conscience, advise Edie to give up on the $663,000 she had paid in federal and state taxes because filing her case "was not good for the movement." She was my client, she had put her faith in me, and I owed it to her to bring her case before the court, as I had promised her I would. I told James, "I'm not going to talk to Mary. Nothing good can come out of that phone call." My fear was that Mary and I would get into an argument that might make the relationship difficult going forward, and I did not want to take that chance. Even if we were filing two separate cases, we were going to have to work together, so I told James that he would have to take care of this problem on his own.

At the same time, I did not want to come on as the bullish outsider, trampling all over other people's turf. To keep the peace, James and I arrived at a compromise: even though our complaint was ready to go, we would hold off filing it until Mary's was ready, too. James made the proposal to GLAD, and after an endless exchange of e-mails, everyone agreed that we would each file simultaneously on November 9, 2010.

We scheduled a press conference at the LGBT Center on West 13th Street, just a few blocks from Edie's apartment. Expecting no more than a couple of dozen people, we booked a room with just a few rows of chairs. While the *Edie & Thea* documentary had played at film festivals all over the world, Edie was still relatively unknown in New York. I could not wait to present Edie and her case to the world.

8

SOMETIMES, PRAYER WORKS

"Thank you all, each and every one of you, for being here today," Edie said to the twenty or so people assembled in a small, somewhat ramshackle auditorium at the LGBT Center in New York. "This case is extremely important to me, and I am grateful for your presence and support." She was, as always, perfectly put together—dressed in a tailored black suit, purple silk blouse, and the circular diamond engagement pin that Thea had given her in 1967. From the moment she began speaking, she won the room over with her charm and dignity.

This was Edie's first public appearance as plaintiff in the just-filed lawsuit, *Edith Schlain Windsor v. the United States of America*—the official case title that had thrown her into a bit of a panic the first time that she saw it. Edie Windsor versus the entire United States? Who did she think she was? As Edie would later explain in the context of describing how coming out is a continuous process, it was one thing to be an out lesbian, but quite another thing altogether to be "the out lesbian who just happens to be suing the United States of America." But, as she would tell a reporter, "I thought, if Robbie's not terrified, I'm not terrified either."

I was far from terrified. In fact, I was thrilled. After long, tedious months of laying the legal groundwork and worrying constantly about Edie's health, I was relieved that we had finally been able to file her case. During the year and a half since Thea's death, the fight for marriage equality had picked up speed: Vermont, Iowa, New Hampshire, and Washington, DC, had all legalized equal marriage, and in August 2010, a lower court in California had ruled in the Boies and Olson lawsuit that Prop 8 was unconstitutional. That same summer, the seventy-eight-year-old federal judge Joseph Tauro ruled in the case Mary Bonauto had brought in Massachusetts, *Gill v. Office of Personnel Management*, that DOMA was unconstitutional, which meant *Gill* was already at the critical circuit court stage. I was impatient to get our case moving—with Edie front and center.

Putting the spotlight so squarely on one plaintiff was an unusual move in this context. In addition to having multiple plaintiffs, most gay rights cases naturally tended to focus on the organizations that brought them—GLAD, the ACLU, Lambda—since they can cogently articulate the relevant policy issues for each particular case. The Prop 8 case, on the other hand, focused on its star legal team of David Boies and Ted Olson. But highlighting our legal team was not going to make this issue matter or win our case. I knew the focus should be on Edie; she would be the spokesperson for our case, and before long, she would become the spokesperson for our cause. Right now, though, she was just an elderly widow whom we wanted to introduce to the world.

The first press conference "was such a small-time affair compared to most everything that happened after that because people didn't know about the case," remembers James Esseks. "They did not understand her story, didn't understand all that much what we were trying to do. It started out in a very rinky-dink context, a small press conference in the LGBT Center, sort of a little gym/auditorium kind of space with Edie, Robbie, and me up front."

James and Edie spoke, laying out Edie's story and the legal basis for our case, and then I took a turn at the podium.

There is no question that I get the best part of this press conference. Why?—you might ask. Because I get to speak this morning about the plaintiff, Edith or "Edie" Schlain Windsor. It is not very often that a lawyer gets a chance to represent their hero. In fact, it's probably a once-in-a-lifetime opportunity.

I had been searching for a good metaphor to describe how I felt about Edie, and, oddly enough for a case about lesbians, I ended up with a sports analogy. "I kind of feel like the kid who has spent years collecting baseball cards who finally gets to meet his or her favorite, all-star home run hitter. That's exactly what it feels like to have the honor and privilege of representing Edie Windsor." I then launched into what was to be a central theme for the rest of the case:

> We are lucky enough to live in a world that has changed for the better in many ways. So many who did not have rights, including women and gay men and lesbians, now do and many gay people can and do now live their lives openly and with dignity . . .
>
> [I]t is worth remembering that when Edie moved to New York to get her master's degree in mathematics from NYU in the 1960s, no one and I mean no one could be openly gay and pursue a career in any but a few very narrow professions.
>
> That's why when Thea proposed to Edie she did so with a circular diamond pin rather than a ring so that Edie could wear it at her job at IBM and not be "out" at work and risk what might happen if people knew she was a lesbian.
>
> Thea did that in 1967, you heard me correctly—in 1967— two years before the Stonewall rebellion that led to the modern gay rights movement. Take a moment and think about that. In 1967, the idea that two women would be able

to get legally married to each other anywhere in the world much less in the United States was beyond comprehension. That Thea and Edie had the inner conviction, self-worth, foresight and bravery to get engaged at that time is one of the many reasons why Edie is such a hero.

We were finally off and running, although when we found out which district court judge we'd been assigned, I feared it might be more like off and strolling. Judge Barbara Jones was a solid, fair, and moderate judge who I thought would rule our way on the merits of the case, but unfortunately she was known for taking her time in civil cases. I had argued several other cases in front of her, so I knew she was far less tough on the parties about timing in civil cases than other judges in the Southern District. Considering the state of Edie's health, I had hoped for a more aggressive judge—someone who would order the parties to proceed quickly on a "rocket docket"—but when that did not happen, I decided we had better try to give Judge Jones every reason to speed it up.

So on November 22, 2010, less than two weeks after we filed our complaint, I wrote Judge Jones a letter explaining Edie's ongoing health issues.

Given the fact that the fraction of blood pumped by the ventricles of Edie's heart (or her ejection fraction) is very low (40%), her ongoing coronary disease, as well as the fact that she has a rapid heartbeat (or ventricular tachycardia), the decision was made to surgically implant an AICD (or an automatic insertable cardioverter defibrillator) in her chest to prevent sudden cardiac arrest . . .

Edie also carries nitroglycerine tablets with her at all times in order to deal with periodic attacks of angina. Given the circumstances, Edie understandably seeks to pursue this action as expeditiously as possible.

I doubted that this tactic would work, but it was worth a try. We weren't exaggerating any of these medical points—not only had Edie had a serious heart attack after Thea's death, but she had specifically asked me to make sure that I, or someone else, always had her nitroglycerin tablets on hand whenever we were with her at a public appearance. That conversation had a huge impact on me. I was determined to make sure that the court would under-stand the seriousness of Edie's heart condition and the fragility of her health. I truly felt like any time we managed to shave off the process, however slight, might be the margin between Edie living to see her victory—or not.

Three days later was Thanksgiving. Rachel, Jacob, and I were in the Hamptons and I was pretty sure that Edie was as well. I e-mailed her early that morning to invite her over for a lunch of cauliflower soup that I had made from scratch. When she did not reply for a few hours I did not worry, figuring that she probably was not spending Thanksgiving day perched in front of her com-puter. But that afternoon, when she finally did write back, her response—"I had a little heart incident yesterday"—alarmed me. She had become scared being home alone while not feeling well, so a friend had arranged a car service to take her back to the city on Thursday morning.

She was feeling better but was emotional. "My heart is full and behaving," she wrote, "and I'm crying for Thea all day and singing my head off at the same time. So I'm incredibly thankful for everyone here and for you and Rachel and Jacob in my life and . . ." She signed off with that ellipsis, and I felt my eyes well up. We just *had* to win this case for Edie.

The following week, on December 3, we received the court's scheduling order laying out deadlines for filing. Though the order went through April 2011, we were scheduled to still be filing various legal briefs and motions by that point. There was no way around it—this process was going to take time. I forwarded the document to Edie, who wrote back, "I'm exhausted. How does one wait three months?"

So on December 8, I sent another letter to Judge Jones. I informed her that Edie was suffering from an allergic reaction that restricted which medications she could take, and she was spending most of her time confined to her apartment. Once again, I asked the judge to expedite the case in any way possible, adding that we wanted to "inform Your Honor of these developments to the extent that plaintiff's health has any bearing on the Court's consideration of the pending motions."

Over the next year and a half, I would write about a dozen of these letters to Judge Jones, practically begging her to speed up the process. The team jokingly started calling them my "Edie has the sniffles" letters, and though I knew there was a risk we might be annoying the judge, I kept sending them. Julie Fink was worried we were overdoing it. "At certain points, Robbie would call me and say, 'Let's send a letter,' and I would say, 'Are you sure? We just sent one,'" she remembers. While I knew that Judge Jones probably saw the letters as irritating at best and little more than a lawyerly tactic at worst, I also knew that they would serve to remind her that Edie Windsor was a person, not just a name on a lawsuit. I was also confident that Judge Jones, being a fair person, would not hold my letter-writing campaign against Edie, even if she was not pleased with me.

With her various physical ailments, Edie was not having a great winter. And as the holiday season approached, mine was about to get much worse, too.

On December 13, Rachel's father, David Lavine, passed away after a difficult battle with multiple myeloma. Rachel's family is very close-knit, and David's death hit everyone very hard. He was a well-known figure in Connecticut politics, an environmentalist who had written and passed landmark legislation protecting wetlands and other natural resources; he was also a charismatic, handsome, and funny man who adored his family and who was one of my biggest cheerleaders. His death was going to leave a deep chasm in all our lives, including that of our four-year-old son, Jacob.

After David died, Rachel and I found ourselves trying to explain to Jacob what it meant, telling him that it was as if Grandpa David had gone to sleep forever, but that he lived on through us and through all the good that he had done in the world. We were not sure how much Jacob would comprehend about the loss, but as a very sensitive and bright child he understood death and its ramifications. And while he grieved for his Grandpa David, he was emphatic that no one else would ever die—especially none of the three of us. His worry lingered, and one night in his bath he turned to Rachel and quietly asked, "Mommy, can God die?"

"No," Rachel answered, "God is eternal. God never dies. God is within all of us and is something more than all of us." In comforting Jacob, we reminded ourselves of what mattered most— love and our belief that we are all part of something much larger than our individual selves. As far as we know, each of us only has one turn at life, and like my father-in-law, I wanted to make mine matter.

Rachel's family followed the Jewish tradition of sitting shiva at her mother's home in Rhode Island, where we had all gone for his burial and funeral service. Afterward, at the end of December, we went out to the Hamptons. I was physically and mentally exhausted. After the stress of the past couple of months, I just wanted to relax with my wife and child, away from the pressures of work and life for a brief time. One evening, with friends over, I decided to build a fire. Distracted and tired as I carried a few logs into the living room, I slipped on a spot of melted snow on the wooden floor and went flying. I crashed hard, breaking my leg and tearing several ligaments. On top of everything else, I would be ringing in the New Year on crutches. In the course of six frustrating weeks, we had shifted from off and running to off and limping.

BY LATE JANUARY, I was walking on my own again, if a bit stiffly and cautiously. I received a call from Jean Lin, the Department of Justice trial attorney assigned to Edie's case, whom I knew from the New York marriage case when she had worked at the New York Attorney General's Office. As the defendant in our case, the DOJ was required to file its brief on behalf of its client, the United States of America, within sixty days of our November 9 filing. The DOJ had requested, and already been granted, a thirty-day extension, pushing their filing to February. Now Jean was calling to ask me for yet another thirty-day extension, so that they could file their brief in March.

Seriously? I thought. I had been sweating over the timeline for days, writing letter after letter urging Judge Jones to get the case moving, and now the DOJ wanted to delay it even more?

"No way," I said. "Not happening."

Jean was surprised, as it was pretty unusual to turn down such a request from the government, particularly at the beginning of a case. But I didn't care. Edie was fragile. We did not have to agree, and I did not intend to.

About ten minutes later, I received another call from the DOJ—this time from someone a little higher up the totem pole. *We really need this extension,* this person said, with some urgency in his voice. *It would be best if you could just agree to it.*

"No extension," I said. "Not going to happen. I'm sorry, but Edie Windsor is over eighty and in poor health. It is not in our best interest to wait." I hung up, annoyed. The DOJ had already had thirty extra days. I assumed they were planning simply to file a motion to dismiss the case, so what possible reason could they have for not having it ready on time? This was absurd.

On January 21, I received one more call. This time, it was from

Associate Attorney General Tony West, then the number three person at the Department of Justice.

"Robbie," Tony said, "I understand two people have called you, and you've refused to agree to an extension." I readily conceded that he was correct and explained why. "Edie's not getting any younger. We need to get this case moving."

Tony paused, then said, "I'm asking you for an extension because we are seriously considering what position the government should take in this case." He told me that he was having discussions about our case with President Obama and Attorney General Eric Holder, and that they needed more time to decide what to do.

I have to admit, I did not believe him. I thought the Obama administration, like any defendant, was simply playing for time, messing with my client and my case, and I was irritated. DOMA was a terrible law, and I suspected that the government attorneys were not thrilled about having to defend it. Still, the government almost always defends its own laws in cases like this, so I felt they just needed to figure out their strategy and get on with the process, rather than holding everything up.

Given my assumption that this was an unnecessary delaying tactic, I decided to make some demands of my own. "Okay, Tony," I said, "I'll give you the extension, but I want something in exchange. I want you to agree that we won't have any standing issues in the case." If Tony agreed, it would mean the government couldn't argue against us on any technical, non–DOMA-related defense, such as claiming that Edie had "not exhausted her administrative remedies" by taking all the necessary steps to get her tax refund from the IRS. I had been suspecting the DOJ might try a defense like this, since they had already done so in the other DOMA cases.

Tony seemed taken aback. "No way," he said. "I won't give you anything." This type of bargaining was not really how things were done in the world of constitutional litigation, but I did not come from that world. I was a corporate litigator, and this was very much how we did things in my world. I was more than happy to negotiate, but Tony shut that down fast.

"Robbie," he said, his voice even. "I'm telling you that the attorney general of the United States of America himself is asking you for this extension."

"Let me think about it," I said. "I'll call you back." I hung up the phone.

I told my law partner Marty Flumenbaum, who sits in the office next door to mine, about the conversation. When he heard what had transpired, he said, "Robbie, are you crazy? The attorney general is asking for an extension on behalf of the president. Give it to them." Clearly, Marty felt there was no room for debate. Reluctantly, I went back into my office and called Tony.

"Okay, Tony," I said. "We'll give you the extension." Tony thanked me, and the conversation could have, and probably should have, ended there. But I couldn't help myself. I needed to remind Tony whose side the angels were on. "Tony," I said with more than a hint of irony in my voice, "I just want you to know that as you and the president deliberate upon this, I'll be praying for both of you."

THE FACT OF the matter was that the Department of Justice was in a particularly uncomfortable position in our case. Regardless of how Judge Jones ruled, we knew there would be an appeal, as the case was about the constitutionality of a federal statute and had much broader implications than just Edie's personal situation. The eventual appeal would be heard by the United States Court of Appeals for the Second Circuit, and unlike other circuit courts, the Second Circuit had not yet decided how it would analyze laws that discriminated against gay people. Every circuit to have addressed this question to date had concluded that only rational basis review should be applied to such laws.

"Rational basis" is the most deferential form of judicial scrutiny. When a court applies rational basis review, it will uphold the law that's being challenged as long as the government can show any legitimate interest to which the law is tied, however loosely. The government need not even show that the reason it advances is one that actually motivated the law. Nor does it need to show that the law does a very good job of serving the alleged purpose. During meetings with our team, I often referred to this as the "spit test," since it really doesn't take much to satisfy it. If the court decided to assess DOMA under rational basis, we still could win, but we would have a much higher hill to climb.

But the Second Circuit had not yet decided whether rational basis review was the right standard for cases involving discrimination against gay people. If the Second Circuit were to decide that some form of heightened scrutiny should apply to cases involving this kind of discrimination, it would be a very big deal, potentially determining the outcome of the case.

"Heightened scrutiny" encompasses two higher levels above and beyond rational basis—"strict" and "intermediate" scrutiny. When a court looks at a law using either one of these heightened standards, as a practical matter, the burden shifts—the assumption is no longer that the law is constitutional; the burden is now on the defendant (usually the government) to show that the law furthers an "important" government interest and that the law is "substantially related" to that important interest. (Under strict scrutiny, the government's interest in the law must be "compelling" and the law must be "narrowly tailored" to achieve that goal.) In other words, under either one of these tests, there has to be (as I often say) a "pretty damn good reason" for the law to exist as well as a strong connection between what the law actually does and what the law was intended to accomplish. If the court chose to assess DOMA under heightened scrutiny, the chances were very high that we would win.

Most laws are considered under rational basis, because our society has the expectation that legislators know what they are doing and do not generally seek to pass unconstitutional laws. Moreover, *all* laws necessarily draw lines, and we obviously can't have a legal system where all lines are suspect. But heightened scrutiny exists because sometimes laws do unfairly target certain groups of people, such as women and racial minorities. The Supreme Court has pointed to four factors that explain when a law that draws these kinds of distinctions should trigger heightened scrutiny:

1. There is a history of discrimination against that group of people.
2. Being a member of that group does not affect a person's ability to contribute to society.
3. Being a member of that group is not a choice (it is immutable); or, if it is a choice, one shouldn't have to choose not to be a member of the group in order not to be discriminated against.
4. The group doesn't have enough power to protect itself from discrimination through the political process.

DOMA was clearly written to deny gay people federal recognition of their marriages. If we could show that gay people, as a group, fit within this framework, then we could persuade the court to assess DOMA under heightened scrutiny. At that point, the government would have to put up an extremely strong argument to keep the law. I believed we would win our case either way, but getting heightened scrutiny would certainly be a tremendous benefit.

Of the twelve circuit courts in the United States at that time, most had already decided cases that established the precedent that laws affecting gay people should be considered under rational basis. This made the situation easier for the DOJ; its lawyers could just follow that precedent in writing their briefs in the other DOMA cases. In fact, that's exactly what the DOJ had done in Mary Bonauto's *Gill* case in the First Circuit. But because the Second Circuit had no precedent, the DOJ would be forced to take a position. If the DOJ declared in its brief that DOMA should be considered under rational basis, it would be making a strong—and politically unpalatable—statement that gay people did not need or deserve such protection.

James Esseks, on behalf of the ACLU, had already been in discussions with the Justice Department about this issue for a year and a half. As he describes it, "We wanted to put the government in a box. We knew it was not easy for them, but we wanted them to know, 'This is coming.'"

In those meetings, gay rights advocates had been lobbying hard for the government to change its stance on DOMA—partly because of the tone-deaf, insensitive brief that the DOJ had filed back in June 2009 in an earlier DOMA case. In that brief, the government had defended DOMA, which was its responsibility. But what took gay rights advocates by surprise was the language that the DOJ lawyers used.

In one section, the DOJ drew parallels between the plaintiffs' case and (1) an incest case involving an uncle and niece, and (2) a case involving a sixteen-year-old bride. DOMA, the DOJ argued, "permits States to choos[e] to recognize or reject same-sex marriages . . . it adopts on the national level, and permits on the state level, a wait-and-see approach to new forms of marriage."

Incensed by the government's arguments, John Aravosis and Joe Sudbay put up a fiery post on AMERICAblog on June 12 entitled "Obama defends DOMA in federal court. Says banning gay marriage is good for the federal budget. Invokes incest and marrying children." Aravosis and Sudbay called the brief "despicable, and gratuitously homophobic." They then went on to argue: "Before Obama claims he didn't have a choice, he had a

choice. Bush, Reagan, and Clinton all filed briefs in court opposing current federal law as being unconstitutional. . . . Obama
could have done that."

For months, James and others had been working behind the
scenes, doing the difficult, unglamorous work of lobbying to
achieve that result. At a minimum, they wanted to convince the
DOJ to change the way it was defending the law. Best-case sce-
nario, they wanted to convince the DOJ not to defend it at all.

Others were coming on our side, too. On February 13, the *New
York Times* ran an editorial called "In Defense of Marriage, for
All," which concurred with these arguments, declaring that "The
1996 Defense of Marriage Act is indefensible—officially sanc-
tioned discrimination against one group of Americans imposed
during an election year. President Obama seems to know that,
or at least he has called on Congress to repeal it. So why do his
government's lawyers continue to defend the act in court?"

We had given the government lawyers their extra thirty days.
What they would do with that time was anybody's guess.

THE FOLLOWING WEEK, while I was on spring break with my family, I received an e-mail from Brian Martinez at the DOJ asking
about my availability for a call with Tony West. James Esseks,
Mary Bonauto, and Gary Buseck of GLAD were on the e-mail,
too. Seeing that, I felt a surge of excitement. Why would Tony
West need to talk to all of us? There was no reason I could think
of, unless . . .

I sent a quick e-mail to Andrew Ehrlich, now a Paul, Weiss
partner. "I think they are going to tell us they're not defending,"
I wrote. Andrew replied minutes later with "Holy sh*t!!!" As I
dialed in for the call, my hands were shaking.

Once we were all on the line, Tony broke the news I had
not dared to hope for—the government would refuse to defend
DOMA. He told us that President Obama, Attorney General

Holder, and he himself had discussed the matter at great length and had decided that the law was unconstitutional and that they would recommend that the court consider it under heightened scrutiny. Some of the others on the call started asking technical questions, but all I could think was *Who cares about that? They're not defending!* I don't think I have ever been more surprised about anything in my entire life. I literally had tears streaming down my face.

At the end of the call, after Tony had gone through all the logistics about how the DOJ would be announcing their dramatic change in policy, he asked, "Robbie? You remember that thing you said to me before on our call—about praying for me and the president?"

"Yeah," I said. "Of course." I felt a little chagrined, remembering my prior glib tone.

"Well," he said, "I just want *you* to know, Robbie, that *sometimes*, prayer works."

It is almost impossible to overstate how important this decision was for our side—or how brave President Obama had been to make it. It is extremely unusual for the government to decline to defend federal laws, especially when doing so might come at a political cost. In all the back-and-forth with the DOJ, I had remained cynical. I knew what I thought the administration *should* do, but I never dreamed that they would actually do it.

But this ended up being an important lesson for me. In the incredibly fast-paced world that we live in today, with instantaneous news feeds, tweets, and Facebook posts, it is all too easy to fall prey to cynicism, to assume that everything that is done by the president or his administration is part of some Washington, DC, inside game and is not based on principle or policy. And while I generally am allergic to making direct comparisons between the LGBT civil rights movement and the African American civil rights movement, given their stark historical differences,

I think it is no coincidence that it was, in fact, three African American men—President Barack Obama, Attorney General Eric Holder, and Assistant Attorney General Tony West—who made the decision not to defend DOMA. How could they, in good conscience, sit down and write a brief claiming that gay people are not discriminated against? Or that being gay has anything to do with one's ability to contribute to society? Or that gay people can choose not to be gay? Or that gay men and lesbians have so much political power that they don't need to rely on the courts to enforce their constitutional rights? Gay people clearly needed the assistance of the courts to obtain their basic civil rights, and these three courageous men were not willing to argue otherwise.

After I hung up the phone, I hurriedly wrote an e-mail to our team. My hands were still shaking, so it was a bit of a mess:

WE ARE NOT ALLOWED TO TELL ANYONE FOR
2 HRS
DOJ not defending. Subject to heightened scrutiny and DOMA fails. Obama's decision. Will be released in 2 hrs. ltrs to Congress and statement by AG Decision by Obama I'm crying. President will continue to enforce statute pending judicial decision.

That e-mail led to a funny moment—one that perfectly illustrates how far we still have to go to secure rights for everyone. Julie Fink, the associate who had recently come out as a lesbian, had gone on vacation that week with her girlfriend (now wife), Katie. Here's Julie's description of what happened next:

We had just arrived in Jamaica and were standing on line for customs. I had not even thought to check how Jamaica treated gay people, so while we were standing there, I looked it up on my phone.

I turned to Katie and said, "Oh my god, we're in one of the top ten worst countries to be if you're gay. You can literally be killed legally by the government." I told her we'd just have to play it cool, get rooms with two beds. I just—I hadn't really thought about it.

And then right after I got off that web page, I went to check my email, and there was an email from Robbie saying it's still kind of a secret, but the government's going to announce that they're not defending DOMA. And I'm looking at this email, and I just start crying. And Katie says, "What's wrong?"

And I whispered, "Don't worry about it! We'll talk about it later!"

The timing was unbelievable.

The DOJ was stepping down. But now, who would defend DOMA in our case? The answer ended up being not that surprising, although the lawyer who ultimately took on the case was in for some surprises himself.

9

SUPERIOR DANCE

Once President Obama had decided not to defend DOMA, the House of Representatives stepped into the breach. On March 9, the House's Bipartisan Legal Advisory Group (BLAG) voted in a 3–2 party-line vote to defend the law, with House Democratic leaders Nancy Pelosi and Steny Hoyer casting the two dissenting votes. We could have filed a motion opposing BLAG's standing to defend DOMA on behalf of Congress, but we didn't since I was actually pretty happy about it. From the moment the DOJ stood down, I believed that we would win—but our victory would only be seen as truly legitimate if we had a real adversary on the other side of the case.

While there was a lot of discussion within BLAG about exactly how their defense of DOMA would take shape, I did not care that much about any of that, figuring that these were just technical issues the government would work out. I was more interested in finding out who BLAG would choose as its lawyer to represent them in the case. After several weeks and much speculation, BLAG announced on April 18 that it had chosen Paul Clement, a highly regarded conservative attorney with the King & Spalding law firm, to defend DOMA.

BLAG's choice was inspired. Clement was not only a member of the Supreme Court bar, he had also served as the solicitor general for three years under President George W. Bush. He had a reputation as an extremely gifted appellate lawyer. One of the attorneys on our team, Jaren Janghorbani, had watched Clement argue in front of the Supreme Court during her clerkship there, and in her opinion he was "one of, if not the very best" oral advocates she had ever seen. Right now, *Windsor* was just a district court case, so bringing in a lawyer of Clement's caliber was a bit like hiring Itzhak Perlman to play the fiddle at your kid's bar mitzvah.

My Paul, Weiss colleague Neil Kelly fondly remembers that on the day we learned that BLAG had retained Paul Clement, Neil and I, never ones to let moss grow on trees, called Clement's office at King & Spalding. His assistant answered the phone and, taking a message for him, asked me to spell my last name. According to Neil, I spelled out "K-A-P-L-A-N" for her and then, muting the telephone, looked over to Neil and said, "I am the Jewish lesbian from New York City who's going to win this case."

If—and this was a very big if at that point—our case actually made it all the way to the Supreme Court, Clement would be an intimidating opponent. For the moment, however, we were at the trial court, and I felt I had the advantage there. Clement was not really a trial lawyer, but I was. And the Southern District of New York and the Second Circuit were my home courts. For now, I felt confident moving forward, and what happened next gave me even more confidence.

Just one week after Clement took on DOMA's defense, King & Spalding filed a motion that they had changed their mind and would not, in fact, be defending DOMA in court. The firm's chairman, Robert Hays Jr., said in a brief statement that the "process used for vetting this engagement was inadequate." Given this formal language, I had the sense that no one at the firm had anticipated the huge backlash that occurred when the fact that they were defending DOMA became public. From the moment BLAG announced its choice, King & Spalding came under heavy fire from LGBT rights groups, including HRC, which was the most prominent and vocal critic. It apparently contacted many of the firm's clients—including some Fortune 100 companies—to let them know the firm was taking the antigay side in such an important case.

This backlash left King & Spalding in a terrible position. It did not look good for them to defend an antigay law, but it also did not look good for them to abandon a client once they had taken it on. A few hours after the firm's announcement, the situation got even messier when Paul Clement made an announcement of his own, stating that he was leaving King & Spalding for another firm and would in fact continue to defend DOMA. He publicly released a copy of his impassioned resignation letter, which read, in part:

> I take this step not because of strongly held views about this statute. My thoughts about the merits of DOMA are as irrelevant as my views about the dozens of federal statutes that I defended as Solicitor General.
>
> Instead, I resign out of the firmly-held belief that a representation should not be abandoned because the client's legal position is extremely unpopular in certain quarters. Defending unpopular clients is what lawyers do. The adversary system of justice depends on it, especially in cases where the passions run high . . . I recognized from the outset that [DOMA] implicates very sensitive issues that prompt strong views on both sides. But having undertaken the representation, I believe there is no honorable course for me but to complete it.

Clement obviously wanted his decision to be viewed as taking the ethical high road. But if honor requires completing one's representation of a client in the face of public criticism, this leaves open the question whether to take on a particular client in the first place. Since I am 100 percent confident that Clement has zero issues with treating gay people fairly, why did he want to take on this case?

I believe the answer to this question lies, at least in part, in the surprisingly dramatic difference in cultural and legal views of LGBT rights between 2011 and today. At the time that Paul Clement took on DOMA's defense, only five states permitted same-sex marriage. As I write this in 2015, thirty-seven states, covering approximately 72 percent of the U.S. population, allow it today—and there is an excellent chance that by the time this book comes out, the Supreme Court will have ruled that all fifty states must permit it. We have seen a true sea change in attitudes, a shift so fast and complete that it took most Americans (myself included) by complete surprise. When Clement agreed to defend DOMA, it is very likely that he believed the battle over same-sex marriage could still swing either way. After all, in 2011, you could be opposed to marriage equality and still be considered a moderate. Clement was often mentioned as a potential candidate for the Supreme Court, so naturally he (like most lawyers) would welcome the chance to argue such a high-profile case.

Yet even at that time, there were signs that a major shift in public opinion was under way. In December 2010, largely due to the efforts of the Department of Defense's counsel, my friend and former Paul, Weiss partner Jeh Johnson, as well as those of my high school prom date, Aaron Belkin, the U.S. Congress repealed the military's Don't Ask, Don't Tell policy—meaning that in 2011, openly gay people would finally be allowed to serve in the U.S. military. Jeh and I had worked together on the Tokyo case back in the 1990s, and he and I have been close ever since. He's an amazing lawyer, but more than that, he is a great public servant; he is now serving as the Secretary of Homeland Security. With respect to Don't Ask, Don't Tell, Jeh led a national listening tour within the Armed Forces, going to military bases all over the country to ask service people their thoughts, and as a result wrote the report recommending repeal of the legislation. Jeh is truly an unsung hero of the gay rights movement. But now that Don't Ask, Don't Tell was finally dead and gone, how could we allow gay people to fight and die for our country but not allow them to marry the people they loved? Very soon, Americans would start to see the absurdity of that disconnect. In fact, in May of that same year—just one month after King & Spalding withdrew from the DOMA defense—a Gallup poll showed that for the first time, a majority of Americans supported marriage equality.

With any luck, Clement and his team's job would only become more challenging as time went by. And the BLAG lawyers made it more difficult for themselves by virtue of a few missteps early in the case.

DURING A CONFERENCE call between our team and the BLAG team on May 5, one of their lawyers asked us for documentation regarding Edie's first marriage. *Really?* I thought. *This is how you plan to defend DOMA?* Apparently, they believed that the fact that Edie had once briefly been married to a man showed that being gay was a choice. I knew, however, that the details of Edie's first marriage were actually a very powerful argument for our side. In fact, I was so thrilled that BLAG wanted to get into this issue that I actually did my own version of the *Saturday Night Live* Church Lady's Superior Dance with my colleagues in my office, as soon as the call ended.

We asked Edie to tell us the whole story, which we later recounted in a supplemental affidavit to the court.

Before I met Thea, shortly after I graduated from Temple University in 1950, I married a man in Philadelphia.

He was my older brother's best friend, whom I had long

looked up to and respected. He and my brother were friends throughout high school and "hung out" together at our house. They both served as soldiers in World War II—my brother in the Air Force, and his friend in the Army in Europe. The friend often visited my family when he was on leave during the war. During all those years, I had a bit of a crush on him; and he thought of and treated me as a "kid sister."

When the war ended, he and I started college together. By that time, I had matured into a woman, and he had noticed. He began asking me out on dates, and I accepted his offers. Although I had had the feeling that I was attracted to women, and not men, since I was a young girl, I never considered the possibility of consummating those feelings with anyone, and I did not want to. In the context of the homophobia that was so prevalent in the 1950s, I certainly did not want to be a "queer." Instead, I wanted to live a "normal" life.

I cared very much for him, and I was able to convince myself that I could have a life together with him. He was exactly what most girls wanted in a man. He was big, handsome and strong, yet sweet. I think that if I had been straight, he would have been the love of my life. We went to all the dances together and did the things that couples did back then, which did not include physical intimacy prior to marriage.

During our third year of college, he asked me to marry him, and I accepted.

Soon after the engagement, I met and developed, for the first time in my life, strong romantic feelings for another person, a female classmate of mine at Temple University. I fell deeply in love with her.

I did not know what to do next, but I had such terribly strong feelings for this woman that I decided I needed to break off my engagement. I told my fiancé that I was not ready to get married. Inside, however, I knew that I needed to figure how to deal with my love for this woman.

Of course, times were very different then—people did not even talk about being gay or the possibility of having a life with someone of the same sex. I associated my same-sex attractions with shame, and I did not want to be "queer." In fact, people tried to reassure me that I was not destined to be "queer." I therefore tried to stick it out with my fiancé.

Although I would get jealous when I saw two women together on the street on a Saturday night, what I thought I really wanted was to be like my older sister—to have a husband, children and lead a "normal" life. Because of the intense social pressure and homophobia, even the woman I fell in love with in college was not interested in staying together in a relationship with me.

Meanwhile, this man persisted and kept asking me out. I loved him and so did my whole family; everyone thought we made a great pair. My time with him was wonderful in many ways, although not romantically, as I soon discovered after we were married in May 1951.

After the wedding, it did not take long for me to realize that I could not fulfill any of his or my own expectations for the relationship. I couldn't love him the way a wife should love her husband, and, after a few months, I told him so. I also explained that I was yearning for women and that I needed something else in my life. I explained to him that he deserved much better, and that I wanted him to have someone in his life for whom he was the most desirable person imaginable.

And so, with a heavy heart, I moved back in with my mother. My husband and I soon divorced on March 3, 1952.

Edie Windsor had every reason in the world of the early 1950s to want to be straight and married: societal pressure, family expectations, the commitment of a good man whom she adored. But she simply could not do it. As Edie recounted in her interview with Nina Totenberg of NPR, "I told him the truth. I said, 'Honey, you deserve a lot more. You deserve somebody who thinks you're the best because you are. And I need something else.'" As Edie told me this story, I remembered my own feelings while in college, when I had been so desperate not to be gay that I thought, *Maybe I should just marry a man and make do.* But like Edie, I knew in the end that I just could not do that to another person. It would be not only dishonest, but cruel.

If BLAG thought that Edie's first marriage and divorce proved gay people could choose their sexual orientation, I was more than happy to help them make that blunder. As a matter of fact, Edie's first marriage proved exactly the opposite—that she had no choice about being gay. We entered Edie's marriage and divorce certificates from Philadelphia into the record, and I felt encouraged that BLAG seemed to be off the mark in its preparation for the case—an impression that only grew as we moved deeper into the discovery phase.

BY THE TIME Paul Clement came on board, five long months had passed since we had filed Edie's suit, and virtually nothing had happened; despite my "Edie has the sniffles" letters, we had made no progress in actually moving the case forward. Between the DOJ's two thirty-day extensions, the appointment of BLAG, and the kerfuffle between Clement and King & Spalding, we had faced delay upon delay, none of which were the result of anything we had set in motion, so I was even more desperate to get the process moving. We set up a conference in early May with the BLAG lawyers and Magistrate Judge James Francis, who was handling scheduling and other pretrial matters on behalf of Judge Jones, to discuss the schedule. I was a woman on a mission.

Normally, the process in a case like this is both rigidly defined

and predictable. Typically, the first thing that happens after a complaint is filed is that the defendant files a motion to dismiss the case
on the ground that the plaintiff has failed to plead valid causes of
action. The plaintiff then files a brief opposing dismissal. Then,
assuming the court denies the motion to dismiss, both sides engage
in discovery, which involves producing documents, taking depositions, and compiling the affidavits and briefs that will explain the
facts of the case for the judge. At the close of discovery, either or
both sides can file a motion for summary judgment based on the
evidence marshalled during discovery, which the judge may or
may not grant. As a result, both sides already knew how this case
would unfold, but I hoped that in this conference, we could at least
urge the magistrate judge to help it unfold as quickly as possible.

"We're ready to go," I told Judge Francis. "If BLAG files their
motion to dismiss according to schedule, we can both oppose it
and at the same time file our own motion for summary judgment
immediately after that." In other (nonlegal jargon) words, *Let's get
this show on the road!*

You could practically hear the tires screeching to a halt as the
BLAG attorney told the judge, "We're not ready." I believe I
actually let out a groan. The defense did not care how long this
process took—and why should they? In court cases, delay is often
the rule, not the exception, particularly for defendants, so this was
just business as usual. BLAG wanted more time, and we could not
file our motion until they had filed theirs, so we were stuck; there
was literally nothing we could do to speed up the process. Unless
we just threw the process out the window altogether.

"Fine," I said. "If you guys aren't ready to file your motion to
dismiss, then we'll file our motion for summary judgment first. We
all know what the arguments are, so what difference does it make
which order we go in? Let's just do it this way—it will save time."

The BLAG lawyers looked stunned, as if I had suggested per-
forming the final crypt scene in a production of *Romeo and Juliet*

before the balcony scene. In the buttoned-up world of judicial process, a move like this was beyond unorthodox—it was extraordinary. But at this point, I cared far more about timing than about process. I did not know if switching the order of filings had ever been done before, but why not try it?

James Esseks was stunned, too, saying later that the move put everything "kind of ass-backwards." But fortunately, Judge Francis liked my idea. He actually seemed irritated that BLAG had asked to delay the case again, so he went a step further and set up an expedited schedule: we would exchange written discovery requests by June 3, and the discovery process had to be finished by July 11. This gave BLAG's attorneys only a couple of weeks to depose our experts, which they were not happy about. Despite their protests, Judge Francis held firm. I was ecstatic. At long last, we might actually be able to get this case moving. We left the conference ready to plunge into discovery.

Doing discovery in a civil case is a bit like undertaking an archaeological dig. It can be slow and tedious work, akin to sifting through mountains of dirt (or in today's world, gigabytes of data) to find valuable pottery shards. But doing discovery well is often the key to winning cases.

I had learned an important lesson from our mistakes in the 2006 New York marriage case, when we had failed to submit experts on our side to bolster our arguments. This time, we made sure to compile affidavits that covered all the bases. They included affidavits from UCLA psychology professor Letitia Anne Peplau, pointing out that sexual orientation exists and is stable over time; Yale history professor George Chauncey, demonstrating that gay people have been subjected to discrimination; and Cambridge child psychology professor Michael Lamb, concluding that children raised by same-sex parents do just as well as children raised by opposite-sex parents.

We also submitted affidavits from Harvard history professor

Nancy Cott, explaining that marriage has changed dramatically over time and has always been the purview of the states, rather than the federal government; and from Stanford political science professor Gary Segura, demonstrating that gay people as a group do not possess a meaningful amount of political power. By contrast, BLAG decided against using any of their own expert witnesses at all.

Our expert affidavits would serve to strengthen our argument to Judge Jones by establishing a firm factual record upon which we had built the case. We worked closely with the experts to compile their affidavits, after which BLAG would have a chance to question our experts at depositions, in hopes of finding cracks in their arguments. Unfortunately for their side—but luckily for us—Paul Clement did not do the depositions himself. Instead, he sent a brand-new attorney from his firm to take the depositions of our expert witnesses.

During the depositions, this young BLAG lawyer seemed nervous and ill-prepared. Granted, he was facing a difficult task, trying to poke holes in the arguments of academics who were among the foremost experts in their fields. Often he seemed to be throwing whatever he could at the wall in the hope that something might stick. With Harvard professor Nancy Cott, our expert on the role of the states in marriage, for example, he veered into polygamy during the nineteenth-century in the Utah Territory, the marriages of freed slaves during Reconstruction, and the regulation of Native American affairs by the federal government. Cott calmly refuted all his points, and he then tried out a few more tropes about the supposed slippery slope of polygamy before giving up. If anything, Cott's position was stronger after her deposition than before it.

Sometimes it seemed as if the BLAG lawyer was just going through the motions. While questioning Stanford professor Gary Segura, however, he actually went a bit off the rails. Segura was our political science expert, so the BLAG lawyer was trying to elicit a response showing that gay people actually had a significant degree of political power. But the way he did it was somewhat curious, to say the least.

"I have a good friend, who is a celibate, chaste gay man," the lawyer said. "He believes that gay marriage should be banned. And would his interests be different from the rest of gays and lesbians? How would you analyze that?"

This was an odd question for a deposition (even one in this case), to say the least. While I could not figure out where he was going with this, I saw no reason to prevent Professor Segura from answering the question. "Objection to the form," I said, and then turning to Professor Segura, "You can answer," I said. He replied:

> I would say [that] [t]here are individuals with lots of different positions on lots of different matters. When I am looking at what a group's interest is, I would look for the consensus viewpoint among the largest percentage of that population. In this case, I think your friend is very, very out of the mainstream of thinking of others who would self-identify as gay or lesbian.

At this point, I glanced at the BLAG lawyer and saw that his face had flushed deep red. I was not sure where he was going with this, but the exchange seemed to be striking a personal chord. Even though we were on opposing sides, I had no interest in embarrassing him or seeing him sweat, so I jumped in. "At some point I need to take a break," I said. "Let me know when would be good for you."

"Now is a good time to take a break," the young lawyer croaked. I wish I could say that he regained his composure afterward, but unfortunately he never really did. It was one of the odder depositions I had ever experienced.

In defense of that young attorney, it was not easy being on the pro-DOMA side of the table, from either an evidentiary or a strategic standpoint. Even though President Obama had declined to defend the law, the DOJ was still technically a party to the case, so several of their attorneys came to the depositions. They would sit on BLAG's side of the table, but they always came over to us beforehand to shake hands and say things like, "Sorry about this. Obviously, we're with you." During lunch breaks, the DOJ lawyers would often join us, while the BLAG attorneys would sit off by themselves.

At this point, I had enough confidence in our arguments that I was willing to give BLAG whatever they wanted, as long as it kept the process moving. I would say, "Listen, whatever documents you want, just ask us. We'll give you everything." To my surprise, the BLAG lawyers did not ask for much. Although they could have asked to depose Edie, they chose not to. They probably believed it would look bad for them to interrogate an eighty-two-year-old widow in hopes of denigrating her forty-four-year-long relationship with the now deceased love of her life—a wise call on their part.

In the nuts and bolts of trial preparation, we were clearly ahead. Meanwhile, outside the conference rooms where our team was building her case, Edie was also starting to gain attention in the battle for public opinion.

OUT MAGAZINE'S JANUARY 2011 profile of Edie was the first in what was to become an avalanche of coverage. That spring, a Boston-based lesbian publication called GO magazine included Edie in its "100 Women We Love" issue, and the ACLU announced that it would award its Roger Baldwin Medal of Liberty to Edie, who would be honored along with Constance McMillen, a young lesbian who had sued her Mississippi school district for barring her from attending the prom with a female date. Writer Jill Hamburg

Coplan also contacted us, hoping to do an interview with Edie for an extensive profile in New York University's alumni magazine.

When I e-mailed Edie to ask if she wanted to do the interview, she responded with weariness. In a June 7 e-mail, she wrote, "I feel overdone and I don't have a lot to say publicly . . . I just don't have the energy. Right now, I'm stalling doctor's appointments until I finish the whole Pride month activities . . . Just too much."

Edie's e-mail worried me because she usually relished her public appearances. She loved giving speeches, and she seemed to truly enjoy plunging headlong into crowds, sometimes with an enthusiasm that outstripped her sense of self-preservation. But she was in her eighties now, with the vast catalogue of minor ailments that age brings, not to mention her ongoing heart trouble. I was constantly worried about her health and safety, especially since her activities and profile increased the deeper we got into the case.

One thing I did to alleviate my anxieties in this regard was to begin asking some of the younger associates to serve as Edie's "body person." Whenever Edie went anywhere related to the case, whether it was down the street or across the country, someone on our team would accompany her. At first, she did not seem to mind. In fact, she enjoyed being escorted by Paul, Weiss associates. But later, as time went on, Edie began to chafe at being "handled." She would say, "I'm going to the bathroom," and then disappear for half an hour. Alexia Koritz called this "giving us the slip," and Edie became very good at it. "She didn't like the idea of someone taking care of her, really," Alexia remembers. "Once, at Georgetown law school, we were getting her lunch and she just took off to see students and talk to them."

Jaren Janghorbani remembers that one of the perennial battles that everyone fought with Edie was to prevent her from taking the subway. "You'd arrange for the black car, then pick her up, then take her to where you needed her to be, making sure everything was taken care of," she says. "But Edie never wanted to do any of that. She just wanted to get on the subway. She didn't want to sit in traffic. She did not want to wait for the car. We all used to joke about it, like, 'Robbie's going to kill us if we lose Edie on the subway.' The last thing we needed to do was get into trouble with Robbie for taking our beautiful old client onto the subway and losing track of her." Edie was not trying to make life difficult for the associates; she just wanted to do her own thing—even if that thing meant heartburn for whoever was traveling with her.

On the other hand, traveling with Edie gave people on the team a chance to really bond with her. In June, when Edie flew to Orlando to accept the ACLU award, Julie Fink went with her. "This was not a normal Paul, Weiss assignment, to be a fifth-year associate who's flying to Florida to accompany your client to get an award," Julie remembers. But although it was an unusual assignment, Julie found herself grateful for the time she spent with Edie.

On the flight down, they did math puzzles together and talked for hours. "It was great to talk with Edie about her relationships, and her and Thea, and how they met," says Julie. "We just got to know each other very well. It's not a normal client-lawyer relationship, the relationship we all have with each other—whether it's Robbie and Edie, or me and Edie, or Jaren, or Alexia, or anyone else. The whole team was more like a family than anything else."

At the ACLU event, Julie played bodyguard to Edie, who was greeted like a rock star. "Everybody wanted to buy Edie a drink," Julie recalls. Edie happily obliged, accepting (though not always drinking) the only alcohol she's not allergic to, vodka, and posing for photographs with everyone who asked. Her fame was growing and her story was getting out, which could only help us. More than ever, I believed that if people came to know Edie well and learned the details of her four decades with Thea, they would come to see DOMA as an unfair, discriminatory, antigay relic.

For that reason, I wanted to make sure that every one of our court filings focused on Edie's personal story as much as possible.

Which is why, around that same time, I gave Julie another unusual assignment. One of the briefs drafted by our side felt too lawyerly to me. "The draft of this brief is terrible. It's not up to Paul, Weiss standards," I told Julie. "I want more feeling in it, more emotion. I want a brief that is in keeping with the greatest traditions of this law firm." She did not say anything, so I said, "Listen, you need to 'Julie this up.' Go have a drink somewhere, take Jaren with you—get drunk if you have to—but fix this brief."

Julie took my advice, literally. She called Jaren and invited her to Ted's Montana Grill, a restaurant across the street from the office. Over beer and pickles, they talked at length about the filing, with Julie finally deciding that "I wanted someone to read this legal document and cry. These women devoted their whole lives to each other. Thea was sick for thirty years, and Edie took care of her. Whatever relationship you, the reader of this brief have, this is the one you'd rather have. And the government has discarded it."

The next draft of the brief was brilliant, as was so much of the work the team did. On June 24, we filed our five expert affidavits, as well as our motion for summary judgment. I happened to be on a family trip to Israel with Rachel and Jacob, and though I did not mind being away for the filings, I was sorry to miss another big event that happened to take place that very same day.

WE WERE SITTING at a restaurant in the Neve Tzedek (ironically, in Hebrew, "abode of justice") neighborhood of Tel Aviv, enjoying a meal of Israeli-style Spanish tapas, when my BlackBerry buzzed. I looked at the message and let out a whoop of joy: the New York legislature had just passed the Marriage Equality Act, making it legal for gay New Yorkers to marry. Five years after I had lost the *Hernandez* case, forcing Edie and Thea—and countless other gay New Yorkers—to travel to Canada to wed, same-sex couples would finally be able to marry in our own home state.

We had known that there was a fierce battle going on behind the scenes in the New York legislature because one of Rachel's and my closest friends, and one of New York's top political consultants, Emily Giske, was leading the charge. (My former client Danny O'Donnell, perhaps at least in part because of our defeat at the Court of Appeals in 2006, had over the years become one of the most prominent legislative sponsors of the bill.) Emily had been sending me a series of e-mails that, in her own inimitable style, became terser and terser as time went on. I could always tell how the political situation was changing by the number and volume of e-mails that Emily sent—the fewer and briefer the e-mails, the better the chances of passage. But I do not think that anyone else outside of Albany had any realistic conception that the legislation might actually pass in 2011. Just a year and a half earlier, the state senate had rejected a marriage equality bill by a vote of 38–24—a resounding defeat that we had watched, heartbroken, on closed-circuit TV in a conference room at Paul, Weiss. And in late 2010, when then–Governor David Paterson had floated the idea of trying to pass a marriage equality bill during the legislature's lame-duck session, he had given up when it was clear the votes simply were not there.

So, while I had every confidence in my friend Emily's political skills, I had tried not to get my hopes up. The news that New York had just become the sixth state to extend marriage rights to gays and lesbians was incredibly gratifying, and it was also good news for our case.

The fact that we were bringing a DOMA challenge in a state that did not permit marriage between same-sex partners had always been a bit of a wrench in our case. From a technical, legal standpoint it was not an impediment, since New York did officially recognize such marriages when performed in Canada. From a perception standpoint, however, it certainly was not the strongest fact for our case. Now that New York was permitting marriage—and even better, by legislative vote rather than by court order—we were instantly on stronger footing.

Governor Cuomo, who had played a key role in championing marriage equality, signed the legislation into law that very same day, Friday, June 24—the first day of New York City's Pride weekend. Rachel and I wanted more than anything to be back in New York for the parade that Sunday, but we were not scheduled to leave Tel Aviv until the 28th. We did check out a few earlier flights online, but with the time zone differences and the length of the trip, we simply could not make it back in time. I was very sorry we would miss the parade and the community outpouring of joy, but at least I knew that when we did get back, we would be returning to a changed New York. Edie's case would be stronger than ever.

Late that night, I received an e-mail from my law partner Andrew Ehrlich, who had worked with me on the 2006 *Hernandez* case and was the very first colleague I had brought in to help with Edie's case. "We have come a long way since that terrible morning we got the *Hernandez* decision," he wrote. "Thank you for letting me be part of the journey. Congratulations."

The dominoes appeared to be falling our way—which is perhaps why BLAG, two weeks later, began flailing a bit in their filings, making claims that went beyond unlikely and into the realm of the absurd.

10

PROFESSOR DIAMOND AND CAPTAIN UNDERPANTS

I f Thea had been "Theo"—in other words, if she had been born a man rather than a woman—then Edie, upon being widowed, would not have had to pay a single penny of estate tax on her inheritance. This was a simple fact, true in all fifty states, and it was a pillar of our case. If we could establish this fact to the satisfaction of the court, then we could focus our argument on the fact that DOMA, and DOMA alone, was the reason why Edie was forced to pay those taxes.

In a court case, however, you cannot just say that a statement is a fact. Establishing an undisputed fact for purposes of a case can be a two-step process: first, the plaintiff files "requests for admissions," laying out the factual groundwork for the case. Then the defense responds by either admitting or denying the truth of each fact asserted, with the goal of eliminating unnecessary argument over elements of the case that everyone can and should be able to agree on. In its response to our filing, which asked BLAG to admit as fact that Edie would not have paid those taxes if Thea had been a man, BLAG asserted that they were "without sufficient knowledge or information to admit or deny whether this hypothetical estate would have been entitled to the marital tax deduction."

It was a pretty disingenuous answer, and not their only one. When we asked BLAG to admit that "lesbians and gay men have experienced a history of unequal treatment in the United States because of their sexual orientation," BLAG replied that the statement was "undefined and vague." In fact, of the twenty-eight requests for admission we filed, BLAG failed to provide any meaningful response to twenty-three of them, stating over and over again that the terms and phrases we used were "undefined," "vague," or both.

To a certain extent, this was just lawyers lawyering. Court battles commonly go this way, with no side wanting to cede an inch of territory to the other side. I didn't mind most of BLAG's posturing, because I had fully expected them to reject a certain number of our requests as a matter of course. But the two that rankled were their refusal to acknowledge that Edie paid those taxes solely because Thea was a woman, and their insistence that they had no idea what we meant by "discrimination." We answered with a sharp letter to Magistrate Judge Francis, skewering BLAG for its nonresponses:

> [T]here is clearly nothing even remotely vague about terms like "discrimination," "unequal treatment," "stereotypes," "denied jobs," or "terminated from jobs." . . . These phrases are not part of some technical or scientific jargon, are common English words, and mean precisely what their plain language indicates. . . .
>
> Moreover, it is simply not plausible that the House of Representatives does not understand what the term "discrimination" means in light of the fact that there are numerous federal statutes directly addressed to prohibiting discrimination (albeit none that would protect gay men and lesbians).

Ten days later, the magistrate judge issued his order: BLAG would not have to respond to most of our requests for admission, because the issues presented were too complex. "Any complete answer to the questions posed here could fill volumes and would not serve to streamline the litigation," he wrote. Magistrate Judge Francis did, however, order BLAG to admit or deny our central point—namely, that Edie would not have had to pay any estate taxes if Thea had been a man. BLAG ultimately did admit that this was true, an admission that would play a big role later at the Supreme Court. Our case was getting stronger—and then, once again, BLAG made a misstep that we were able to exploit.

One of BLAG's core arguments in the case was that being gay was a choice rather than immutable. This was the reason they had asked for documentation of Edie's first marriage—they wanted to show that Edie supposedly had a choice about being a lesbian since she had once been married to a man. In the discovery process, rather than asking experts to file affidavits in support of their argument, BLAG chose instead to cite published articles. One was by a researcher named Lisa Diamond, an associate professor of psychology and gender studies at the University of Utah, who had written a book called *Sexual Fluidity: Understanding Women's Love and Desire.*

I had never heard of Lisa Diamond, but when I Googled her, I made several surprising discoveries. First, she had been publishing articles about lesbians and lesbian sexuality for years, not the typical résumé of a person who wants to be part of a DOMA defense. As I scrolled through her list of publications, awards, and grants, I became convinced that she was more likely on our side than BLAG's. Then I found the holy grail: a 2008 interview in the *Salt Lake Tribune* where she explained that her research had been misused by an antigay group called NARTH:

If NARTH had read the study more carefully they would find that it is not supported by my data at all. I bent over backward to make it difficult for my work to be misused,

and to no avail. When people are motivated to twist something for political purposes, they'll find a way to do it.

It was astonishing. Diamond had stated plainly that she did
not want her research being used to bolster antigay arguments
about "immutability," and yet the BLAG attorneys either did not
know this fact or chose to ignore it. Unless Diamond had suddenly changed her mind over the last year or so, BLAG had just
made a crucial mistake—one that I could hardly wait to take
advantage of.

I decided that we should contact Diamond ourselves, in the
hope that she might be willing to repudiate BLAG's use of her
research in our case. It is unusual, and risky, to contact an academic whose work is cited by your opponent. You have no idea
how she or he might react, and the conversations are not considered privileged, because that person is not your expert or your
client. Here, however, the potential benefit clearly outweighed
the risk. Instead of making the call myself, I asked my Paul, Weiss
partner Craig Benson to do it, to keep things under the radar in
case Professor Diamond did not respond well. Craig called her
on August 18, leaving a voice mail message letting her know that
BLAG had cited her work and asking whether she would be interested in filing an affidavit to counter BLAG's claims.

She shot back an e-mail that same day. "Craig, just listened to
your message," she wrote. "You are correct, they are misusing my
work (and as you mentioned, it's not the first time . . . grrrrr!!!). I can
do the affidavit—let's talk by phone tomorrow about the details."

Over the next week, we worked with Professor Diamond to
prepare and file a short affidavit—one that BLAG had no idea
was coming. In it, Professor Diamond slammed the opposition,
declaring, "BLAG misconstrues and distorts my research find-
ings, which do not support the position for which BLAG cites
them . . . BLAG has incorrectly characterized my research." And,

in case it was not already abundantly clear, "Counsel for BLAG never requested that I serve as an expert witness for them in the above-referenced lawsuit. If they had so requested, I would not have agreed to do so."

Later in their brief, BLAG actually had the chutzpah to continue to cite Diamond's work to support the following proposition:

> Plaintiff's claim runs headlong into the different definition of the terms "sexual orientation," "homosexual," "gay," and "lesbian" . . . These differing definitions show that these terms are amorphous and do not adequately describe a particular class.

In response, we included in our brief what is probably one of my favorite passages in any of our briefs in the case:

> Perhaps most surprising, is BLAG's assertion . . . that there is no such thing as a "class" of gay men and lesbians . . . [W]hat BLAG appears to be saying is that because academics in the field do not uniformly agree upon the precise definition of terms like "gay" or "lesbian," what constitutes a homosexual sexual orientation is too amorphous for lesbians and gay men to constitute an identifiable class of persons for purposes of the United States Constitution.
>
> We respectfully would ask the Court to take a minute or two to pause on this statement given the reality of life today in the United States. When a relative, friend, or colleague says that he is gay, is it really credible (or even intellectually honest) for BLAG to argue that it is impossible to know what that person is talking about?

SO FAR, IN the battle of filings, we were outflanking BLAG pretty well—except for one thing. I was still troubled that BLAG got

away with refusing to admit that gay men and lesbians had historically experienced discrimination in our country. It seemed obvious and incontestable to me, but following the magistrate judge's
order, at least technically for the purposes of our case, it was still
up for debate. I wanted to make the point clearly and inarguably,
so I turned to Edie.

"BLAG is making the argument that discrimination against
gay people was never that bad," I told her. "Do you have any stories where you felt discriminated against? Anything at all?"

I had asked her this question numerous times as we were preparing her complaint, and she had always responded that nothing
negative had ever happened to her because of being gay. It just did
not seem plausible to me, but no matter how I phrased the question, or how many times I asked her to keep thinking about it, she
always came up blank. Then one day, she mentioned offhandedly
that an FBI investigator had interviewed her in the 1950s while she
was still at graduate school in mathematics at NYU. She had been
afraid the interviewer would find out she was "queer," she told me.

"Edie, that's exactly what I'm talking about!" I blurted. "Tell
me the whole story."

Edie was surprised.

That kind of experience had been so commonplace that she
had not even registered it as discrimination. Despite all of her
own political activism for LGBT rights over the subsequent sixty
years—the computer programs she had set up for New York
City's LGBT Center when it first opened up in the 1980s and the
lobbying that she and Thea did for full marriage rights via the
Empire State Pride Agenda, New York's statewide LGBT advocacy group, among others—Edie still took it for granted that this
was just how things were. She was afraid and she hid because she
knew that most people would strongly disapprove of her lesbianism and penalize her for it. Right or wrong, good or bad had not
really entered into the equation for her. She had just adapted to

what was, since there was no way she could change any of it—either the homophobic society of the 1950s or her own lesbianism.

I now understood that her attitude had been a necessary means of survival for Edie—and for so many other LGBT people of her generation. Without that understanding on her part, she never would have managed to have the dignity to create such a happy and successful life for herself. Now that I understood her psychological as well as her historical frame of reference, I could finally unlock her full history. "Tell me everything," I said again, and she did. We submitted it in an affidavit to the court on September 15, 2011.

BLAG makes statements in its opposition papers seeking to minimize the seriousness of the discrimination that existed against gay men and lesbians in the twentieth century. As a result, I would like to tell a story about something that happened to me personally to add some context concerning what things were really like for gay men and lesbians when I was young.

After [my husband] and I got divorced, I moved to New York from Philadelphia, where, in 1955, I began working on a master's degree in applied mathematics at NYU.

In order to cover tuition, I worked as a secretary at NYU. I took some computer classes and later sought a technology-related job. I eventually got a job as a research assistant, programming NYU's Univac computer, which was devoted to United States Atomic Energy Commission work. Consequently, I had to get "Q" security clearance—a particularly high level of security clearance—in order to perform my duties.

While I was waiting to obtain this clearance, I received a letter from the FBI requesting that I attend a meeting with them. Although they explained that I did not need a lawyer for this meeting, it immediately occurred to me that the meeting was really about my homosexuality. In other words, I expected to be asked if I was a "queer."

Not only did I worry that I might not get the necessary security clearance if they found out that I was "queer," but I was also very concerned that being "queer" was actually illegal. After I went to the trouble of doing some research, I came to understand that, for women, all that was illegal in New York at that time was impersonating a man. So, I went to the interview dressed even more "feminine" than I usually did—wearing a dress with crinolines and high heels.

There was no question in my mind that I would be completely honest, even though I knew doing so would likely mean that I would lose the job that I loved. At the time, I was especially frightened because the FBI had asked my building superintendent whether there were people coming and going from my apartment. My superintendent told me that he had told them in response: "just a bunch of college girls." As a result, I thought for sure that the FBI was "on to me."

As it turned out, the FBI was only following up on a false lead. Fortunately for me, and to my great relief, the FBI agents asked a series of questions about my sister's friends in the teachers' union, but did not ask me any questions about whether I was a lesbian. And in the end, despite all my fears and anxiety, I received my "Q" security clearance.

It turns out, of course, that Edie's fears were completely justified. Not only was this the height of the McCarthy period, in which gay men and women were being outed and fired from their government jobs every day, but it was actually a felony then to be gay and employed in any capacity by the federal government. In fact, even companies with federal government contracts (such as IBM, where Edie later worked) were prohibited under the law from having gay employees.

Bit by bit, we were using every tool we had to chip away at BLAG's argument. Both sides filed so many motions, affidavits, memos, and other legal paperwork that it was not until the end of October—nearly a year after we had first filed Edie's lawsuit—that all the filings were finally finished. Judge Jones did not typically ask for oral argument in civil cases, so there was nothing more to do except wait. And wait. And wait.

The leaves on the oak trees near Edie's West Village home turned gold and red, then fell to the ground. Winter descended on Manhattan, and amid the snow and ice storms, I worried even more about Edie's health. We kept up our letter-writing campaign to Judge Jones, asking her again and again to please expedite her decision, but to no avail. Then, as winter began to give way to spring, I received the call I had been dreading. On March 6, 2012, Edie suffered a heart attack.

She was admitted to the cardiac unit at Mount Sinai Hospital on the Upper East Side, and as soon as I heard the news, I rushed out of the office to go see her. I had recently spent a great deal of time at Mount Sinai, visiting our close friend Emily Giske, who had undergone chemotherapy there, so I took my usual route—swinging by Eli Zabar's deli on the way uptown to pick up sandwiches. Edie's condition was stable, so the least I could do was to make sure that she had something good to eat while she was stuck in the hospital.

When I arrived, Edie was deep in discussion with a doctor about whether or not to agree to a certain procedure. Edie was understandably reluctant since, following Thea's death, her heart had stopped after stents were implanted. Although the doctor tried to persuade Edie that the technology was better now, she refused. I really could not blame her, considering what had happened. Yet, at the same time, given that the doctor was recommending the procedure, I tried to convince Edie to change her mind.

Over the nearly two years that I had known her, I had developed a maternal feeling toward Edie. Despite the fact that she is almost twice my age, at times she can be as impulsive as a teenager, and she approaches life with an openness and trust that have felt to me, at times, like naïveté. I often found myself wanting to protect her, and never more so than when she was feeling ill or otherwise vulnerable. "Listen, Edie," I said. "If you were my mother, I would tell you to trust your doctor." She just shook her head. "But you're not my mother, so you can make your own decision," I said.

When I first met Edie, she had told me that her doctors had said she only had a year or two to live. I wanted to do anything we could to help extend her time, partly because I am a bit like the dog in one of my son's favorite books when he was younger, *A Dog Needs A Bone*, partly because I am the kind of person who wants to fix every problem, but also because I cared so deeply about Edie. Sitting in her hospital room and seeing how tired she looked as she nibbled the edges of her sandwich, I felt like my own heart was about to burst.

And then something unexpected happened. As we talked, Edie started taking care of me.

I began talking about my almost-six-year-old son, Jacob, telling Edie about the difficulties of being the parent of a child who had what we later learned was severe dyslexia. Edie knew Jacob, of course, and she was so sweet and loving with him that he had quickly grown to love her back as another close family member. Edie had always wanted children, but it just was not feasible for a lesbian couple in the 1960s to have kids. That reality often made me feel sad for Edie, especially watching how she lit up like a Christmas tree whenever Jacob was around.

Edie is just amazing with him. Jacob loves having someone read to him, and Edie would come over and read him the entire series of *Captain Underpants* books—which are just what they sound like but even more so—for two hours. That's about an hour and forty-five minutes longer than I can stand reading *Cap-*

tain Underpants. She would also bring him huge bags of chocolate, handing them to him on the sly whenever she came over. One year for his birthday, she made him a card as tall as he was, with pictures of them together. Another year, for Hanukkah, she made a poster-size card of Jacob dressed as Judah Maccabee with a ledge of tiny lamp bulb candles for the menorah—enough for the full eight-day holiday. Edie is like a third grandmother, always wanting to spoil Jacob and infinitely patient with him. And Edie's love is not unrequited. Jacob adores her in return.

Jacob is a wonderful and very loving son, but as anyone with kids knows, parenting can be challenging. As Edie listened to me pour my heart out about the ups and downs of our family life, she gave me thoughtful advice and offered much-needed words of support. I had never considered opening up to her about my own problems, but thanks to those hours sitting together in the hospital, I did—and it enabled me to see another side of her. She calmed and comforted me that day, and I was grateful to her. Rachel and I had always tried to treat Edie like family, but after that day in the hospital, it felt like she truly *was* family.

Edie spent a couple of days in the hospital, and though we were all relieved when she got to go home, I could not help but worry, knowing she could have another heart attack at any time. I was desperate for Judge Jones to release her decision, but the weeks kept ticking by. Then, in early May, Vice President Joe Biden unexpectedly entered the fray, making the whole debate a lot more interesting—and a lot trickier for President Obama.

VICE PRESIDENT BIDEN was in the middle of an appearance on *Meet the Press,* discussing the economy and the ongoing 2012 presidential campaign, when David Gregory threw him a curveball. "You know," he said, "the president has said that his views on gay marriage, on same-sex marriage have evolved. But he's opposed to it. You're opposed to it. Have your views—evolved?"

"I am absolutely comfortable with the fact that men marrying men, women marrying women, and heterosexual men and women marrying one another are entitled to the same exact rights, all the civil rights, all the civil liberties," Biden replied. "And quite frankly, I don't see much of a distinction—beyond that."

The vice president had just blown up the administration's official position, whether he meant to or not. He realized quickly that he had gone further than he had intended, judging from his halting response to Gregory's next question: "In a second term, will this administration come out behind same-sex marriage, the institution of marriage?"

Biden replied, "Well, I—I—I can't speak to that. I—I—I—I don't know the answer to that." He was clearly thrown, having inadvertently put the president in a difficult position. Now, President Obama would have no choice but to address the contentious issue of gay marriage. As President Obama later joked, "He probably got cut a little bit over his skis, but out of generosity of spirit." Biden's statement made headlines all over the country, including this gem in the *New York Post*: "Going Rogue: Joe Biden Endorses Gay Marriage, *Will & Grace*, and a Dick Cheney Style of Out-Gaying His Boss." Biden, joking that he's a "good skier," later explained that when he saw the president in the Oval Office that Monday after *Meet the Press*, President Obama just started laughing, totally embracing what Biden had said.

Three days later, President Obama characteristically rose to the occasion. In an interview with morning-show host Robin Roberts, he hit all the crucial points:

I have to tell you that over the course of several years, as I have talked to friends and family and neighbors, when I think about members of my own staff who are in incredibly committed monogamous relationships, same-sex relationships, who are raising kids together, when I think about

those soldiers or airmen or marines or sailors who are out
there fighting on my behalf and yet feel constrained, even
now that Don't Ask Don't Tell is gone, because they are not
able to commit themselves in a marriage, at a certain point
I've just concluded that for me personally, it is important
for me to go ahead and affirm that I think same-sex couples
should be able to get married.

(Apparently President Obama didn't know that Roberts was gay
during the interview; Roberts came out publicly as a lesbian two
years later.)

With these words, Barack Obama became the first sitting U.S.
President to support marriage equality. His statement was the lat-
est, greatest advance in what had become an amazing run for our
side. In February, the Ninth Circuit Court of Appeals ruled that
Prop 8 was unconstitutional, setting up a possible appeal to the
Supreme Court. Weeks later, Washington and Maryland became
the seventh and eighth states to legalize marriage equality. (The
New Jersey legislature passed marriage equality, too, although
Governor Chris Christie vetoed the measure.) And in one of the
four DOMA challenges under way across the country, *Golinski v.
Office of Personnel Management*, District Court Judge Jeffrey White
in California had ruled that DOMA was unconstitutional.

Golinski was now the second of the four DOMA cases to win
at the district court level. Like the *Gill* case in Massachusetts,
Golinski was immediately appealed, sending it up to the Ninth
Circuit court level. (The fourth case, Mary Bonauto's *Pedersen v.
Office of Personnel Management*, was still at the district court level
in Connecticut.)

By now, it was clear that the DOMA fight would go all the way
to the Supreme Court—and that the justices would choose one of
these four cases to hear. The Supreme Court would want a case
that already had a circuit court decision, so timing was now more

crucial than ever. We needed Judge Jones to make her decision, and make it fast, and then get a quick decision at the circuit court level, if we had any hope of getting to the Supreme Court at all.

Judge Jones, however, still did not feel any pressure to move quickly. On the contrary, she knew this was a historic case, so she continued to take her time. By late May, more than seven months had passed since she had all the filings in hand. Because our "Edie has the sniffles" letters obviously had not worked, there was nothing we could do now but watch with frustration as the other DOMA cases moved forward. On May 31, the First Circuit Court of Appeals released its decision in *Gill*, ruling unanimously that DOMA was unconstitutional. As the first case to receive its circuit court–level decision, *Gill* now looked like the front-runner to go before the Supreme Court.

It is important now to note two things. First, nobody deserved to argue a DOMA case at the Supreme Court more than Mary Bonauto, the undisputed architect of the marriage equality movement. Second, a victory over DOMA would be a victory for all of us, no matter whose case went to the Supreme Court. That said, we wanted the justices to choose *Windsor*, for several reasons.

The most important one was that there was a serious complication with *Gill*. When that case was filed in March 2009, Elena Kagan was not yet on the Supreme Court. She was then the solicitor general of the United States. In that capacity, she was likely involved in discussions concerning the many meetings in which gay rights advocates (such as James Esseks) were trying to persuade the DOJ not to defend DOMA. This was a big red flag: how could Justice Kagan sit in judgment on a case in which she'd been involved? In fact, Justice Kagan had made it clear during her Senate confirmation hearings for the Supreme Court in the summer of 2010 that she took her recusal obligations seriously, telling Senator Patrick Leahy, "I would recuse myself in any case in which I had played any kind of substantial role in the process."

The last thing we needed was an eight-justice court, bereft of Justice Kagan's vote. In fact, *Gill* and *Golinski* both had been filed while Justice Kagan was the solicitor general, meaning both were at risk of having her recuse herself. But because we filed *Windsor* in November 2010, after Justice Kagan was already on the Court, our case did not have that problem. (We now know that these concerns were well taken. When the final orders were issued in all four DOMA cases in the summer of 2013, Justice Kagan recused herself from both *Gill* and *Golinski*.)

I also wanted the justices to choose *Windsor* because I believed Edie's story would go beyond the legal arguments to touch people's hearts. And let's be honest: I wanted the chance to represent a client before the Supreme Court. Who wouldn't? I relished the thought of arguing an important historical case on such a grand stage.

The truth is, I have never shied away from a stage, even as a kid. One of Jacob's favorite stories about me involves a formative incident at the Red Raider Day Camp, where I spent my summers as a kid in Ohio. One morning, when I was about seven, I went out with my fellow campers to pick blackberries. When it seemed like all the good ones had been picked, I became greedy. Charging deeper into the brush in search of some magical cache of berries, I stepped on a hive of yellow jackets. An angry swarm surged toward me, and before the counselors could rescue me, I was covered with stinging red welts. My hands were so swollen that I could not move my fingers.

Because I was so badly stung, there was talk that I should be sent home early. But in the 1970s, there were different standards of child safety, and the counselors probably did not want my parents to see me like that, so they came up with a plan. "If you stay until the end of the day," they told me, "we'll make you Camper of the Day." Camper of the Day! This meant I would get to go up onto a little stage in front of the whole camp to receive the award.

So, like the hyper-ambitious little second grader I was, I agreed. The comforts of home and immediate medical attention meant far less to me than winning that award.

Jacob loves when I tell him this story, and although it's funny, it reveals something about me that is still true. I love to win, whether it's corporate litigation, a pro bono case, or a game of Scrabble. At this moment, I wanted more than anything to have the chance to win Edie's case in front of the Supreme Court. And because I had the loving support of Rachel and Jacob, I knew that I could win. (My mother has repeatedly pointed out to me during the course of our daily phone calls that, had I not met and married Rachel, I never would have been involved in this issue, much less had the courage to bring Edie's case.) But the longer it took Judge Jones to make her decision, the more it looked like we would not have that opportunity.

Then, as if spurred by the First Circuit making their decision, Judge Jones suddenly released her decision. On June 6, 2012, she issued a concise, clear opinion with not a single extra word or phrase concluding that DOMA was unconstitutional, even under rational basis scrutiny. In response to BLAG's primary argument that it was okay for section 3 of DOMA to discriminate against married gay couples because of an interest in promoting "uniformity," Judge Jones had this to say:

> [I]t bears mention that this notion of "consistency," as BLAG presents it, is misleading. Historically the states—not the federal government—have defined "marriage" . . . The federal government neither sponsored nor promoted that uniformity . . .
>
> Yet even if Congress had developed a newfound interest in promoting or maintaining consistency in the marital benefits that the federal government provides, DOMA is not a legitimate method for doing so.

Judge Jones has acknowledged that the First Circuit ruling played a part in her thinking. "When the First Circuit came out with the state's rationale for deciding that DOMA was unconstitutional, we took great advantage of that. It was a rationale that we knew we were going to rely on," she said. She added, "I couldn't imagine a better plaintiff [than Edie], and it was a story Robbie told very effectively in the papers . . . [I]t's always important to present your plaintiff in a way where, when you put the papers down you think, 'That person should win this case.'"

Now we just had to get things rolling in the Second Circuit Court of Appeals. The day Judge Jones's ruling was handed down, we began pressing BLAG to file its appeal. I scheduled a call with the BLAG lawyers, and following some discussion they agreed to file their notice of appeal just two days after the decision. We then filed a motion with the Second Circuit, proposing what James Esseks called "the most aggressive briefing schedule I had ever seen."

BLAG was not happy. Although they had agreed to the idea of an expedited schedule, this was what one of their lawyers called "warp speed." BLAG quickly filed a motion opposing the schedule, calling it "radically expedited" and "patently unreasonable."

Even some of the attorneys on our side were surprised at how hard we were pushing. "I remember looking at the schedule that Robbie wanted to propose, and I'm thinking, 'They're never going to accept that,'" James recalls. "And Robbie said, 'Well, this is what we're proposing.' And we didn't get exactly that, but it was not all that far off in the end." Ultimately, despite BLAG's objections, the court agreed to a very aggressive schedule, with oral arguments scheduled for September.

In the meantime, U.S. Solicitor General Donald Verrilli Jr. soon made it clear which of the DOMA cases he preferred that the Supreme Court take. And ours was not one of them.

Here I am "talking" with my parents on my first birthday in 1967, just a few months after Edie and Thea became engaged.

Aaron Belkin and me at our high school prom in Cleveland in 1987.

Sitting at Chief Judge Kaye's desk (which previously belonged to Judge Benjamin Cardozo) during my clerkship.

Rachel Lavine and Emily Giske marching for the Gay & Lesbian Independent Democrats at New York's Gay Pride Parade in 1995. New York Assemblymember Deborah Glick and LGBT activist Tom Schuler are with them.

Edie and Thea in August 1969, two years into their forty-year engagement. *Courtesy of Edie Windsor*

Edie at her job writing software for IBM. *Courtesy of Edie Windsor*

Edie and Thea at their Toronto wedding in 2007. *Photograph by Virginia Moraweck*

Rachel and me walking with our parents at our wedding in September 2005.
© *Dana Siles Photographer*

Rabbi Jan Uhrbach marrying us under the chuppah at Rachel's parents' house in Rhode Island.
© *Dana Siles Photographer*

Arguing the New York marriage case in Albany in 2005.
AP Photo / Tim Roske

Practicing my answers with Pam and James at the Stanford moot. *Photograph by Joshua Kaye*

Our Passover Seder in Washington, DC, two nights before my Supreme Court argument in *Windsor*. *Photograph by Joshua Kaye*

Julie Fink, Walter Rieman, Pam Karlan, Andrew Ehrlich, Josh Kaye, Colin Kelly, and Mary Bonauto in the early morning outside the Supreme Court before the *Windsor* oral argument. *Photograph by Dianne R. Phillips*

Edie, Jaren, and myself walking into the Supreme Court on March 27, 2013. *Photograph by Kathryn Barrett*

Edie hugs Jacob and his cousin Ari on the courthouse steps after the *Windsor* oral argument, with Pam Karlan looking on. *Photograph by Adam Lavine*

Edie and me reading Justice Kennedy's opinion on a laptop in my apartment shortly after it came down. *Photograph by David S. Allee*

James Esseks of the ACLU being lifted in a chair at our victory celebration dance party on June 29, 2013. *Photograph by Lindner Studio*

My Mississippi clients talking to Edie after my Fifth Circuit argument on January 9, 2015. *Photograph by Alexia Koritz*

Edie and Jacob mug for the camera. *Photograph by Rachel Lavine*

Rachel, Jacob, and me in Central Park. *Photograph by Jo Moser*

11

PERFECTLY PLEASED

In Latin, the word *certiorari* is a present passive infinitive; it means "to be informed." When the Supreme Court justices grant certiorari, or "cert," in a case, it means that they have agreed to hear it. Most of the Supreme Court's docket consists of cases raising legal issues that arise repeatedly, so the Court often has to choose from several cases which ones to hear. When the legal issue involves the constitutionality of a federal statute, the solicitor general usually steps in to make a recommendation to the justices as to which case the SG thinks they should take.

On July 3, 2012, the solicitor general filed two cert petitions, one recommending that the Supreme Court take the *Gill* case, and the other recommending *Golinski*, most likely as a backup if Justice Kagan decided that she had to recuse herself in *Gill*. I, of course, was not a happy camper about the fact that two other cases had received the solicitor general's seal of approval, and not ours. What really troubled me, however, was that *Golinski*, like *Windsor*, did not yet have a circuit court decision. If the solicitor general was going to take the unusual step of filing a petition for cert before judgment, I didn't see why he should prefer the *Golinski* case over Edie's.

I was irked but also encouraged: if the solicitor general was willing to overlook *Golinski*'s lack of an appellate decision, then that should not hold us back, either. I decided that we too should file our own petition for cert before judgment.

With this step, however, our legal team would be entering unfamiliar territory. Bringing a case in a trial court or arguing an appeal before a circuit court is one thing, but the Supreme Court is another matter altogether. Like any court, the Supreme Court has its own quirks, rules, and customs that can be very different from those of the lower courts. It even has its own loose collection of a few dozen lawyers who argue a disproportionate number of its cases.

A Reuters report examining Supreme Court cases between 2004 and 2012 noted the enormous influence of this group: In that period of time, 17,000 attorneys filed cert petitions before the Supreme Court. Of those, a small group of sixty-six were six times more likely to get their cases accepted. To quote Muriel Spark's Miss Jean Brodie, these lawyers are the "crème de la crème," or "the elite of the elite." Reuters noted that "although they account for far less than 1 percent of lawyers who filed appeals to the Supreme Court, these attorneys were involved in 43 percent of the cases the high court chose to decide."

While I had great confidence in our case and in our team, my instincts told me that we needed help. For starters, none of us had ever filed a petition for cert before judgment (which is a rarely used procedural mechanism in any event), and we weren't exactly sure how to go about doing it. We needed to get someone on board quickly who knew the ins and outs of the Supreme Court—a kind of "local counsel" for the high court, ideally a member of the Supreme Court bar. But who? Jaren and I discussed the issue and decided that we did not want a lawyer from another firm, because that could get awkward. We both preferred an academic, ideally one who was gay. That narrowed the field considerably, and we quickly zeroed in on a Stanford law professor by the name of Pamela Karlan.

On paper, Pam was perfect. She specialized in civil rights cases and had worked for the NAACP Legal Defense Fund in the 1980s, where she litigated voting rights cases throughout the South. She had also clerked for Supreme Court Justice Harry Blackmun, who, before he died, publicly gave Pam credit for writing much of the dissent in the infamous *Bowers v. Hardwick* case, which had upheld a Georgia antigay sodomy law in 1986. At Stanford, Pam was cofounder of the Stanford Supreme Court Litigation Clinic, which typically handles several cases a year before the Supreme Court, and she brought her Stanford law students in to work on these cases. In fact, the Stanford clinic has taken part in more Supreme Court cases than all but a few private law firms.

Pam is the real deal. She is known for her brilliant mind, not to mention her prodigious work ethic, and had been repeatedly mentioned as being on the short list of potential Supreme Court nominees. What impressed me most, though, was a comment that she had made in 2009 about why she would probably never be nominated to the Supreme Court: "Would I like to be on the Supreme Court? You bet I would. But not enough to have trimmed my sails for half a lifetime." Here was a woman who, like me, speaks her mind. Pam is a clear-eyed, unafraid, openly gay genius who knew her stuff—exactly the kind of person I wanted on our team.

The solicitor general's brief came out on July 3. The next day, even though it was the Fourth of July holiday, I decided to go ahead and e-mail Pam. While I am definitely not known for doing anything at a slow pace, in this case, we really had no time to waste.

Reading my rather terse e-mail now, it is a wonder I thought anyone might suddenly throw aside their hot dogs and Fourth of July fireworks to respond.

Professor Karlan:

I am a partner at Paul, Weiss and counsel to Edith Windsor in the estate tax DOMA challenge pending in the Second Circuit. (Decision by SDNY Judge Barbara Jones on rational basis grounds was issued last month.)

I was wondering if you had any time to discuss some issues with us. I very much apologize for e-mailing you on the July 4th holiday; unfortunately, the issues are somewhat time sensitive.

Thanks so much in advance for your time; any help you can provide us will be greatly appreciated.

Best regards,

Robbie Kaplan

Pam read this scintillating e-mail while standing at her kitchen sink in Palo Alto, dressed in biking clothes for her morning ride—which she graciously postponed in order to talk with me on the phone. "Yeah, sure, I'd love to help," she said. Just like that, we signed on the newest *Windsor* team member who became our not-so-secret weapon.

MONDAY, AUGUST 6, 2012, was one of those unbearably hot and sticky summer days in Washington, DC. Jaren Janghorbani, Joshua Kaye, James Esseks, and I plunged into the humidity, traveling to the capital for a meeting at the solicitor general's office as part of our ongoing quest to get Edie's case heard by the Supreme Court. At Jaren and Julie's suggestion, I had added Josh, a fabulous lawyer and person, who had recently come back to Paul, Weiss after completing a judicial clerkship.

With Pam Karlan's help, we had filed our petition for cert before judgment on July 16, but the chances the justices would choose *Windsor* were still very low. It is very rare for the justices to receive petitions for cert before judgment, and even rarer for them to grant one—in Pam's estimation, they only hear such a case once every few years at best. And, of course, our position was made weaker by the solicitor general's filings recommending that the court take *Gill* or *Golinski*, but not *Windsor*. (The likely reason why the solicitor general had chosen *Golinski* was because the district court in that case had decided the issue on heightened scrutiny grounds—the DOJ's preferred argument—rather than on a rational basis, as Judge Jones had in our case.) Still, the justices would not be making their decision until the fall, which meant that we had time to try to persuade the solicitor general's office to change its mind and back *Windsor* instead. That was what this meeting was all about.

We gathered in a giant conference room at the Department of Justice, and as at any government meeting in DC, there were dozens of lawyers present. The meeting was run by Principal Deputy Solicitor General Sri Srinivasan, a sober-minded son of Indian immigrants who would later be appointed to sit on the DC Circuit and was widely reported to be on President Obama's short list for the Supreme Court. Sri was the person we needed to persuade, and we wasted no time telling him the compelling facts of Edie's case.

As everyone knew, of the nine Supreme Court justices, the one whose vote likely mattered the most was Justice Anthony Kennedy. Four justices—John Roberts, Antonin Scalia, Clarence Thomas, and Samuel Alito—were solidly conservative in outlook and voting records. Four others—Ruth Bader Ginsburg, Stephen Breyer, Sonia Sotomayor, and Elena Kagan—were considered to be reliably liberal. Justice Kennedy was therefore the deciding fifth vote in most high-profile cases, the justice we needed to convince in order to win.

I strongly believed that of the four pending DOMA cases the justices could choose to hear, Edie's was likely to resonate the most with Justice Kennedy. After all, Edie and Justice Kennedy were contemporaries in age, and I thought that her stories of FBI interviews and McCarthy-era fears were sure to be familiar to him. An article in *Time* magazine had reported that when Justice

Kennedy taught at the McGeorge School of Law in Sacramento in the 1960s, one of his closest friends was a closeted gay man, which meant that he would probably find the facts of Edie's story compelling. I brought all of this up at our meeting and reiterated the other strong points of our case: the fact that Edie's tax-bill injury was so straightforward; that she was such an appealing plaintiff; and that there was no chance she and her spouse could split up during the case.

But Sri and the other government attorneys did not seem to be very interested in the facts. They wanted a case that had a circuit court decision, plain and simple. *Gill* had one, but the possibility of a Kagan recusal loomed over that case. *Golinski* and *Pedersen* did not have one, and of course neither did *Windsor*. And Sri was unmoved by the fact that we had filed a petition for cert before judgment, since the solicitor general had already done that for *Golinski*, which was then still pending in the Ninth Circuit.

In fact, in one sense, the government's cert before judgment petition in *Golinski* had backfired from a procedural standpoint. Once the Ninth Circuit judges became aware of it, they decided to stay the case rather than issue a decision. The government's chances of persuading the Court to hear *Golinski* thus actually decreased. At our meeting, Sri assumed that the same thing would happen with *Windsor*. "How do you know the Second Circuit won't just stay your case?" he asked me.

"They won't," I said. "Believe me, I may not be a Supreme Court practitioner, but I do know my home court in the Second Circuit. Not only are they not going to stay the case, but we are going to get a very fast decision."

Sri raised his eyebrows. He did not seem to believe a word I had said, but I forged ahead. "I am a New York lawyer," I told him. "That's what I do. You guys know the Supreme Court, but I know New York courts. We are going to get a very fast decision from the Second Circuit, you will see."

I believed and hoped that I was right, because that was our only chance. Three weeks after our meeting in DC, the solicitor general filed another brief, once again advising the Supreme Court in no uncertain terms to take either *Gill* or *Golinski,* with the *Windsor* and *Pedersen* cases pretty much an afterthought, to be considered only in the unlikely event that the Supreme Court rejected the other two.

Our poor position in the four-way race to the Supreme Court was not only disheartening, it was threatening to hurt our chances before the Second Circuit. I found this out in August, when I contacted George Washington University law professor Alan Morrison, who had come up with an ingenious new argument as to why DOMA should be struck down.

Alan's daughter, Nina, is a lesbian and a good friend of ours, as well as a highly regarded criminal defense attorney, so Alan had been interested in the DOMA challenges from the very beginning. He had called Mary Bonauto soon after she filed *Gill* in 2009, offering to help out in any way he could.

As Alan plunged deeper into the issues surrounding DOMA, he came to a profound realization. "I had an insight," he says, "that DOMA was not only mean-spirited and vicious, but it had other negative consequences, too: it meant that all the federal laws and rules about ethics simply didn't apply to same-sex couples." In other words, if a married lesbian was working for the federal government, DOMA ensured that her wife wouldn't be subject to any of the disclosure laws, recusal rules, or conflict of interest regulations with which married federal employees normally must comply. This was not only nonsensical, it was contrary to sound public policy and even national security.

"I realized that this was important, because it showed how irrational DOMA was," Alan says. "No rational person could have meant to do that." Alan asked Mary if he could write an amicus brief about this for *Gill*, and she readily agreed.

Shortly after that brief was filed, Alan came to a second realization. "The same thing was true about bankruptcy and tax," he says. "There were huge loopholes in the tax laws, for example, that allowed same-sex couples to engage in tax avoidance in ways that opposite-sex couples couldn't." In other words, DOMA made it possible for same-sex couples to flout all kinds of laws, an unintended, and heretofore mostly unnoticed, consequence. Alan added these arguments to his brief and filed it in the Ninth Circuit in support of *Golinski*.

When I read Alan's briefs, I was struck by how powerfully they articulated a completely different anti-DOMA argument—one that might appeal to more conservative judges. I e-mailed Alan right away to ask if he would file a brief in the Second Circuit for us, too. He told me he was very busy and suggested I just cite his existing briefs, so he would not have to write a new brief for us. The reason he was begging off was apparent: he didn't think *Windsor* had a chance of making it to the Supreme Court.

Stubborn as always, I decided to call Alan and give him the same pitch that I had delivered to Sri. "Listen," I said, "this case is moving fast. We're going to get a decision soon, and we really need your brief." Thankfully, Alan said yes, and his was one of the seventeen amicus briefs filed on behalf of *Windsor* in the Second Circuit. We also had briefs filed by 145 members of the House of Representatives; the American Psychological and the American Psychiatric Associations; the Partnership for New York City; the states of New York, Connecticut, and Vermont; the city of New York, and others—all pulled together with lightning speed, in time for filing before the September oral argument.

I was worried about the oral argument in the Second Circuit because we already had two strikes against us. The first was that the three-judge panel that would hear our case included two conservatives: Chief Judge Dennis Jacobs and Judge Chester Straub. We knew Judge Straub was unlikely to vote our way, and I suspected that Chief Judge Jacobs might not, either. Judge Jacobs was a frequent speaker at Federalist Society functions who had never, to my knowledge, decided that a federal statute was unconstitutional outside of the criminal context. Jaren, who had clerked for Chief Judge Jacobs, did believe we would get his vote, although she admitted that this was more of a gut feeling than anything supported by his record.

The second strike was that the oral argument was scheduled for September 27, the day after Yom Kippur.

For those unfamiliar with Jewish holidays, Yom Kippur is the Day of Atonement, considered to be one of the holiest days of the Jewish year. It is a day of repentance, and most Jews—even those who are not particularly religious—spend twenty-four hours fasting and reflecting on their sins of the past year. Thus, from sundown on September 25 to sundown on September 26, I would be observing Yom Kippur, which meant no work, no studying, no eating. This was not, obviously, the best way to prepare for an oral argument, but I am far too religious (and superstitious) to mess around with God.

As a child in Cleveland, I had been told countless times the story of the Los Angeles Dodgers pitcher Sandy Koufax, who sat out the first game of the 1965 World Series because it fell on Yom Kippur. Legions of baseball fans were aghast that one of the best pitchers in the league would choose to miss a World Series start, but for American Jews of my parents' generation, Koufax's decision was nothing short of heroic. When I learned that our oral argument would fall on the day after Yom Kippur, the first thing I thought of was Sandy Koufax, and the second was to begin drafting a request for the court to change the date. That request was denied, so instead of spending the day before the oral argument reading, practicing, and otherwise preparing, I did the next best thing: Rachel and I took Edie to Yom Kippur services.

We went to Congregation Beit Simchat Torah, the LGBT

synagogue where Rachel and I had first met thirteen years earlier. On High Holy Days, so many people want to come to services there that the congregation meets at the giant Jacob K. Javits
Convention Center on Eleventh Avenue. There must have been
five thousand people at services that day, and we spent hours
there, praying and reflecting. Although she is Jewish, Edie does
not know a lot of the religious rituals and customs, so I helped her
read the Hebrew prayers and follow along. Then she and I were
invited to open the Ark.

In a synagogue, the Ark is a large cabinet where the Torah,
the sacred scrolls considered by most religious Jews to be either
inspired by or the actual words of God, are kept. At certain points
in Jewish services, the Ark is opened for the Torah scrolls to be
placed for reading, walked around the congregation, or simply so
that the entire congregation can see the scrolls during important
prayers. These are moments of great holiness, and being invited
to open the Ark is considered to be a great honor. Edie whispered
to me, "How do I do this?" I whispered back, "Don't worry. Just
follow me." The two of us walked up to the Ark and opened the
doors together, a moment I would not have traded for any extra
time preparing an oral argument.

THE NEXT MORNING, September 27, Edie and I walked with our
team into the Thurgood Marshall Courthouse in Lower Manhattan for the oral argument. And as soon as it began, everything I
had anticipated about how the argument would go went right out
the window.

Paul Clement argued first for BLAG, and I split the *Windsor*
argument with Stuart Delery, one of the highest-ranking gay
officials at the DOJ. Unlike Supreme Court arguments, where
the attorneys are given little time and the justices pepper them
incessantly with questions, each side received a leisurely forty-
five minutes. This was the first time I had met Paul Clement in

person. I walked over to introduce myself and I remember notic-
ing that all he had in front of him was a single piece of paper in a
manila folder, which he presumably intended to use as the outline
for his argument. Wow. That was impressive. What surprised me,
however, as Clement's argument unfolded, was that Chief Judge
Jacobs seemed eager to focus on whether DOMA should be considered under rational basis or heightened scrutiny.

As I sat listening at the counsels' table, I began wondering:
Was it possible that Chief Judge Jacobs was actually considering
whether to rule on heightened scrutiny? No federal court had
ever done that in a gay rights case, so this was an exciting—and
unexpected—development. We could win our case either way,
but we were pretty much guaranteed to win if the panel decided
to apply heightened scrutiny to DOMA.

When it was my turn to step to the podium, I was prepared
to take any opportunity I could to urge the panel in that direction. But first, I wanted to open by sending a specific message to
Chief Judge Jacobs. After all, he was the judge who, in an earlier
talk at the Federalist Society, had criticized lawyers who "use
public interest litigation to promote their own agendas, social and
political." He obviously did not approve of cases brought solely to
advance social causes, so I wanted to make clear that he understood that this was not that type of case.

> Good morning. This case presents a single question, is
> Section 3 of the Defense of Marriage Act, or DOMA,
> unconstitutional as applied to Edith Windsor, an eighty-
> three-year-old lesbian widow who had to pay a $363,000
> estate tax bill and wants her money back. Judge Jones held
> that it was.

This case was about Edie Windsor and an unfair tax burden,
no more, no less. I went on to argue that "this case is not about

the federal right to marry. It is about circumstances where states define marriage, and where DOMA explicitly said we are going to leave that to the states." In dividing up our oral argument time, we had decided that Stuart, arguing for the United States, would address the heightened scrutiny question, but I did manage to make a few salient points when Judge Christopher Droney asked me which level of heightened scrutiny (strict or intermediate) applied here.

> [W]e believe that being gay or lesbian is closer to being an African American than it is to being—I hate to get so personal about this, than being a woman, because there is nothing about being gay or lesbian that has anything to do with an individual's ability to perform in society and that's essentially what I believe the courts are looking at . . .

When the oral arguments were over, I felt pretty confident that we would win—and now there was even a sliver of hope that we might win on heightened scrutiny. If that happened, it would likely propel our case directly to the Supreme Court. If, that is, the decision came down quickly enough.

Three weeks later, on Thursday, October 12, I was sitting in my apartment slogging through a tedious task. Each October, Paul, Weiss partners are required to submit a report to all the other partners at the firm describing everything they did in the previous year. Those annual reports are then circulated to each of the other Paul, Weiss partners so that everyone can read them. I'm generally not a procrastinator, but I hate doing this report and always put it off until the last possible minute, so I had stayed home that morning in order to force myself to get it done.

When my phone rang, I stopped what I was doing to pick it up. It was Colleen McMahon, the former Paul, Weiss partner who had led the Jury Project and introduced me to Chief Judge Judith

Kaye all those years ago. Colleen was now a federal district court judge and a close friend.

"Robbie, what in the hell are you doing at home?" she asked me.

"I'm writing my report," I said, confused as to why she was asking.

"The Second Circuit has ruled," she shouted. "You won."

What? This did not seem possible. After all our weeks and months of rushing, rushing, rushing, I was caught totally off guard by how quickly the Second Circuit had released its decision. Releasing an opinion just three weeks after oral argument was insanely fast, even for New Yorkers.

To my shock and delight, the court had ruled for Edie on the basis of heightened scrutiny, the first federal circuit court decision ever to explicitly apply that standard to a law that discriminates against gay people. As Jaren would later put it, "No judge, much less no conservative judge, had ever said heightened scrutiny should apply to sexual orientation. And here was this older, white male conservative judge doing it. He just said, 'Of course this applies.' And he was right."

As I raced through Chief Judge Jacobs's opinion, I was stunned at its eloquence and how persuasively it advanced the arguments for our side. The court's opinion declared it "easy to conclude that homosexuals have suffered a history of discrimination." That history was unconnected to gay people's worth, for while there are "some distinguishing characteristics, such as age or mental handicap, that may arguably inhibit an individual's ability to contribute to society, at least in some respect," being gay "is not one of them." The court's opinion also recognized that "there is nothing amorphous, capricious, or tentative" about being gay, thereby rejecting any suggestion that sexual orientation was a choice. And finally, the court answered the question of whether gay people "have the strength to politically protect themselves from wrongful discrimination." They did not, the court declared; gay people "are not in a position to adequately protect themselves from the discriminatory wishes of the majoritarian public."

Assessed under this heightened standard, DOMA had no chance of surviving. Even the other side had admitted as much, as Judge Jacobs wrote: "At argument, BLAG's counsel all but conceded that [the] reasons for enacting DOMA may not withstand" heightened scrutiny. This opinion was a resounding affirmation that laws that treated gay people differently simply because they are gay needed to be scrutinized more carefully by the courts.

Judge Jacobs also demolished the "slutty heterosexuals" argument—the very argument that Judge Robert Smith had employed in 2006, when he wrote the *Hernandez* opinion denying gay New Yorkers the right to marry. Six years had passed since that decision, enough time for another conservative, Republican-nominated New York judge to deem the argument nonsensical in the context of DOMA:

> DOMA does not provide any incremental reason for opposite-sex couples to engage in "responsible procreation." Incentives for opposite-sex couples to marry and procreate (or not) were the same after DOMA was enacted as they were before. Other courts have likewise been unable to find even a rational connection between DOMA and encouragement of responsible procreation and child-rearing.
>
> DOMA is therefore not substantially related to the important government interest of encouraging procreation.

In a paragraph foreshadowing one of the major arguments that would be made in the marriage equality cases post-*Windsor*, Chief Judge Jacobs concluded that *Baker v. Nelson*, a 1971 case in which two gay men in Minnesota sought to marry, that the Supreme Court had dismissed for want of a substantial federal question, did not foreclose Edie's case: "Even if *Baker* might have had resonance for Windsor's case in 1971, it does not today . . . In the forty years after *Baker*, there have been manifold changes to the Supreme Court's equal protection jurisprudence."

In his concluding point, Jacobs dispatched in a single paragraph the argument that gay people should not have the right to marry out of a respect for either religious beliefs or "tradition." He even inserted this zinger at the end, referring to St. Paul's Chapel across the street from the federal courthouse in Manhattan:

> Our straightforward legal analysis sidesteps the fair point that same-sex marriage is unknown to history and tradition. But law (federal *or* state) is not concerned with holy matrimony. Government deals with marriage as a civil status—however fundamental—and New York has elected to extend that status to same-sex couples. A state may enforce and dissolve a couple's marriage, but it cannot sanctify or bless it. For that, the pair must go next door.

I did not know whether to laugh, cry, or shout with joy. The opinion was brilliant, even though Chief Judge Jacobs clearly had rushed to draft it. He had included almost nothing about the facts of the case, which was unusual, and the first printed opinion of the case even had different typefaces for the majority opinion and the dissent. The court had raced to get this decision out, and given the DOMA petitions at the Supreme Court, I believed I knew why.

Now that *Windsor* had its circuit court decision—and a decision that invoked heightened scrutiny to boot—our case became the front-runner to be heard by the Supreme Court. *Gill* was the only other case with a circuit court decision, but it was likely that Justice Kagan would have to recuse herself from hearing it. In an instant, all of our hurrying and fretting and nudging had paid off. Now, if the Supreme Court decided to take a DOMA case, it would most likely be *Windsor*.

One week after the decision, Sri Srinivasan called me to discuss the latest DOMA case "rankings." We had been planning to file a new brief with the solicitor general's office, but Sri told me that "without being definitive, given our policy, I don't think you need to be filing anything. We are planning to file a supplemental brief tomorrow."

"Great," I said. "And what will our new ranking be?"

"I believe you will be perfectly pleased," Sri replied. He told me that their prior reasons for not preferring *Windsor* had been "taken care of" by the Second Circuit decision, and we then went on to discuss a few points about the opinion, but the one thing that stuck in my mind after I hung up the phone was that phrase: "perfectly pleased."

On October 26, the solicitor general's office filed its brief recommending that the Supreme Court take *Windsor*. Our whole team was jubilant, and in the midst of all the high-fiving at the office, I made sure to call Pam Karlan at Stanford. "Did you see the brief?" I said.

"I'm perfectly pleased!" she said.

Now we had just one more step to get to the Supreme Court: the justices had to actually agree to hear our case.

THE SUPREME COURT is a secretive and occasionally mysterious institution. It is difficult, if not impossible, to know what goes on behind closed doors, so at that point all we could do was hope that when the justices met to decide which DOMA case to take, they would choose Edie's.

These meetings, called conferences, typically happen a few times a month during the Supreme Court's term, which runs from October to June. The justices meet in a private room at the Court and discuss the cases up for consideration, and if four justices vote to hear one case, it will be heard. The justices can also decide to combine more than one case on the same issue, lumping them together and letting the attorneys sort out among themselves who should make the oral arguments.

We had been advised that the justices would be considering the four DOMA cases at their November 20 conference. So that afternoon, a group of us—including Edie, of course—huddled together in a windowless Paul, Weiss conference room equipped with a big screen. Some people had brought in their laptops, which were slightly faster than the big-screen Internet setup, and everyone kept refreshing the SCOTUSblog home page to get the announcement. It felt a little absurd to be getting such important news from the Internet, but we knew that SCOTUSblog would have the information first. So there we sat, all of us hitting *refresh, refresh, refresh* or staring at the big conference-room screen until our eyes were bugging out of our heads.

And then the announcement! Our excitement was snuffed out in an instant as we read that the justices had declined to make any decision, punting the DOMA question to their next conference. It is not uncommon for the justices to take several conferences to decide whether to hear a case, but that knowledge did not make the waiting any easier. We all shuffled back to our offices, deflated.

The next conference was scheduled for Friday, November 30, and just as before, we all gathered in the windowless conference room. *Refresh, refresh, refresh* . . . and . . . here we go! Once again, no decision.

At this point, Edie was getting pretty frustrated. What was taking so long? We knew that the Supreme Court was inclined to take a DOMA case, partly because Justice Ruth Bader Ginsburg had said as much in a September appearance at the University of Colorado at Boulder. In response to a student's question about equal protection for gay men and lesbians, she replied that she could not answer that question, as "I think it's most likely that we will have that issue before the Court toward the end of the current term." Because it is pretty rare for justices to give such hints, her statement was seen as confirmation that the court was planning to take a DOMA case.

It was possible that the justices needed more time to consider procedural questions. Would they hear the DOMA case based on the merits only? Or would they decide to consider the jurisdictional issue—meaning whether the Court even had jurisdiction in this case, given that the DOJ had declined to defend and BLAG had stepped in? The justices were not simply deciding whether they would take a case and which one it would be; they also had to decide which legal questions they wanted to answer.

And of course the justices were also discussing another high-profile gay rights case at the same time. Ted Olson and David Boies had won their Prop 8 case, *Hollingsworth v. Perry*, in the Ninth Circuit on February 7, 2012, so it was also up for consideration. Although both cases were about marriage equality, the issues in *Perry* were very different from ours so we knew that the justices would not combine the cases. But would they choose to hear *Perry* at all? And if so, would they schedule our cases to be heard around the same time? All these questions needed answers, and the justices appeared to be taking their time in answering them.

The next announcement was scheduled for Friday, December 7, and once again we all gathered in a conference room at Paul, Weiss. Our whole team was present, as well as James Esseks and Edie. Surely we would get a decision. If not, I thought that Edie and I might both collapse from stress and anticipation.

As James describes it, "We were just sitting there and waiting and waiting and waiting, and we're all frustrated and antsy and we can't keep still." *Refresh, refresh, refresh* . . . And then someone said the magic word: "Granted." Jubilation broke out in the conference room. The justices had chosen to hear not only *Perry* but *Windsor.* We were heading to the Supreme Court!

Someone brought in a bottle of champagne, and we popped the cork and poured it into water glasses. Since Edie is allergic to champagne, someone went out to find vodka for her. In the meantime, she had a sip of juice while we toasted, ecstatic that three and a half years after she had experienced the crushing indignity of having her marital relationship denied, her case would be heard by the highest court in the land.

We had a strategy prepared in anticipation of this moment and had to start e-mailing and making calls to put it into motion. But before that happened, there were two important people I needed to speak to first.

The first call I made was to Mary Bonauto. Mary had worked harder than anyone to defeat DOMA, and the truth is, if her *Gill* case had not had the Justice Kagan recusal problem, it most likely would have been the DOMA case going to the Supreme Court. Mary had been instrumental in the entire campaign to topple DOMA, and her help would be critical at this stage as well. "Mary," I said, "would you help us run the amicus effort?" I knew that Mary would have the insight and connections to help us compile an outstanding selection of amicus briefs, and I wanted her to be part of our team. Fortunately, she said that she would be happy to do it.

The second call I made was to Pam Karlan. Pam had already been a tremendous help in our effort to get cert. Now, with *Windsor* heading to the Supreme Court, we were going to need her insights, intelligence, and sense of humor more than ever. I dialed her number, and when she picked up, I yelled, "Get ready to get your hair blown out! We're going to Washington!"

That evening, Rachel and I hosted a pizza party at our apartment to celebrate. Our whole Paul, Weiss team came—Julie, Josh, Jaren, Andrew, and Alexia; James Esseks was there, and Emily

Giske, hero of the New York marriage equality legislation, along with her wife, Annie Washburn. Edie was there, too, sipping a vodka on the rocks, her blond bob as perfect as ever. Brendan Fay, the activist who had helped Edie and Thea get married back in 2007, was there, too, as was Eddie DeBonis, Brendan's friend who had originally put Edie and me in touch in the first place.

In fact, this was the first time that Edie, Brendan, Eddie, and I had ever been in a room together, so we started talking about how our paths had all come to cross in this fantastically auspicious way. We found out in the next moment that there had been a little less fate in our being brought together than Edie and I had originally thought when Eddie said, "I have a confession to make." At the time Eddie had asked me to consider taking Edie's case, he told Edie he had contacted several lawyers on her behalf. As we all stood together in the middle of this celebration, he said, "Now I can tell the truth. Robbie is the only person I called."

We all clinked glasses—one of many times that night. It was one of those rare, fleeting moments in life when you are present enough to know that you are part of something momentous, something far larger than yourself. I was still flying high a few hours later when I checked my BlackBerry to find an e-mail from Marty London, the Paul, Weiss partner who, all those years ago, had entrusted me with that big Tokyo case when I was an eager young associate. Marty had become my mentor and great friend. He had come to cheer for me during the Second Circuit argument. Marty's e-mail made me laugh, even though it contained no text and only this subject line: "Ok, babe, on to the Show!"

12

BE OUR GUEST

Not long before the justices agreed to hear *Windsor*, I had an important conversation with Pam Karlan. We knew that our case was probably the favorite at that point, and for the first time I started thinking seriously about how it would feel to have the privilege of arguing Edie's case before the Supreme Court. I was thrilled, of course, but I was also too neurotic and compulsive not to have second thoughts.

While I had confidence in my legal skills, I was born and bred as a Paul, Weiss trial attorney and was not a repeat player at the Supreme Court. I was also extremely conscious of the fact that the Supreme Court is unlike any other court in America, and that any lawyer who lacks experience bringing cases there is probably at a distinct disadvantage. In fact, just a few weeks earlier, I had tortured myself by reading an article in which Justice Kagan seemed to say that lawyers who have never argued a Supreme Court case probably should defer to those who have, an assessment that had caused me more than a few nights of insomnia. As much as I wanted to argue this case, I had an obligation to Edie Windsor to provide her with the best legal representation possible. And as hard as it was to acknowledge, perhaps this meant that I should not be the one to argue her case.

I called Pam, whose instincts and advice I trusted completely by then. "Listen," I said, "I want you to know that I am considering whether or not to argue our case if we get to the Supreme Court. If I don't do it, I'm going to recommend to Edie that you do." I took a deep breath. "Given that," I said, "what do you think I should do?"

Most members of the Supreme Court bar, if handed such an opportunity to argue a historic case like *Windsor*, would not think twice before answering yes. In fact, many lawyers would probably angle to take the case over, whether it was offered to them or not. But Pam is not like most other attorneys, or even most other people for that matter. She has incredible integrity and is enormously generous not only with her time and mind but in ensuring that those who work with her receive their moment in the sun.

"Robbie, there is no question that you should argue it," she said. "This is your case. You know it better than anybody else."

Yes, Supreme Court arguments were different from those in other courts, Pam explained, but there was nothing that I could not learn or adapt to. For one thing, SCOTUS oral arguments were shorter, and they tended to be more about playing defense rather than actively persuading the justices to vote one way or another. In most cases, the justices have already made up their minds by reading the briefs; the oral arguments are really about damage control. Occasionally, one justice might try to lobby another through the questioning at the oral argument, but that was not really a strategy lawyers could plan for. "It's really a conversation among the justices more than anything else," Pam told me. "We'll make sure that you're fully prepared."

Pam had argued seven cases in front of the Supreme Court and had second-chaired almost two dozen more. If she had said the word, this oral argument would have been hers. But instead she was a total mensch, telling me, "You are perfectly capable of doing this. Whatever you don't know, you can learn."

After this conversation with Pam, I reported what she had said to Brad Karp, the chair of Paul, Weiss. Brad told me that I would have his unwavering support, which certainly helped to assuage at least some of my anxiety. I now felt at least a little more confident about arguing before the Supreme Court, although I wished there were some way that Pam and I could both argue Edie's case together.

A few weeks later, when the Supreme Court granted cert, the justices handed us that opportunity. The order instructed us to brief and argue not only the question of whether DOMA was constitutional, but a new question as well: "Whether the Executive Branch's agreement with the court below that DOMA is unconstitutional deprives this Court of jurisdiction to decide this case." Essentially, the justices wanted us to address whether the DOJ's decision not to defend DOMA meant that the Supreme Court no longer had jurisdiction (or authority) to hear Edie's case.

This jurisdictional issue was a bit of a curveball. I was not sure how to tackle the question, but fortunately Pam had plenty of expertise in this area, so she immediately volunteered to work with her Stanford students to prepare the brief on it. Because the justices were asking us to address two questions, we could also divide up the oral argument. After consulting with Edie, I asked Pam if she would be willing to argue the jurisdictional question in front of the justices. I was thrilled to make this offer, not only because she so richly deserved it, but also because she would be saving me from having to brief and argue a completely new issue that I knew little about. Pam readily agreed to do it.

I felt extremely lucky and grateful to have Pam on our team, all the more so because starting in January, she was not even supposed to be in the United States. When the Supreme Court agreed to hear *Windsor* on December 7, Pam was less than a month away from flying to Italy with her partner, Viola Canales, for Stanford's winter quarter. She had been taking Italian language classes for months and was really looking forward to teaching Stanford undergraduates in Florence. Of course she could have worked with us from Italy via computer, but the four Stanford students she wanted to bring into the case (Elizabeth Dooley, Michael Baer, Bailey Heaps, and Nico Martinez) could not have done so without Pam. She wanted to give those students the opportunity to work on a major Supreme Court case from the ground up. And she and Viola knew how important the case would be for LGBT rights. So Pam called the head of the Italian program and got permission to postpone her stint in Florence.

Pam and the students went to work on the jurisdictional brief, while the Paul, Weiss and ACLU teams, James, and I started working on the merits brief. And, of course, Mary Bonauto was working to organize our amicus briefs, a gargantuan task that required not only great effort and organizational skills but great tact as well, because everybody and their grandmother suddenly wanted to file one for us, whether we believed it helped our case or not. We needed to make sure that we put together a meaningful cross-section of arguments without overwhelming the justices—a task at which Mary proved to be extraordinarily adept. Unfortunately for the justices, but lucky for us, BLAG did not have the same success on the amicus front.

ON THE MORNING of Saturday, December 8, less than twenty-four hours after the Supreme Court granted cert in our case, I received an e-mail from a woman named Margie Phelps. "Dear Counsel," it read. "Pursuant to Supreme Court Rule 37, I am writing to request your consent to my client, Westboro Baptist Church, filing an amicus brief in the above case . . . Please advise if you will grant your consent."

In Supreme Court cases, both sides almost always give permission for amicus briefs to be filed, and while most lawyers file a letter with the Court granting blanket permission, Pam and I had decided that we wanted to wait to approve each request individually so that we would know exactly who would be filing on the other side.

"Please advise if you will grant your consent." Are you kidding? I thought when I read the e-mail. As Lumière sings in the Disney movie *Beauty and the Beast* (one of Jacob's and my favorites), *"Be our guest."* We definitely wanted the Westboro Baptist Church to file a brief in support of the constitutionality of DOMA. Westboro was the infamous church in Topeka, Kansas, whose parishioners showed up at protests and funerals bearing "God Hates Fags" posters. Church members had picketed the funeral of gay hate-crime victim Matthew Shepard, but they were all over the map: they had also picketed or otherwise protested the funerals of the victims of the Sandy Hook Elementary School shootings, the victims of the Boston Marathon bombing, and an assortment of U.S. soldiers killed in Iraq. Most reasonable people considered the Westboro congregants to be hateful, if not downright crazy. Of course, that was exactly the kind of opposition we wanted.

I forwarded Phelps's e-mail to Pam without comment, and she shot back, "I wonder whether the argument will be that national security requires reversal [of DOMA] because otherwise God will continue to kill American troops overseas. Having these folks file will remind Justice Kennedy of what bigots think."

Five minutes later, Pam sent me another note that made me laugh out loud: "Plus, she sent it on Shabbat!!"

Pam's legal expertise was vital to our case, but we also grew to depend on her wicked sense of humor. In the midst of a difficult moment or a confounding problem, she could always lighten the mood with a wry joke. And she was at her wittiest in response to the blizzard of bizarre amicus briefs filed in support of the other side.

On January 24, 2013, she sent me an e-mail with the subject line "Calling Dr. Freud" to point out a "staggeringly badly written sentence of the brief filed by psychiatrist Paul McHugh: 'Professor Diamond's seminal research on the fluidity of female sexuality was summarized in a widely-praised book published by Harvard University Press.' This is what George Orwell was writing about in 'Politics and the English Language' when he warned against using dead language."

On January 29, after reading the brief filed by the group known as Parents and Friends of Ex-Gays & Gays (PFOX), she begged, "Promise me if I start to write like this that one of you will fly out to Stanford and smother me." In response to the brief filed by Helen Alvaré, a conservative Catholic law professor who was a well-known opponent of birth control, she wrote, "You'd think the fact that we don't ever use contraception would at least warm this lady's heart toward us."

The list of amicus briefs filed in support of DOMA was long, with most coming from expected sources: the National Association of Evangelicals, Concerned Women for America, the National Organization for Marriage, the Family Research Council, the Coalition for the Protection of Marriage. These organizations had been fighting against marriage equality for years, and their arguments were variations on the same predictable themes. To a certain extent, this was what we would be doing, too—collecting amicus briefs from organizations such as Freedom to Marry, the Family Equality Council, Empire State Pride Agenda, Lambda, GLAD, and others who had spent years advancing the cause of marriage equality. But we wanted to reach beyond that circle, too—far beyond it. We decided that it was strategically important to pursue amicus briefs from organizations that were not normally associated with LGBT rights to show the breadth and depth of support for what was, at its core, not just an LGBT issue but a human rights issue.

Mary called this going after the "unusual suspects," and we went after them hard. We already knew we could get amicus briefs from LGBT churches, but I decided that we needed to go after the mainstream churches and religious organizations. Wouldn't that carry even more weight? In my view, one mistake that the

LGBT rights groups had made in the past was to cede religion to the antigay side. The United States Conference of Catholic Bishops were filing an amicus brief in support of DOMA, so we decided to approach the bishops of the Episcopal Church, hoping to persuade them to file in support of Edie. The church's New Hampshire diocese had elected openly gay Gene Robinson as a bishop in 2003, so they were not strangers to taking a pro-equality stance. Even so, this was a mainstream church, not an activist group.

Thanks in large part to Mary's tireless efforts, we ended up with an impressive list of amici for the mainstream religious amicus brief. Not only did the Bishops of the Episcopal Church in ten states and Washington, DC, sign on, but nineteen other churches did too, including a branch of the Evangelical Lutheran Church in America, the United Church of Christ, and groups of Methodists, Presbyterians, and Quakers, as well as a number of Jewish congregations. Most impressive, though, was the fact that we were able to persuade the Jewish Theological Seminary (JTS) of America to sign on.

It is not unusual for Reform Jewish organizations to support gay rights, but JTS is at the center of Conservative Judaism. Not only that, but JTS had never filed an amicus brief of any kind at the Supreme Court and had only recently begun admitting openly lesbian and gay rabbinical students, so this really was a coup. It had taken many hours of lobbying to get JTS on board, and it never would have happened without the help and efforts of the rabbi who had married Rachel and me back in 2005, Jan Uhrbach.

Jan had already demonstrated great courage in fighting for gay rights over the years, even though she is not gay herself. Before becoming a rabbi, Jan had gone to Yale Law School and had made partner at a First Amendment law firm, so she was familiar with the legal issues. As a Conservative rabbi, she was not always in the majority, yet she was never cowed or quieted. When she officiated at Rachel's and my wedding, the Conservative movement had not yet approved of its rabbis doing so. She also fought for JTS to admit openly gay and lesbian students and for the ordination of gay rabbis. At the time, these were pretty radical positions for a Conservative rabbi to take, but Jan believed that God wanted gay men and lesbians to be treated fairly and justly, and she was not afraid to make her views known. She even published an op-ed in the *Washington Post* entitled "A Conservative Rabbi's Case for Marriage Equality," in which she wrote:

> My support of marriage equality is an expression of my faith. It arises from fundamental principles found in the Hebrew Bible and the rabbinic tradition, among them, that each human being is made in the divine image, that affording full dignity to every person is a religious obligation, and that we are commanded to pursue social justice . . .

Jan and her friend Rabbi Julie Schonfeld, head of the organization of Conservative rabbis known as the Rabbinical Assembly, spent hours thinking about how we might get the Jewish Conservative Movement groups to sign in support of the amicus brief. My law partner Daniel Beller, who serves on the board of JTS, made calls. Most Conservative Jewish congregations at that time still did not allow lesbians and gay men to marry in their synagogues. In theory, though, they could still support marriage equality as a civil right, rather than a religious one. The mainstream religious brief, which was written by Jeffrey Trachtman, a partner at the law firm of Kramer Levin (who had been co-counsel with Lambda in the *Hernandez* case), opened with this very point:

> While *Amici* come from faiths that have approached issues with respect to lesbian and gay people and their families in

different ways over the years, they are united in the belief that, in our vastly diverse and pluralistic society, particular religious views or definitions of marriage should not be permitted to influence who the state permits to marry or how legally married couples are treated by the federal government.

The brief then reiterated the point Jan had made in the *Washington Post*: "A vast range of religious perspectives affirms the inherent dignity of lesbian and gay people, their relationships, and their families. This affirmation reflects the deeply rooted belief, common to many faiths, in the essential worth of all individuals. . . . With time, and across traditions, religious Americans have affirmed that the dignity of lesbian and gay people logically and theologically follows from the premise that all persons have inherent dignity."

And in case it was not crystal clear, the brief went on to note that striking down DOMA would not result in any churches or synagogues being forced to perform marriages of which they disapproved, including those between gay people:

> All religions would remain free—as they are today . . . to define *religious* marriage in any way they choose. . . . [By] affirming the [Second Circuit's decision], this Court will ensure that civil law neither favors nor disfavors any particular religious viewpoint, and it will leave individual faith communities free to determine for themselves whether or not to add religious sanction to particular unions.

Accumulating this vast array of mainstream religious groups in support of our case was a tremendous achievement—one that was bound to surprise many people. But that was only one part of our Supreme Court strategy.

We were also fortunate to have an amicus brief filed by 172

members of the House and forty members of the Senate who wanted to see DOMA overturned and to make it clear that BLAG was not representing their views. To have that many congressional signatories on the brief was itself an important symbol of how far we had come, especially since a number of the members of Congress who signed on to the amicus brief had actually voted for DOMA back in 1996.

In addition, we compiled what we called the business brief—an amicus brief signed by 278 employers and organizations representing employers arguing that DOMA was bad for business. Signers included dozens of huge corporations such as Amazon, Apple, Citigroup, Goldman Sachs, Facebook, Levi Strauss, Microsoft, Nike, Oracle, Starbucks, UBS. . . . The list went on and on. Two years after King & Spalding had withdrawn from its DOMA defense just a week after taking the case, the corporate voices calling for equality for gays and lesbians had grown even louder.

Our business brief made the point that DOMA "requires that employers treat one employee differently from another, when each is married, and each marriage is equally lawful. DOMA thus impairs employer/employee relations and other business interests." Like Alan Morrison's brief on ethics laws—which he also filed at the Supreme Court—it argued against DOMA from an unexpected angle. We wanted to make clear to the justices that DOMA was a terrible law not only for the obvious reasons but for many not-so-obvious ones as well.

One of those less obvious reasons turned out to be utterly heart-wrenching, a perfect illustration of just how irrational and cruel DOMA truly was.

We began hearing from a variety of sources that since the repeal of Don't Ask, Don't Tell, gay military personnel had understandably taken the opportunity to get married. But because of DOMA, the federal government—including the military branches—could not legally recognize those marriages. This restriction had led to tragic, unforeseen consequences: when a gay married soldier was killed, the military was not allowed to acknowledge his or her spouse in any way. They could not call the spouses to notify them of the death. At funerals, they could not hand the flag to the widow or widower. This was agonizing to the Pentagon brass and an insult to the dignity and honor of soldiers and their spouses, values that the military holds dear. But under DOMA, there was nothing anyone could do about it.

I was stunned. It had never occurred to me that gay married soldiers, sailors, marines, airmen, and their families were being demeaned—however reluctantly—during the very rituals that were meant to honor their sacrifice to this country. LGBT advocates had been so thrilled when Don't Ask, Don't Tell was repealed, it did not occur to most of us that the existence of DOMA would continue to haunt gay servicemembers' lives and, worse, their deaths. I knew that we had to brief the justices on this point; what better way to show the inherent irrationality of the law?

We ultimately had two amicus briefs covering this issue. One, filed by Outserve-SLDN, included this heartbreaking true story:

> The death of Staff Sergeant Donna Johnson illustrates the real-world impact of DOMA. While on her third deployment in Afghanistan, Sgt. Johnson was killed in October 2012, along with two other married soldiers, when a Taliban suicide bomber drove a motorcycle packed with explosives into their patrol. Because of DOMA, the military did not notify Sgt. Johnson's wife of her death, but instead notified Sgt. Johnson's mother. Sgt. Johnson's wedding ring was not returned to her wife, but was given to her mother along with her personal effects. The flag that draped Sgt. Johnson's coffin was handed to her mother, not to her spouse. And her spouse was denied the spousal death benefits and support services that opposite-sex spouses of fallen soldiers are

entitled to receive, including the opposite-sex spouses of the other soldiers killed in the same attack.

The military's inability to notify the spouses of fallen soldiers of their deaths, to return the soldiers' wedding rings to their spouses, or to extend other benefits to compensate military spouses for their loss—solely because Congress disapproves of the gender of their spouses—is indefensible, and an insult to those who give their lives serving this country.

The stories of people whose lives were scarred by DOMA never failed to move me. The treatment of gay soldiers—who had literally given their lives—and their widowed spouses truly shocked my conscience. We could only hope that they would also move the justices—at least five of them, anyway.

GIVEN HOW IMPORTANT the briefs are in the Supreme Court process, I needed to make our merits brief the most compelling document I had ever written. From the moment that the justices decided to hear *Windsor*, I became obsessed with that task.

The whole team was involved in the process, whether helping with research, talking through strategies, or reading drafts and offering comments. As we came closer to our late February filing date, though, I hunkered down alone. By this point, instead of going into Paul, Weiss, I decided to work in the small room in my apartment I used as a home office, where I wrote and rewrote the document, in order to minimize distractions. For about two weeks, I sat in that tiny room, wearing sweatpants and drinking coffee, hunched over piles of paperwork. I like to edit by hand, so I was surrounded by printouts marked up in pen; I must have rewritten every single word of our brief at least a dozen times.

Ever since we had learned that the Supreme Court had granted cert, my phone had been ringing off the hook with people offering advice. Everyone had an opinion, it seemed, and everyone wanted to be heard. I was certainly open to input, especially since I had never previously been involved in a Supreme Court case. It quickly became apparent, however, that I had to work to separate the helpful advice from the avalanche of random opinions and posturing that suddenly came cascading down upon me. Everyone had a different idea about what arguments we should make (or not make), what cases we should cite (or not cite), and what themes we should emphasize (or not emphasize).

In order to make sure I kept my focus where it needed to be, I wrote the following five words on a Post-it note, which I stuck to my laptop screen: "It's all about Edie, stupid." This was, of course, a play on the famous line from Bill Clinton's 1992 election campaign: "It's the economy, stupid." I wanted to make sure that in all the writing and rewriting, all the back and forth about strategy and tactics and angles, I did not lose sight of the single most important part of our case.

To that end, we opened the brief with Edie and Thea's beautiful love story. It is very unusual for a Supreme Court brief to open with a personal story, but I wanted the justices to truly understand the dignity of these women and of their marriage. We wanted the justices to understand in their minds why DOMA was unconstitutional, and to feel it in their hearts as well. At the very beginning of the brief, we described their lives in this way:

> In the early 1960s, at a time when lesbians and gay men risked losing their families, friends, and livelihoods if their sexual orientation became known, respondent Edith Windsor and her late spouse Thea Spyer fell in love and embarked upon a relationship that would last until Dr. Spyer's death forty-four years later.
>
> The depth, commitment, and longevity of their relationship and eventual marriage are all the more remarkable given the times they lived through. Dr. Spyer was expelled from

college when a campus security guard observed her kissing another woman. Ms. Windsor entered into a brief, and
unsuccessful, marriage to a man in the early 1950s because
she did not believe that it was possible for her to live openly
as a lesbian.

We told the story of Edie's FBI interview, their diamond
engagement pin, Thea's long battle with MS, the couple's eventual marriage, and Thea's death. "They spent their last two years
together as a married couple," I wrote. "Dr. Spyer died of a heart
condition on February 5, 2009. Grief-stricken, Ms. Windsor suffered a severe heart attack and received a diagnosis of stress cardiomyopathy, or 'broken heart syndrome.'" And at that point,
because of DOMA, she was forced to pay more than $600,000 in
inheritance taxes, solely because Thea was a woman.

We then outlined the history of DOMA.

"We've got to do a better job explaining how different this
law is," I urged our team. "We can't let the other side keep making the argument that DOMA is some ordinary law. It's not." At
the same time, we needed to make the argument in a way that
would appeal to the Supreme Court justices—meaning we could
not seem like strident, radical activists. In other words, we had to
make the argument on their terms.

One tricky element, which our team debated at length, was
how to make it clear that DOMA was intentionally discriminatory without branding all the many legislators who voted for
it—or the president who signed it into law—as prejudiced against
gay people. I did not want the other side to be able to accuse us of
finger-pointing, which was the term I used to describe a favorite
strategy of the pro-DOMA side. The essence of this argument is
that by asserting (as was plainly the case) that some of the people
who supported DOMA may not have had the best motives, we
were somehow branding everyone who voted for the statute in

1996 a bigot or homophobe. We needed to convey that DOMA was passed solely for the purpose of treating gay people differently, whether out of fear, animus, bigotry, misunderstanding, cynical political calculation, or some combination of the above, without seeming to blame the legislators personally.

Pam came up with the brilliant idea of including the most vitriolic quotes from the 1996 debate over DOMA—but, contrary to standard Bluebook citation format, not to identify who had actually said them.

> DOMA sped through Congress in large part because of the strong views many members of Congress expressed at the time about the morality of being gay. The House Report explained that refusing federal recognition to marriages of gay couples reflects "moral disapproval of homosexuality."
>
> During one day's debate, a Representative declared that homosexuality "is based on perversion, that it is based on lust." Another Representative charged that homosexuality was "inherently destructive." At one point, the tenor of the debate led one Representative to observe: "Words have been thrown around. . . . Today, I wrote down . . . 'promiscuity, perversion, hedonism, narcissism . . . depravity and sin.'"
>
> The congressional debate was also filled with predictions of dire consequences if same-sex relationships received legal recognition. One Representative cautioned that marriages between gay couples would "destroy thousands of years of tradition which has upheld our society." Another Representative exclaimed that "[w]e as legislators . . . are in the midst of chaos." Yet another Representative stated that marriages of gay couples legitimized "unnatural" behavior. Two Representatives predicted that failure to pass DOMA would lead to "discussing pedophilia," and allowing marriage between "two men and one woman, or three men, four men, or an adult and

a child." And another Representative warned that no culture that has ever embraced homosexuality has ever survived.

Although Congress did not invite testimony concerning the programmatic or other implications of DOMA, it did schedule witnesses who predicted that the failure to pass DOMA would lead to marriages "between parents and their grown children" and claimed that supporting DOMA was "no more 'homophobic' than it is 'sibling phobic' to oppose incest, or 'animal phobic' to want humans to make love only to their own species."

We also wanted to make it clear to the justices that the animus displayed in these quotes was not a mere relic of the past. If anything, as evidenced by groups like the Westboro Baptist Church, it was alive and well and as colorful as ever, as we explained in footnote 3:

> The continued antipathy to gay people is reflected in the tone and content of many of the amicus briefs submitted in this case in support of BLAG. *Amici* referred to gay men and lesbians as immoral, sinful, radically disruptive to society, abhorred and opposed and a vector of injury and disease. One set of *amici* argues that overturning DOMA will make it more socially acceptable for fathers to leave their families. Another compares the recognition of Ms. Windsor's marriage by New York to the Fugitive Slave Act that forced residents of New York to assist their slave-state neighbors to return slaves who had escaped, back to slavery. Still another analogizes same-sex marriage advocates to pro-slavery advocates of the 1850s.

"Radically disruptive." "A vector of injury and disease." "Pro-slavery." Reading the other side's briefs, you would have thought gay people were a robotic force of pure evil seeking to wipe out civilization as if in one of the superhero or *Transformers* movies that my son Jacob loved. We wanted the justices to see at a glance how shrill and irrational these pro-DOMA arguments were. And from there, our job was to make the case why the statute was unconstitutional.

We argued that the Court should consider DOMA under heightened scrutiny, as the Second Circuit had done, even though we were under no illusion that the justices would actually do that. We therefore needed to make sure that our argument for striking down DOMA under the less-stringent rational basis standard was bulletproof. So we created what I dubbed the "checklist section"—six pages in the middle of our brief that outlined three simple, straightforward red flags for why the Court should be concerned about the constitutionality of DOMA and should rule our way, even under rational basis review.

First, the purpose itself of DOMA was illegitimate. The law, we noted, was passed out of fear or dislike of the unknown: "The very language of its title indicates that DOMA was enacted to defend or 'guard against' people who appear to be different." In constitutional terms, this is called animus, and laws that are infected by such animus are not legally valid.

Second, DOMA had broad impacts that Congress clearly never anticipated. In other words, DOMA targeted gay people and then imposed upon them "disabilities that are so broad and undifferentiated as to bear no discernible relationship to any legitimate governmental interest":

> By amending the Dictionary Act, rather than any specific federal program, DOMA categorically disqualifies gay peo
> ple who are married from all federal rights, privileges, and obligations of marriage, creating a sweeping exclusion that is disconnected from any specific rational justification . . .

The fact that DOMA is *not* a discrete or tailored statute, but instead sweeps across over 1,100 federal statutes that
confer benefits or impose responsibilities on married people
strengthens the conclusion that it fails rationality review.

Third, throughout U.S. history, the states, not the federal government, have always had the right to determine who can marry.
The passage of DOMA marked the first time that the federal government chose to ignore the states' decisions in this area. "Statutes
provoke suspicion when they upset the relationship between the
federal government and the states in novel or unusual ways," we
wrote. "Sometimes the most telling indication for a severe Constitutional problem will be the lack of historical precedent for
Congress' intervention."

Each of these three reasons was different, and each of them
offered a legitimate reason why DOMA should be subjected to, if
not heightened scrutiny, at least more careful consideration by the
Court. My hope was that in enumerating them so plainly in the
checklist section, we could give the justices who were expected
to vote our way plenty of ammunition to sway the others—in
particular, of course, Justice Kennedy.

We ended our brief by asserting that the facts of Edie's case
only reinforced the conclusion that DOMA was unconstitutional:

> In her complaint, Ms. Windsor challenged the marital
> deduction generally available to married couples. If Con-
> gress had passed a discrete statute simply excluding mar-
> ried couples who are gay from the benefits of the estate tax's
> spousal exemption, it would be impossible to discern a ratio-
> nal connection between that exclusion and any of the inter-
> ests that have been advanced on behalf of DOMA.
>
> For example, even if the federal government has a legiti-
> mate interest in encouraging responsible procreation by

straight couples, it would be irrational to think that denying gay couples the benefits of the estate tax deduction would do anything to further that interest. Hardly any straight couples— especially straight couples of an age where their relationship still runs a risk of "produc[ing] unplanned and unintended offspring"—would make decisions about "responsible pro- creation" based on their eligibility for a deduction from an estate tax likely to be levied only decades later and only on a small fraction of the population. And none are likely to be influenced in their immediate procreative or childbearing choices by how that tax is or is not levied on gay people . . .

Finally, while BLAG repeatedly argues that the Court should not "constitutionalize" the issue because "the dem- ocratic process is at work," the question presented here is a narrow one: is there a sufficient federal interest in treat- ing married gay couples differently from all other married couples for all purposes under federal law? There is not. By suggesting that the Court cannot or should not answer this question, BLAG fails to recognize that the protections of the Fifth Amendment are abiding. DOMA is impossible to reconcile with the promise of impartial governance that the Constitution's guarantee of equal protection extends to all of our Nation's citizens.

After weeks of migraines, sleepless nights, and endless rewrites, we finally had a brief we were happy with, and on Sunday, February 24—two days before the filing deadline—our whole team gathered in a huge conference room at Paul, Weiss for the final read-through. We had poured our collective blood, sweat, tears, and souls into this document, and this was our last chance to catch typos or any odd- sounding sentences. We decided that the best way to do so was to actually read each and every word of the brief out loud.

That day, Rachel was busy with another project and our plans for child care fell through. So I brought six-year-old Jacob with me to a conference room at Paul, Weiss, handed him an iPad loaded with movies, and placed an oversized pair of earphones on his head. Then, with the whole team seated around a conference table, I asked everyone to read one sentence each, going around the table, as if we were reading from the script of a new play by my friend Terrence McNally. This turned out to be a surprisingly effective way to read through the brief, and it ended up being one of my favorite moments in the whole case.

The brief was seventy-seven pages long, so the process took us a little over three hours. As we were reading, Jacob watched his movies, and every once in a while he would get so excited by something he had seen on the screen that he would want to share his thoughts about the scene with all of us. He quickly settled back down each time, but just as we reached the very end of the brief, Jacob actually leapt off his chair in the middle of one of his favorite Tintin movies and exclaimed, "The problem is, they're *running out of gas!*" We all cracked up. It was the perfect note to end on.

We filed our brief on February 26, 2013, and that same day, after reading the final brief, Colleen McMahon sent me a note. "The editing is simply superb," she wrote. "There's not an extra word or phrase. It's as close to flawless as any brief I've ever read."

This was extraordinary praise coming from someone I admired as much as Colleen, not to mention a federal judge, so I forwarded the note to Pam with the comment, "OK, I'm ready to retire."

Pam replied with her usual dry wit and an always-welcome reference to one of my favorite Broadway musicals: "What a wonderful email," she wrote. "And did you ever see Sondheim's *Merrily We Roll Along*? One of the characters says something like 'and after you hear this song, you'll want to swallow poison because there will be nothing left to live for.' Seriously, like the videos say, 'Things get better.' This is a high point, but it won't be the only one."

13

TO DE-GAY OR
NOT TO DE-GAY

On the morning of March 4, Pam boarded a flight in California to come to New York City for our first moot court session. She had a connecting flight in Charlotte, North Carolina, and when she turned on her cell phone in the airport there, she saw it lighting up with multiple voice mail messages. As she started listening to them, she realized that they all said essentially the same thing—"I'm so sorry, Pam," or "Pam, I'm terribly sorry." The problem was, Pam had no idea what all these people were talking about.

She called me at the office, and when I picked up the phone, I too said, "I'm so sorry." At this point, completely exasperated, Pam asked, "Why in the world is everyone feeling so sorry for me?"

It turns out that while Pam had been in the air, the Supreme Court had issued an order dividing up the lawyers' time in the upcoming *Windsor* oral arguments. For the merits arguments, as the parties had already agreed and proposed to the Court, BLAG would get thirty minutes, and the solicitor general and I would each get fifteen minutes. But for the jurisdictional issues, a Court-appointed Harvard Law School professor named Vicki Jackson would get twenty minutes, BLAG would get fifteen minutes, the solicitor general would get fifteen minutes, but counsel for Edie Windsor would not get any time at all.

The Court had taken the step of appointing Vicki Jackson to argue as amica (or "friend") for the Court because everyone in the case agreed, albeit for different reasons, that the Court did have jurisdiction to resolve the constitutionality of Section 3 of DOMA. President Obama and the DOJ had taken the position that, while they agreed DOMA was unconstitutional, out of a respect for Congress they would not give Edie her money back until the Supreme Court had decided the issue in her favor. Edie, of course, wanted the Supreme Court to decide the case so that she could get her refund check from the IRS. And BLAG took the position that it was the appropriate party to defend DOMA in court and that the decision of the Second Circuit should be reversed. So the Supreme Court appointed Vicki Jackson to be the one lawyer to argue that there was no jurisdiction.

In other words, the Court had decided not to allot any time at all for Pam to argue the issue. In terms of the case, this was probably a good sign, since it seemed unlikely that the Court would find there to be no jurisdiction if they were not going to give Edie any argument time. But it was incredibly disappointing that Pam wouldn't get to participate in the oral argument.

When she heard the news, Pam was crestfallen. This was a historic case, and she had been excited to have the chance to argue it. Pam had been preparing for weeks and had even invited her eighty-one-year-old aunt, who lived in New York City, to come watch her at the first moot court. But now there was no reason for her aunt to do so because Pam wouldn't be arguing anyway. "I thought, there goes my moment in the sun," she remembers with whimsy in her voice.

And then, as a pure coincidence, Pam ran into a group of her friends who also happened to be at the Charlotte airport at that time. They were fellow civil rights lawyers flying home from Selma, Alabama, where they had been taking part in an anniversary commemoration of Martin Luther King's historic march

from Selma to Montgomery. Seeing and talking to her friends
not only boosted Pam's spirits but clarified her perspective. "I
thought, I'm a civil rights lawyer," she said later. "This is a long
struggle, and whether I get to argue this case or not is not the
biggest deal in the world." This is classic Pam, always keeping
priorities clear and thinking of the greater good no matter what.

By the time she arrived in New York for the moot court, Pam
was her usual centered and supportive self—which was fortunate
for me, since the first moot was not exactly a resounding success.

BECAUSE I HAD never argued a Supreme Court case before, I was
constantly being bombarded with advice. People were coming
out of the woodwork, wanting to help, convinced I would screw
up, or simply wanting a stake in a piece of history. That is to be
expected in any Supreme Court case, especially one as important as *Windsor*. My inexperience at the Supreme Court obviously
made me nervous, but I hoped that the moot court sessions would
help me to get a solid grip on which arguments were working and
which were not in my oral argument.

In a moot court, a lawyer faces a panel of "judges" (usually
other lawyers) to practice his or her argument. The panel asks
questions, often mimicking the tone or style of the real judges
or justices who will be hearing the case, while other people are
sometimes invited to watch, take notes, and offer constructive
criticism or suggestions on how to improve. That is the ideal sce-
nario, anyway. But our first moot was, to put it mildly, not ideal.

The moot took place in a large room at NYU's law school,
and when I walked in I was astonished by how many people were
there. At one end of the room there was a long table behind which
the judges would sit, and in front of that table, at the very center
of the room, there was a lectern for me to use while I argued. I
was literally encircled by dozens of people sitting in rows of seats
around the room.

Waiting to begin, I obviously felt enormous pressure. I was painfully aware that a number of accomplished Supreme Court advocates—some of whom were there that day—were wondering to themselves, *Why in the world is Robbie Kaplan arguing this case?* I had come to learn and work on my strategy, but I also felt that I had something to prove. What I had hoped would be a tightly focused exercise felt, from the very beginning, more like a lopsided contest, like one between gladiators in the Roman Coliseum. (I probably should have begun with the traditional saying used by the gladiators before they began to fight that I remembered from my high school Latin class: *Morituri te salutamus*, or "We who are about to die salute you.")

"The nature of moots," James Esseks explained, "is that you get a lot of very opinionated people telling you with great conviction that you have to do 'x' and you can't do 'y,' and all the advice is different. You have to sort through it and figure out what you're going to do. And while some points do come through consistently, a whole lot doesn't." In other words, from the moment I started, I would have to assess which of the many conflicting pieces of advice to follow and which to discard.

I stood in front of the moot panel and began my oral argument. "My client Edith Windsor met her late spouse Thea Spyer in 1963. They were fortunate enough to be able to spend the last two years of Dr. Spyer's life together as a married couple. When her spouse died—"

"But not in New York," one panelist interjected.

"Excuse me?" To be honest, I really hadn't expected to be interrupted in the first three seconds of my argument. First of all, that's not what is typically done in moot courts, since you want to have a chance to work on your actual opening. Second, although the Supreme Court justices are notorious for interrupting lawyers, even they were not likely to cut someone off before she had even completed her third sentence. We then veered into a ten-minute detour about whether Edie and Thea's marriage was recognized under New York law (it clearly was), and then I was able to continue my opening.

Things didn't get much better from there, because it soon became clear that I was not the only one in the room who felt the need to prove something that day. "People were asking these very esoteric questions," recalls Julie Fink. "I don't think they were questions that anybody really expected."

"It was an odd panel to have for Robbie's first moot," Pam remembers. "Lots of academics. And academics often have their own theories of what cases are actually about, so they're not usually the most helpful people to moot in front of."

I parried a lot of questions, but unfortunately not too many that were likely to come up in front of the actual justices. I tried to get through the main points of our argument but kept getting bombarded with questions from left field, right field, and from completely out of the ballpark. The moot was truly all over the map, with the moot court judges at times seeming far more concerned with having their own theories heard than helping me to prepare for my oral argument.

After a lengthy back-and-forth with the panelists, my oral argument, such as it was, ended. We then moved on to the debriefing session, where the panelists and observers could offer their critiques and suggestions. That's when things really started to veer off course.

At least one extended discussion was based on one panelist's theory that DOMA was really analogous to a hypothetical restriction on who could ship cargo on freight trains. The panelist suggested that even though the issue was obviously not addressed in our briefs, we should argue that marriage is like a public utility that everyone should have equal access to and that the government must therefore offer it on equal terms to everyone. This was a pretty far-out theory, one that was unlikely to resonate with anyone but the most staunch libertarians, but I had to respond to it anyway. Others suggested similarly odd strategies, in comments that James Esseks later noted were "even less connected to the real concerns the Supreme Court might have than the questioning had been." And several people suggested that we take the focus off of Edie, minimizing the facts of the case and concentrating only on prior case law.

My frustration—and that of the whole *Windsor* team—was growing. All around the room, the crowd of observers were shifting uncomfortably in their seats, aware of the disconnect between our strategy and the panelists' questions and comments. Fortunately for me, given my job as a litigator who argues for a living, I have developed pretty thick skin over the years. But a comment from one lawyer really sent our team over the edge:

> You shouldn't get into facts . . . your low-hanging fruit is all the things that are irrational. Make it about an irrational federal statute. De-gay the case. De-gay this case.

De-gay the case? This seemed absurd. From the very beginning, our strategy had been to make the whole case about Edie and Thea—about their dignity as a couple, their unequal treatment, and the overt discrimination of DOMA. There didn't seem to be any legitimate way to "de-gay the case," and even if there was, I had no interest in doing so.

But the lawyer was not finished. Several others on the panel had already suggested that we model our argument on *City of Cleburne v. Cleburne Living Center*, a case decided by the Supreme Court in 1985. In that case, the city of Cleburne, Texas, had denied a permit for the Cleburne Living Center (CLC) to build a group home for mentally disabled people. Lawyers for the CLC argued that the justices should apply heightened scrutiny in the case, because mentally disabled people have historically suffered from discrimination. In the majority opinion, written by Justice Byron White, the Court found in favor of CLC, but on rational basis, rather than heightened scrutiny.

Cleburne was clearly relevant to our case, since it was one of the relatively few times that the Court had found legislation to be unconstitutional while applying rational basis review, rather than heightened scrutiny. And because the Court was not expected to apply heightened scrutiny in *Windsor,* we needed to be prepared to win on rational basis review as well.

While I had no objection to discussing how best to strategically employ *Cleburne,* the strategy that was being recommended was, in my opinion, misguided since it downplayed the importance of Justice Kennedy's gay rights decisions in *Romer* and *Lawrence.* Here was the attorney's suggestion:

> *Cleburne, Cleburne, Cleburne.* This is a *Cleburne* case . . . *Cleburne* reverse-engineers the animus. It never says people hated the mentally retarded people in the neighborhood . . . Cars on the street? These people drive less than frat boys. Noise? These people party less than frat boys . . . *Cleburne* just walks back all the reasons and says why they don't possibly connect to the statute. So it's a disconnect. *Cleburne, Cleburne, Cleburne,* disconnect, disconnect, disconnect . . .

At this point Edie, who was sitting in the room watching the scene, was starting to get confused and upset. Not only was she seeing the lawyer she trusted get picked apart, she was hearing a bunch of strangers insist rather vehemently that we should argue her case as if it were one about mentally disabled people. Over the past two and a half years, as far as Edie was concerned, the litigation process had been incredibly smooth, with victories in both lower courts and little to no dissension among our team. Now, all of a sudden, we were in a large room with a lot of people Edie didn't know telling us that we were going about everything completely wrong.

It seemed clear to me that many if not most of the people in that room did not really believe that we would win at the Supreme Court. Even members of our own team were worried. "I think the low point was the first moot," Julie Fink remembers, "because I was concerned about us. I realized that we had a huge responsibility here, and it was possible it might not work out well." The whole exercise was demoralizing, and to top it off, a lawyer then addressed Edie directly as if Edie were an overwrought diva, flatly informing her that the case ultimately was not really about her and that Edie needed to accept that. It was one thing to pick on me—that was par for the course and what the moot court was all about. But picking on Edie was, in my view, completely out of bounds. This part of the discussion only served to further unsettle Edie—and now to make me angry.

When the moot was finally over after an exhausting two and a half hours, I approached Alan Morrison, who was on the panel and who had always offered helpful feedback. "What do you think?" I asked. I wanted to hear what he had to say before giving him my own opinion. Alan, to my enormous relief, said exactly what I had been thinking. "You can't 'de-gay' this case," he said. "That's what it's about. You have to embrace it. You got a huge amount of conflicting advice here today, and now you have to go back and think about what *you* want to do, not worry about the fact that you can't make everybody happy." This was great advice, and I planned to follow it. But first I had to take care of Edie, who was upset and bewildered by what had just occurred.

Pam, James, and I walked Edie back to her apartment—just a few blocks across Washington Square Park from NYU—and tried to calm her down. At every stage of the case, Edie had always expressed the utmost confidence in our team and our strategy, so the fact that the moot had left her feeling shaken was significant.

"Listen, Edie," I said. "Our strategy is the right one. People have their opinions, but we're not changing. This moot was about a whole bunch of other things that actually have nothing to do with winning the case." Edie nodded, but she still seemed doubtful.

"The first moot is always pretty rocky," Pam told her. "But don't worry. It's still early, and we'll have many more before the oral argument."

It took about an hour, but the three of us were finally able to reassure Edie. And while I believed everything we were telling her, deep down I had also been thrown. Friends as well as colleagues had been there at the moot along with dozens of law students, and I had seen the look on their faces. As we sat with Edie in her living room, all I could think was, *I've really got a lot of work to do.* Our next moot was scheduled to take place at Stanford University one week later, and there were several more scheduled after that, so I feared that if I did not do well at Stanford, there might truly be cause for concern.

There was, however, one big upside to that disastrous first moot: it ended up bonding our whole team. When we examined what had happened, there was remarkable unanimity about what advice we agreed with and what advice we thought was misguided. Our discussion of that moot crystallized our collective thinking about how to argue the case, which was absolutely crucial given how little time we had left—in just three weeks I would face the Supreme Court justices. Most of all, it required us to reexamine and reaffirm our bedrock principle: "It's all about Edie, stupid."

IN ADDITION TO the first moot court fiasco, I had plenty of other things weighing on my mind. By this point, I was certain that someone on the other side would ask me whether we thought Bill Clinton was a homophobe, since he was the president who had signed DOMA into law back in 1996. In fact, I'd been worrying about this issue ever since we had filed Edie's case at the district court, which is why I had suggested back then that we try to get President Clinton to file an affidavit for our side. Several of the ACLU lawyers on our team thought that was a bad idea, and although we went back and forth about what to do, I ultimately decided to let it go, since it didn't seem worth the effort at that point.

That is where the matter stood until the Supreme Court granted cert in *Windsor*. I then decided that we really needed to try to get President Clinton involved. I called a friend of mine who is close to the Clintons and, using my best Jewish mother guilt strategy, said, "I need you to ask the president something for me. I can't believe I have the *chutzpah* to say this, but I want you to tell him that, like everyone else, he too is going to have to meet his Maker one day, and I'm sure that he's not proud about signing DOMA into law. But if he's ever going to express that regret, he's got to do it now. Because if he does it after the oral argument, it won't do us any good."

My friend said that she would pass this along, and on March 7, I was delighted to see that the *Washington Post* was running an op-ed by Bill Clinton entitled "It's Time to Overturn DOMA." It was a full-throated and moving repudiation of the statute by the very president who had signed it into law.

> In 1996, I signed the Defense of Marriage Act. Although that was only 17 years ago, it was a very different time . . . As the president who signed the act into law, I have come to believe that DOMA is contrary to those principles [of freedom, equality, and justice above all] and, in fact, incompatible with our Constitution . . .
>
> When I signed the bill, I included a statement with the admonition that "enactment of this legislation should not, despite the fierce and at times divisive rhetoric surrounding

it, be understood to provide an excuse for discrimination." Reading those words today, I knew now that, even worse than providing an excuse for discrimination, the law is itself discriminatory. It should be overturned . . .

Americans have been at this sort of a crossroads often enough to recognize the right path. We understand that, while our laws may at times lag behind our best natures, in the end they catch up to our core values.

This moving statement from President Clinton solved my "Is Bill Clinton a homophobe?" problem. But as I would soon find out, it probably led to other questions at my Supreme Court argument that I had not been able to predict.

A few days later, on March 11, we flew to California, and whatever jittery nerves I was still feeling after the NYU experience were calmed even further once I got to Stanford and watched Pam Karlan in action with her four law students, the same students who had helped write our jurisdictional brief and were now working on a reply to BLAG's opposition to it.

Upon my arrival, I found Pam and her students gathered in a small conference room, their eyes glued to a large screen where the brief was projected. With each section, the students would discuss edits, and Pam would ask questions and guide them. She often had her own views about how the document should read, of course, but the students were true colleagues in developing the arguments and the team worked to reach a consensus. Pam was so dedicated to making sure that her students got the most from the experience that she pulled an all-nighter that night, working on the brief until the early hours of the morning.

Seeing those students working so hard for our case was inspiring, and once the moot court got into full swing, I felt even better. The Stanford moot was incredibly helpful, full of productive comments and constructive criticism from "judges" like Pam's colleague Jeffrey Fisher, without all the odd posturing that had happened at NYU. By the time we finished, I was feeling confident and battle-ready again. *We're going to be okay*, I thought. *I can do this*. I was lucky, however, that the Stanford moot happened before going on to the next one.

We knew going in to the oral arguments that our strategy was very different from the strategy in *Perry*, the case about Prop 8. In fact, that was the primary reason I had proposed to the *Perry* team that we do a joint moot. Mary Bonauto had already been working closely with them in organizing the amicus briefs, making sure that there was nothing inconsistent that could be damaging to either case. This was trickier than it seems because even though both cases were about marriage equality, they had different goals from a legal perspective. In *Windsor,* we simply needed the Court to defer to the judgment of states like New York or Massachusetts that allowed gay couples to marry, while in *Perry,* the plaintiffs needed the Court to overrule most states' explicit prohibitions on same-sex marriage. Thus, as a practical matter, the scope of what we were seeking in *Windsor* was much narrower than it was in *Perry*. I wanted to make sure that I did not do or say anything at oral argument that might inadvertently hurt the *Perry* case.

Not surprisingly, given the difference in scope, there were plenty of other differences between our strategies. We focused our case on the lives and dignity of gay people, who deserve to be treated the same as everyone else. In contrast, *Perry*'s team saw their case as being more about the dignity of marriage. In the opening of their brief, they cited arguably the greatest Supreme Court decision in U.S. history, *Brown v. Board of Education*, the 1954 case that declared that "separate, but equal" in the American public schools was unconstitutional. There was no way that Pam and I would have cited *Brown* on the first page of our brief. *Brown* was a huge leap forward in American constitutional law. We certainly didn't want the Court to see *Windsor* as requiring such a huge leap—we wanted them to see it as a small, easy, moderate step forward.

We had already had a number of intense meetings with the *Perry* team and its allies, including Mary Bonauto, James Esseks, longtime marriage advocate Evan Wolfson, HRC head Chad Griffin, and Hilary Rosen, who had been brought in as a communications consultant for both cases. We would go around and around in circles, discussing our cases, legal tactics, and press strategies. I always ended up saying, "Look, do whatever you want in *Perry*. But when it comes to *Windsor*, please don't talk about it in such broad terms. We need to keep the messaging about the cases separate, so when you talk about *Windsor*, please don't say anything about a fifty-state victory or compare it to *Brown v. Board*." I desperately wanted to be able to control the message, because I did not believe we would gain anything by being seen as part of one big ball of wax with the *Perry* case.

My fears in this regard were not unfounded. In Jeffrey Toobin's profile of Justice Ginsburg published in *The New Yorker* just a couple of weeks before oral argument, Justice Ginsburg appeared to raise on her own the possibility of there being a connection between the theory she had articulated in a famous lecture that she'd given at NYU about *Roe v. Wade* (the case that first recognized a woman's right to have an abortion) and the issues concerning same-sex marriage. In that lecture, Justice Ginsburg had posited that the Supreme Court had decided *Roe* too soon and had not given enough time for the political process to make more progress in terms of legalizing abortion. Toobin concluded that "[Justice] Ginsburg's arguments against Roe . . . strongly suggest that she has no interest in rendering a fifty-state ruling establishing a right to same-sex marriage," which is what they were seeking in the *Perry* case. I was very worried about the exact same thing.

Because our cases were coming before the Supreme Court at the same time, however, *Perry* and *Windsor* were inextricably linked—and sometimes conflated—in the minds of the American public and the media no matter what we did. The *Perry* team seemed to view this as a good thing, most likely because they believed that our case had a better chance of winning than theirs. By contrast, I did not see any benefit for us in being linked with *Perry*, so I wanted to stay as independent from them as we could. I wanted to see Prop 8 overturned, of course, but I would have been much happier if the Court had not heard our cases together. (*Perry* oral arguments were scheduled for March 26 and *Windsor* for March 27.) I couldn't help but worry about the possibility that a random exchange in *Perry* might harm Edie's case, or vice versa. This was yet another example of the human delusion so many of us suffer from that we actually can control everything in life; as it turned out, the fact that the *Perry* and *Windsor* cases were argued a day apart probably made it easier for the justices to rule the way they did in *Windsor*.

I had proposed a joint moot court with the *Perry* team so we could get a clear sense of each other's oral arguments. In theory, at least, this was a good idea.

The moot was held in the Washington, DC, offices of Ted Olson's law firm, Gibson Dunn, just two days after our team returned from Stanford. I was a little bit jet-lagged, but that was not my biggest problem. The real issue was that Ted Olson argues Supreme Court cases unlike any other lawyer on the planet. Ted has rock-star status, even among the elite Supreme Court bar, which means he can, and does, get away with things that nobody else can.

Ted's legal career has spanned five decades. He started as an associate at Gibson Dunn in 1965, making partner just six years later, and in the 1980s he was an assistant attorney general under President Ronald Reagan. Ted has argued more than sixty cases at the Supreme Court—including his successful representation of George W. Bush in the contested 2000 presidential election.

When Bush became president, he nominated Ted to serve as solicitor general, a post Ted held for three years.

Anyone who has argued multiple Supreme Court cases is treated differently at the Court, but Ted's résumé elevated him even higher. Put simply, justices will give him the benefit of the doubt on points where less experienced lawyers might get hammered. I knew he was admired and respected, but I didn't fully grasp the status he enjoyed until the day of our joint moot.

Ted graciously offered to go first, and it was incredible to see how deferential the "justices" were with him. In his responses to their questions, he rarely seemed to feel the need to elaborate—he would just offer up simple statements and leave it at that. Sometimes he didn't really answer the question at all.

For example, in one exchange with his fellow SCOTUS attorney Lisa Blatt, Ted basically swatted away questions about the slippery slope toward incest:

LISA BLATT: Why can't I marry my sister if I want to marry her?
TED OLSON: Incest statutes.
LISA: If I don't have sex with her, can I marry her?
TED: In cases of close relatives, there may be certain state interests that are not in this case.

Later, he parried questions about bestiality with the same nonchalant brevity:

LISA: So I can marry my cat?
TED: No, maybe the state can say that you cannot marry the cat.
LISA: You can't tell me why I can't marry my cat?
TED: No, because that is not what the case we brought is about.

I watched these exchanges in awe, but during the debrief, when a few people suggested that I should try to argue more like

Ted, I knew that that was a terrible idea. No other lawyer in the country could ever answer the justices' questions the way that Ted Olson does. In fact, to his credit, Ted said as much himself. "You know Robbie can't do that," he told the group. "She'll get eaten alive." I appreciated Ted's candor in that moment, and it reinforced what I already knew. I had to argue this case on my own terms, regardless of what anyone else might say to try to convince me otherwise.

The first thing I did after the moot was to call my friend Annie Washburn (Emily Giske's wife) to find out what she was making for Shabbat dinner that night. I was delighted to learn that we would be having Annie's famous roast chicken. In fact, that was probably the high point of my day—I thought about that roast chicken practically the entire train ride home.

Over the course of six formal moots and many more informal practice sessions with my team, I grew increasingly comfortable with the quirks of arguing in front of the Supreme Court. Normally when I argue cases in the lower courts, I go into a kind of *schmeichel* mode—a Yiddish word meaning "to butter up." I try to subtly charm the judges, to persuade them, to have an intellectual discussion with them about the legal or factual issues, even to try to get them to laugh. That strategy wouldn't work at the Supreme Court, in part because I had so little time, in part because I would be getting questions from up to nine different justices, but mostly because of the tenor of the Court itself. I had to learn to give shorter answers that repeated my main points over and over instead of arguing to persuade the justices. I practiced arguing more defensively, making sure that I wasn't giving the other side anything to use against us. Because I was the only openly gay attorney arguing on either *Perry* or *Windsor*, I also wanted to make sure I kept my emotions as separate as I could from my argument.

Whenever I was in doubt, I would come back to Edie. Her story was so compelling, and the injustice she had suffered so obvious, that it gave me a safe place to land if we got into the weeds on any issues. During the final two weeks before the argument, we spent hours practicing, in conference rooms, on trains, at the gym, over dinner, in bars—whenever I was with anyone on our team, no matter where we were, we would go over potential questions and answers about the case, trying to cover all the bases of what I might be asked. I wanted my responses to come from muscle memory, and I needed to be able to stay on message no matter what was thrown my way.

One of the jokes on our team was that I could simply answer almost any of the justices' questions with the phrase "already married, already gay," because anyone who was adversely impacted by DOMA was, by definition, both, and there was nothing that the Court could do to change either fact. Edie and Thea had absolutely, incontrovertibly been legally married—no one disputed that. They were also, of course, incontrovertibly gay. So if straight married couples deserved the protections of the more than 1,100 statutes that affected them, how could anyone logically argue that Edie and Thea didn't deserve them too? The only way to claim that they deserved to be treated differently was to assert that their marriage was somehow different. But it wasn't, of course. There aren't different categories of marriages in this country. There's just marriage.

"Already married, already gay." We were convinced that this was the way to win our case, which is why the suggestion to "de-gay" *Windsor* had felt so wrong at the first moot. In fact, we ended up turning that recommendation into a joke, too—a silly joke, but one that always made us laugh. At a meeting, someone would point to me or Julie or Alexia and intone in a pseudo-foreign accent: "De gay! De gay!" This was based on the white-suited character Tattoo played by Hervé Villechaize in the TV show *Fantasy Island*, who would race to the bell tower and shout, "De plane, de plane!" when the plane with guests arrived at the beginning of every episode. For some strange reason, we always found this hilarious, although by that point it was entirely possible that we would have found practically anything hilarious, given how slap-happy we all were.

I HAD NEVER seen a Supreme Court oral argument in person, so a few weeks before ours was scheduled to take place, I took the train down to Washington, DC. I wanted to get a feel for the courtroom and watch the justices in action, to get a sense of their demeanor and tone.

Because I had already been admitted to the Supreme Court bar, I was allowed to sit in the special front section that is reserved for such lawyers. The first thing I noticed was two women in full military uniforms sitting right in front of me, huddled together discussing the case, which as I recall had something to do with government immunity in medical malpractice claims. Overhearing a few stray comments, I soon realized that one of the women was a lesbian and that she was married. This was the first moment when I realized that we were going to win. Seeing this openly gay uniformed servicewoman sitting at the Supreme Court talking about her marriage in a case that had nothing to do with gay rights, I knew we had come way too far to be turned back now.

A few weeks later—just about a week before the *Windsor* oral argument—I returned to the Supreme Court. This time I had been graciously invited by a Court employee to come get a feel for the lectern, a grand old antique with a manual crank on the side to move its podium up and down. Josh Kaye came with me, and we were both thrilled and grateful to have the opportunity to explore the Court and get a feel for its history. It was also a nice break from our near constant preparation routine.

The Supreme Court employee walked me up to the lectern, and I put down my bag and papers, straightened my jacket, and stepped up to it. I imagined myself standing there in front of the justices, making an impassioned argument for the dignity of gay people . . . but the podium was a bit too high. I reached for the crank to adjust the height. "STOP!" the employee shouted, jolting me out of my law-geek fantasy. "Don't touch that!" I'm not sure why I wasn't allowed to touch the crank, as other lawyers have; one was even commanded to do so during an oral argument by Justice Ginsburg, who was distracted because the podium was at the wrong height. Whatever the reason, I cautiously backed away slowly from the lectern; the last thing on earth that I wanted to happen was for me to break a historic antique at the Supreme Court a week before my argument.

After a few moments, the employee led us out of the courtroom. And that was when I got what seemed like an odd question: "Will you need any help getting out of the Court on the day of the argument?" I turned, initially confused. "Thanks so much, but although Edie is hard of hearing and will need the help of a special hearing device, she can walk just fine on her own, so I don't think we will need any other help," I said. I thought about it further and asked, "Actually, I'm not sure what you mean?"

It turned out that another lawyer on the case had asked for help getting out the back door after oral arguments, and I knew instantly that there was only one lawyer who that could be. Apparently Paul Clement, the BLAG lawyer who was arguing in favor of the constitutionality of DOMA, had been asked by his client to leave as unobtrusively as possible, presumably so that he wouldn't have to confront the packs of media on the Court's front steps. This was the second moment when I couldn't help thinking, *We are going to win this case.* Josh and I looked at each other and smiled—he knew just as well as I did what this meant.

"No, thank you," I replied. "I'm pretty sure that Edie will want to go out the front door that day."

14

ALREADY MARRIED, ALREADY GAY

About ten days before the oral argument, Julie Fink, Josh Kaye, and I moved from Manhattan to a hotel in Washington, DC, near the National Mall. Other members of the Paul, Weiss team—Jaren, Alexia, Colin, and Andrew—would join us there the week before the argument. Pam Karlan took up residence at another hotel, just a few blocks away from the Supreme Court, since it was her tradition to walk over to the Supreme Court building on the morning of arguments.

We were in the home stretch now, tying up loose ends as I continued to practice. Morning, noon, and night I repeated to myself the points we wanted to make and responses to potential questions from the justices. The rest of the team kept researching, digging up helpful facts about which states had enacted which laws, when they had done so, how many people were affected by them—anything that had the remotest chance of being helpful. It was as if I were cramming for the biggest oral exam of my life. Actually, that's exactly what it was.

There were other details to take care of, too. I had a closet full of suits at home in New York, but I was far too superstitious to simply wear any old outfit to argue my first case at the United States Supreme Court. I had to look right, so I asked my friend

Emily for advice, and she referred me to someone she knew at the Ralph Lauren store on Madison Avenue.

I went in for a fitting, and, to be honest, I chose the fabric and style as if I were deciding between an iced latte or a cappuccino at the coffee shop on our corner. Mary Murray, the saleswoman, laughed and said, "I've never seen anyone make decisions so quickly." But I knew what I wanted: a dark navy suit with pinstripes (conservative, which was appropriate for the Supreme Court) and a silk round-collared, cream-colored blouse. Of all the issues I needed to spend time worrying about at that point, clothing was not high on my list.

Shoes, however, were another matter. I had bought two new pairs—one a somewhat flashier pair of Gucci pumps, the other a more conservative pair from Ferragamo. The Guccis were more comfortable, but I still couldn't decide which pair to wear. Once we got to Washington, Pam suggested I should ask her own personal style consultant: NPR's legendary Supreme Court correspondent Nina Totenberg.

Pam and Nina were old friends, and Pam, who tends to focus on matters of the mind far more than those of fashion, occasionally would get clothing advice from the always fashionably dressed Nina. "I'll bring her over," Pam said. I laid my suit out on the bed, put the shoes on the floor next to it, and ordered up a pot of tea from room service. If we were going to meet to discuss Supreme Court fashion, we might as well be civilized about it.

When Pam and Nina arrived, I poured each of them a cup of tea and then gestured toward my outfit. "So, what do you think?" I asked. "The Ferragamos are more conservative, which might be more appropriate for the Court . . ."

Nina just laughed and said, "Robbie, I am positive that the justices will not be able to see your shoes." I knew she was right, since I would be standing behind the historic lectern that I had already seen. But still, given my state of high anxiety, almost any and every detail somehow seemed crucial—or at least important, anyway. We did not discuss any legal strategy or details of the case, but I told Nina I was planning to go with the Ferragamos, and she nodded. From then on, whenever we e-mailed back and forth about developments in the case, we would joke about my shoes.

In fact, Nina even ended up using my shoes as a detail in a blog post just after the oral argument, writing, "Lawyer Roberta Kaplan, representing DOMA plaintiff Edith Windsor, wore conservative Ferragamo pumps for her argument, deciding against the jazzier Guccis, with a bigger brass buckle. Neither is what I would call racy." As she told me later, she received a lot of praise for her amazingly detailed reporting on this issue.

That same week, I woke up one morning to find an unexpected and very welcome op-ed in the *Washington Post*. George Will, one of the leading conservative pundits in the country, had written a piece entitled "DOMA Infringes on States' Rights." In it, Will advanced what was called the federalism argument against the constitutionality of DOMA. Will had taken his cue from some prominent law professors led by Ernest Young of Duke and Randy Barnett of Georgetown (who had also led the constitutional arguments against Obamacare). They had submitted an amicus brief on our side arguing that DOMA was unconstitutional because it violated the Tenth Amendment, which provides in relevant part that "the powers not delegated to the United States by the Constitution nor prohibited by it to the states, are reserved to the states." In other words, Will urged the justices to strike DOMA down not because it failed to respect the equal dignity of married gay couples like Edie and Thea but because Congress did not have the constitutional authority to pass it in the first place, since only the states, not the federal government, can regulate marriage.

Following this argument, Will argued that each state—regardless of whether it had voted to allow marriage equality (like New York) or had instead voted to ban it (like Mississippi)—should get to make its own decisions about this issue. As he wrote, "By striking down DOMA—by refusing to defer to Congress's usurpation of states' powers—the court would defer to 50 state governments, including the 38 today that prohibit same-sex marriage."

Will's reasoning, of course, was not the same as ours. We wanted the justices to find DOMA to be unconstitutional, of course. But we wanted them to do so on equal protection grounds since DOMA discriminated against gay people, not because it offended the Tenth Amendment conception of states' rights. It wasn't inconceivable, however, that the federalism argument that Will was making might actually convince one or more of the more conservative justices to vote our way. After all, states' rights is an important issue to many conservatives, and certain of the justices had made it clear in their opinions that they were strong believers in this view of the relationship between the states and the federal government. It is interesting to consider whether some of these conservatives, who undoubtedly have LGBT children, siblings, or friends, were supporting us on states' rights grounds because doing so allowed them to avoid the equal protection arguments. In an ideal world, I wanted to win Edie's case for the right reasons—but we don't live in an ideal world and a win was a win, so I was happy to see Will's op-ed.

The closer we came to March 27, the better I felt about our chances. Edie soon came down to DC, joining us at the hotel. No matter where we were, people would stop her for pictures and to wish her good luck. Facebook and Twitter were awash in HRC's red marriage equality logo. In addition to George Will, much of the conservative establishment seemed to be turning our way as well. The best example of this came a few weeks after our Supreme Court argument, when *Commentary* magazine, a bastion of the neoconservative establishment, published an article contending:

To allow the federal government to formulate a national standard for what has long been a state decision would drive one of the last nails into the coffin of federalism. In *Windsor*, the Supreme Court has an opportunity to reanimate the dying spirit of the nation's many-layered and many-leveled political system. Striking down DOMA and leaving the recognition of gay marriage to the political process in the states is not just the federalist thing to do, it is the conservative thing to do.

These were all encouraging signs, but we kept trying to think of ways to make our case more persuasive, especially to Justice Kennedy.

One thing that is distinctive about Justice Kennedy's jurisprudence is the fact that he is the author of the majority opinions in what were then the two major Supreme Court cases affirming the civil rights of gay people: *Lawrence v. Texas* in 2003, which overturned *Bowers v. Hardwick* and struck down Texas's sodomy law; and *Romer v. Evans*, which in 1996—the year DOMA was passed—decreed that an antigay amendment passed by the state of Colorado was unconstitutional. I had read those opinions over and over again until my eyes were bloodshot, because I wanted to make sure that I had truly absorbed Justice Kennedy's thought process and reasoning.

One passage in the *Lawrence* opinion was particularly appropriate since it spoke to the vexing question of why otherwise open-minded people like President Clinton had chosen in the past to support DOMA:

> Had those who drew and ratified the Due Process Clauses of the Fifth Amendment or the Fourteenth Amendment known the components of liberty in its manifold possibilities, they might have been more specific. They did not pre-

sume to have this insight. They knew times can blind us to certain truths and later generations can see that laws once thought necessary and proper in fact serve only to oppress. As the Constitution endures, persons in every generation can invoke its principles in their own search for greater freedom.

In our briefs, we had taken great care not to point fingers at the lawmakers who had voted for DOMA, and I wanted to do the same thing in my oral argument. It's considered bad form to seem to be overtly lobbying for a particular justice's vote at argument. But rather than citing Justice Kennedy's opinions directly, I could try to echo his language in a more subtle fashion, using his own words and phrases like "times can blind." This served another purpose, too. I knew that in all likelihood, one or more of the justices would attempt to box me in on a point I didn't like or want to be boxed in on. The best thing to do in those moments is to pivot, or redirect the argument back to your own strongest points. Interjecting phrases from the justices' own opinions is a time-honored way to do that, which led my brilliant colleague Jaren to come up with a fantastic idea.

"Why don't we put together a list of all the Kennedy quotes that might be useful?" she asked. We quickly went through his *Lawrence* and *Romer* opinions and pulled out the best phrases we could find, creating a cheat sheet I could use that we called "Kennedy's Greatest Hits." It included the most important passages from Justice Kennedy's opinions in *Romer* and *Lawrence,* such as:

- Sweeping and comprehensive is the change in legal status effected by this law. . . . Homosexuals, by state decree, are put in a solitary class with respect to transactions and relations in both the private and governmental spheres. The amendment withdraws from homosexuals, but no others, specific legal pro-

tection from the injuries caused by discrimination, and it for-
bids reinstatement of these laws and policies.

- It is not within our constitutional tradition to enact laws of this
  sort. Central both to the idea of the rule of law and to our own
  Constitution's guarantee of equal protection is the principle that
  government and each of its parts remain open on impartial terms
  to all who seek its assistance. Equal protection of the laws is not
  achieved through indiscriminate imposition of inequalities.

- For many persons these are not trivial concerns but profound
  and deep convictions accepted as ethical and moral principles to
  which they aspire and which thus determine the course of their
  lives. These considerations do not answer the question before us,
  however. The issue is whether the majority may use the power
  of the State to enforce these views on the whole society through
  operation of the criminal law. Our obligation is to define the
  liberty of all, not to mandate our own moral code.

- It suffices for us to acknowledge that adults may choose to enter
  upon this relationship in the confines of their homes and their own
  private lives and still retain their dignity as free persons. When
  sexuality finds overt expression in intimate conduct with another
  person, the conduct can be but one element in a personal bond
  that is more enduring. The liberty protected by the Constitution
  allows homosexual persons the right to make this choice.

I studied this sheet for hours, quite literally walking around
the streets of Washington, DC, like a crazy person, repeating the
phrases out loud over and over again so that they would be on the
tip of my tongue during the March 27 oral argument. People on
our team even began placing bets on when, or whether, I would
manage to work any of them into my oral argument. Regardless
of the office pool odds, I was determined to do so.

By now I had practiced my answers to the justices' potential
questions to the point where I could practically recite them in

my sleep. Everything was going smoothly, until one unfortunate moment just three days before the argument.

This was our final moot, my last chance to calibrate my answers before appearing in front of the justices. Edie, Pam, the rest of the team, and I met in the evening in a big conference room at the Paul, Weiss offices in downtown DC, and for the umpteenth time, I began laying out our arguments. Very soon, Pam started grilling me on the issue of heightened scrutiny, asking me again and again why laws that treat gay people differently should get heightened scrutiny when laws that treat other groups differently—such as the physically or mentally disabled—clearly did not. She kept pounding on the issue, trying to exploit cracks in my argument, and I suddenly felt exhausted.

"You know what?" I exclaimed, speaking out of turn and no longer in moot mode. "Enough! If I have to during the argument, I'm going to throw handicapped people under the bus." What I meant to say, of course, was that I would try to sidestep this problematic issue if the justices brought it up. It wasn't my job, after all, to look out for the legal rights of other minority groups; it was my job to win our case for Edie Windsor. But unfortunately, and to my deep regret, that is not what I said.

The minute I saw the look on Edie's face, I knew that she was furious. Suddenly, I remembered that Thea had been a quadriplegic. She had spent a quarter century in a wheelchair, with Edie taking care of her and loving her through it all. I had even seen Thea like that myself when I was her patient. And I had just casually blurted out a remark about throwing her, or people like her, under the bus.

I immediately felt sick to my stomach. "Edie," I said, "I'm so sorry. I didn't mean it to come out that way." I tried to explain, but Edie was in no mood to hear it. She was tired, she was hurt, and she was absolutely right that I never should have said what I said.

To quote the Paul Simon song, we as lawyers can sometimes "think too much." We can get so caught up in the gamesmanship and legal technicalities that we lose sight of the real people behind the cases. The look on Edie's face reminded me in an instant that this wasn't about the briefs and PR logos and op-eds; it was about the still-grieving woman standing right there, looking at me with hurt in her eyes. *It's all about Edie, stupid.* How could I have forgotten that?

I felt terrible about upsetting Edie that day—in fact, I still do. But in a strange way, that mistake helped me to remember something vital to our case. I wouldn't forget again what *United States v. Windsor* was truly about.

THE DAY BEFORE my Second Circuit oral argument, Edie, Rachel, and I had gone to Yom Kippur services together in Manhattan, an event that turned out to be incredibly meaningful. Coincidentally, two days before my argument at the Supreme Court, it was time to celebrate another Jewish holiday. Monday, March 25, was the first night of Passover, when Jews throughout the world celebrate the liberation of the Jewish slaves from Egypt more than three millennia ago. We planned a big Seder dinner at the hotel and invited dozens of people—practically anyone and everyone who happened to be in Washington, DC, at the time who had anything to do with the case.

In the Supreme Court's original scheduling order, the oral argument in *Windsor* was supposed to take place on March 27 and the oral argument in *Perry* was supposed to happen on March 26. But Vicki Jackson, the Harvard Law professor whom the Court had appointed to argue the jurisdictional question in *Windsor*, had asked the Court to switch the dates because she had planned a Passover Seder at her home in Cambridge for the evening of March 25. The Court readily agreed, and the switch ended up working in our favor, since we would now be able to hear the

Perry argument first and listen to what the justices had to say before I argued Windsor. It also meant we could have our own Seder and still have one more day for final preparation before the oral argument.

Rachel took on the massive task of organizing our Seder. Passover Seders are comprised of many specific dishes—foods that have symbolic meaning for the religious holiday, and which therefore must be prepared with some precision. Above all, no food that is leavened, which includes bread, pasta, and most cookies or cakes, can be eaten during Passover. This is to commemorate the fact that when the newly liberated Israelites were escaping from Pharaoh's armies, they did not have time to wait for their dough to rise. The restaurant at the hotel was mostly Asian, and at one point I could hear Rachel on the phone explaining, "We cannot have any wontons in the matzoh ball soup!"

It is also traditional at Passover for everyone present at the Seder to read from the Haggadah, the centuries-old text that lays out the order of the Seder and explains the meaning of the holiday. There are many different versions of this text, some longer than others and some with modernizing touches. Over the years, Rachel and I had created our own relatively lengthy Haggadah with social justice and feminist overtones, as well as a lot of poetry and traditional Hebrew from the Torah and the rabbinic literature. I was glad that we had brought copies of our Haggadahs with us, full of prayers and poems about fleeing from slavery (or its equivalent) to freedom and liberty. It seemed especially appropriate considering not only the particular meaning of the Passover holiday but why we were all there in Washington, DC, in the first place.

The Seder was magnificent. The large room was so full that it was practically bursting at the seams with friends and family and the many colleagues who had been so supportive of Edie and our team. My parents were there, as was all of Rachel's family, including our niece and all of our nephews from Massachusetts and California; Pam Karlan and her partner, Viola Canales; Mary Bonauto; Emily Giske; Pam's law students who'd helped with the case; our whole Paul, Weiss team; James Esseks; and Edie. Even the then-girlfriend of Jacob's wonderful nanny Ellie Alvarez came and brought her parents from Israel, since they were visiting their daughter for the holiday.

One of the truly special rituals that we did that night was to go around the table and invite everyone to introduce themselves during the song "Dayenu." In Hebrew, the word *dayenu* means "it would have been enough for us," or "it would have been sufficient." The song is about being grateful for all of the gifts God has given us, such as liberating us from bondage, giving us the Torah (or Jewish law), and allowing us the gift of rest on Shabbat. In other words, had God given us only one of those gifts, it would have been enough. As I looked around at all the faces in the room singing this word *dayenu* over and over again, I had tears in my eyes. This extended family—many of whom were gay people just asking to live their lives with dignity and justice—was what all our work (not to mention the Jewish holiday) was really about.

THE NEXT MORNING, March 26, dawned with overcast skies and freezing temperatures. I woke up early and got ready to head to the Supreme Court to hear the oral arguments in *Perry*, feeling extremely fortunate that as the lawyer who would be arguing on behalf of Edie Windsor, I had been given a ticket to get into the Court for *Perry*. Both arguments were expected to draw massive crowds, so I knew some of my colleagues had woken up before dawn to stand in line at the Supreme Court, since that was the only way to get a seat.

Jaren, Pam, Andrew, James, and Paul, Weiss partner Walter Rieman got to the Court around five a.m., and Pam talked later about the uncomfortable transition that took place once they arrived. Because people had started lining up days before, we had hired "line-standers" to act as proxies, so that the attorneys working on the case would not have to spend a sleepless night on the sidewalk. Hiring line-standers has become common for big cases at the Supreme Court, and many firms do it. But Pam described the surreal scene that unfolded the morning of the *Perry* argument.

> We got over to the Supreme Court at 5 a.m., and the entire lawyers' line was made up of homeless black men underneath tarps who had been sleeping there all night. And there was this white guy with a clipboard, and you went up to him and gave him your name, and then he went and woke up one of these guys. The guy would get up, wrap his blanket around him, and get on a bus, and you would then take his place in line.
>
> And if somebody had been there to take a time-lapse photo of this, you would have seen a line of homeless black men turning into a line of affluent white lawyers over about a two-hour period, and I was just staggered by it.

Especially for a lifelong civil rights lawyer like Pam, who had not only worked at the NAACP Legal Defense Fund but had devoted her entire career to obtaining rights for the socially marginalized, this was a particularly gut-wrenching experience.

When Pam and the others took their places in line, they stood in the freezing temperatures for another several hours. Once they finally got into the Court, I had already taken my assigned seat in the first row next to Amy Howe, a member of the Supreme Court bar who, along with her husband Tom Goldstein, runs the SCOTUSblog website. I could not wait to see how the argument unfolded and what the various justices would have to say about the issues in the case.

Charles Cooper, the attorney defending Prop 8, went first.

Cooper had clerked for Justice William Rehnquist and served as an assistant attorney general under President Reagan before cofounding his own law firm, Cooper & Kirk. He was a Southerner, a rock-solid conservative from Alabama who opposed gay rights. But what almost no one knew at the time was that his own stepdaughter, who had grown up with Cooper as a father figure, had recently told him that she was a lesbian. To my knowledge, Cooper never made any public statement revealing how that news had affected him, but it is hard to imagine that his daughter's coming out had no impact. Later, it was reported that Cooper had helped to organize his stepdaughter's wedding to her girlfriend, which took place a little more than a year after the *Perry* oral argument.

Cooper started his argument by focusing on whether Prop 8's proponents even had standing to defend the measure. This was the more technical, jurisdictional part of the case, but the detailed questioning made it clear that the answer wasn't cut and dried. Then Chief Justice Roberts invited Cooper to address the merits, and that's when things started to get interesting.

JUSTICE SOTOMAYOR: Outside of the marriage context, can you think of any other rational basis, reason, for a State using sexual orientation as a factor in denying homosexuals benefits or imposing burdens on them? Is there any other rational decision-making that the Government could make? Denying them a job, not granting them benefits of some sort, any other decision?

CHARLES COOPER: Your honor, I cannot. I do not have any—anything to offer you in that regard.

I couldn't believe what I had just heard with my own ears. Turning to Amy Howe, I whispered, "Did he just say what I think he said? Did he just concede that I win my case?"

Amy whispered back, "Yeah, I think he did."

Chuck Cooper had just admitted that, other than the right to marry, any statute that treats gay people differently from straight people would be presumptively unconstitutional. As far as I was concerned, the same logic would apply to DOMA since the couples adversely affected by DOMA were already gay and already married. This was therefore a pretty significant concession that DOMA itself was unconstitutional.

After that exchange, I was feeling pretty good about our chances, to say the least. And then things only got better, with the following humorous exchange between Chuck Cooper and Justice Kagan:

JUSTICE KAGAN: If you are over the age of 55, you don't help us serve the Government's interest in regulating procreation through marriage. So why is that different?

COOPER: Your Honor, even with respect to couples over the age of 55, it is very rare that both couples—both parties to the couple—are infertile, and the traditional— [LAUGHTER]

JUSTICE KAGAN: No, really, because if the couple—I can just assure you, if both the woman and the man are over the age of 55, there are not a lot of children coming out of that marriage. [LAUGHTER]

This exchange perfectly summed up the flaws in the procreation argument for denying gay couples the right to marry, although Cooper continued to insist that if one person in the couple—the man, obviously—remained fertile, then the government's interest in procreation was still satisfied. Justice Kagan kept pushing back, until finally Justice Scalia saw fit to interject, to much laughter, "Strom Thurmond was not the chairman of the Senate committee when Justice Kagan was confirmed."

Ted Olson went next, and the first half of his argument went more or less as expected, with Justices Alito, Scalia, and Roberts asking pointed questions, and the other justices periodically interjecting friendly questions. The most interesting part was the following exchange with Justice Scalia:

JUSTICE SCALIA: I'm curious—when did it become unconstitutional to exclude homosexual couples from marriage? 1791? 1868, when the Fourteenth Amendment was adopted? . . . When did the law become this?

TED OLSON: When—may I answer this in the form of a rhetorical question? When did it become unconstitutional to prohibit interracial marriages? When did it become unconstitutional to assign children to separate schools?

JUSTICE SCALIA: It's an easy question, I think, for that one. At the time that the Equal Protection Clause was adopted. That's absolutely true.

But don't give me a question to my question. [LAUGHTER] When do you think it became unconstitutional?

Ted and Justice Scalia went back and forth a bit on the question, but Scalia kept pressing the issue.

JUSTICE SCALIA: Was it always unconstitutional?

OLSON: It was constitutional when we—as a culture determined that sexual orientation is a characteristic of individuals that they cannot control, and that—

JUSTICE SCALIA: I see. When did that happen? When did that happen?

OLSON: There's no specific date in time. This is an evolutionary cycle.

JUSTICE SCALIA: Well, how am I supposed to decide a case then—

OLSON: Because the case that's before you—

JUSTICE SCALIA: —if you can't give me a date when the Constitution changes?

What struck me was that instead of focusing his ire on the "homosexual agenda," as he had in his dissent in *Lawrence*, Justice Scalia was now spending his energy and time attacking Ted. Coming into this oral argument, I wasn't sure how fierce Justice Scalia's questions might get. Afterward, I felt confident that I didn't need to worry unduly about any verbal flame-throwing from him, which was a relief.

When the oral arguments in *Perry* were over, our whole team reconnoitered at the DC Paul, Weiss office to compare notes. The firm had ordered Chinese food (accompanied by boxes of matzoh) for lunch, so when we walked into the big conference room, the table was laden with little white cartons. The Supreme Court had already posted a link to the audio of the argument, so we all sat around the table, scarfing down Chinese food, listening to it. We would stop the audio periodically, discuss how best to answer certain of the questions the justices had asked, and assess whether we needed to change any part of our strategy.

We discussed the exchange between Justice Scalia and Ted, with Jaren suggesting two possible answers: either DOMA was unconstitutional in 1996, when it was passed, or it was unconstitutional from 1791 onward, because it had never been the role of the federal government to step in and override the decisions of the states with respect to marriage. We started debating the issue back and forth, and it was about that time that I glanced down at my BlackBerry and read the first few lines of an e-mail that I had just received.

It was from a lawyer who had been at one of the moots. The e-mail started innocuously enough, just sending "good vibes" for my argument. But as I scrolled down, I saw that the lawyer was proposing to dictate an entire opening argument for me, down to starting with "Mr. Chief Justice and may it please the Court." The e-mail even provided a handy pronunciation guide, referring at one point to "Mr. Clement [Pronounced Cle MENT with accent on Ment]."

That was about as far as I got. In a moment of surprising sanity on my part, I slid my BlackBerry across the table to Pam and said, "I don't think I want to read this. Can you take care of it?"

As Pam read the e-mail, her mouth fell open. The notion that someone who was not part of our team, had never been involved in any of our subsequent strategy sessions, and had no idea what my opening argument even was at this point would write a brand-new one, send it to me less than twenty-four hours before I was about to stand in front of the Supreme Court, and believe that this was actually a productive way to help me was pretty amazing. What was I going to do, just throw all our months of work and preparation out the window? What kind of lawyer would truly think that we weren't as prepared as we could possibly be for this argument?

Pam read the whole thing, then said, "Yeah, I don't think you need to finish this." I asked what we should do, and she said—and this is why I so love Pam—"We could send an e-mail that says, 'Someone has hacked into your e-mail account and is sending bizarre messages. You really need to change your password.'"

I never responded to that e-mail, but one good thing did come out of it. For weeks afterward, whenever people on our team e-mailed each other, they'd include little pronunciation guides such as "It's pronounced WIND-sor" or "That's pronounced fo-CUS, in case you care."

AS I WAS walking into the hotel later that afternoon, my cell phone rang. I took the call while standing in the lobby, and just at that moment, Jacob walked by with his nanny, Ellie. He ran up to greet me, shouting with excitement, but I put my hand out to stop him. "Not now," I said. This was not something I ever did, but these were extraordinary circumstances, although Jacob couldn't have been expected to know or understand that.

Jacob got very upset, and Ellie took him away to try to soothe him. I finished my call and went up to my hotel room to continue working. In fifteen hours, I would be standing in front of the Supreme Court, arguing the most important case of my life, and I intended to work for the rest of the afternoon and evening, with as few distractions as possible, before (hopefully) getting a good night's sleep.

Rachel and Jacob were staying at the hotel in a separate room so that I could have space to work and sleep without interruption. It hadn't occurred to me, but this was very strange for Jacob, who was not used to having his two moms staying in different rooms. We had explained to him why it was necessary, but for a six-year-old logic has little sway over emotion. Not only were we not all staying in the same hotel room together but he had hardly seen me in the last few weeks, and now I had just blown him off when he had been so excited and happy to see me.

I honestly wasn't really thinking about any of this, but about thirty minutes or so after I had gone up to my room, as I was reading through my notes for the thousandth time, my phone rang. It was Rachel.

"Robbie, I need you to come down here right now," she said. "Jacob is really upset."

"I can't," I told her. "I'm still preparing." She told me that Jacob was crying, which was something he didn't normally do. "You need to come down."

"Rachel, I don't have time. I have to read this really important—"

"Enough!" she said. "There are a million people working on the case, but Jacob only has two parents, and he needs you right now." There was no appropriate response other than "Okay, I'll be right down."

When I got to their hotel room, I saw that Rachel was absolutely right. Jacob was as upset as I had ever seen him, sitting on the floor in a corner in the bathroom with his back to us. Seeing him like that completely broke my heart, and I crouched down to try to apologize and to kiss and hug him. But he wouldn't budge until Rachel finally said, "Jacob, how would you feel if you and Eema [the Hebrew word for 'mother,' which is what Jacob calls me] went back to her room and you guys had milk and cookies together?"

At last Jacob turned to look at us. "Really?" he said, sniffling.

"Yes," Rachel said. "We will all go to Eema's room together." This was what Jacob wanted, to have our whole family together, and so the three of us went up to my room, ordered milk and cookies from room service, and cuddled up on the bed to watch cartoons. We watched several episodes of *SpongeBob SquarePants* and *Johnny Test*, and Jacob sat contentedly between Rachel and me, munching on cookies.

As Rachel noted later, this was a perfect metaphor for what the case was about. Children need their parents. They need to know that their parents will be there for them whenever they want them, and getting married is a way to help make sure those relationships are kept safe. By spending that time with my wife and our child, we were embodying what *family* means in the truest sense of the word. In fact, in retrospect, I really can't think of a better way to have spent my final afternoon before my Supreme Court argument.

15

SKIM MILK

At 6:35 a.m. on March 27, 2013, I sent Pam the following e-mail from my hotel room: "The blowout is happening. In case you were concerned." This was not some coded secret message about last-minute SCOTUS strategy, it was literally true—I was referring to the fact that at that very moment, my friend David Milligan was in my hotel room giving me a very big, very Washington, DC–style hairdo. My e-mail, of course, was a follow-up to the joke I had made back in December when we learned that *Windsor* was going to the Supreme Court. At approximately 6:40 a.m., Pam characteristically responded in kind, noting that she was "confident that you will have the biggest hair in the whole damn room." As for her own hairdo, she observed that "I'm sprayed to a fine lacquer . . . see you over at the Court."

Emily had arranged for our transportation, so Rachel, Emily, Edie, Edie's friend Virginia Maraweck, and I all piled into a big black car for the short ride over to the Court—or what we thought was going to be a short ride. The Court was literally less than two miles away from our hotel, mostly a straight shot along the National Mall, but somehow the driver ended up on the highway, heading out of Washington, DC. *Really?* This was how my big day in front of the Supreme Court was starting off? I thought I was going to have a heart attack. Soon enough, however, the driver exited the highway and we were there.

Already, there was a huge crowd of people, reporters, camera crews, and police gathered outside the Supreme Court building. We walked into a side entrance, went through security, and made our way to the cafeteria, where Pam had suggested that we should all meet that morning. From the moment we walked in, however, people started mobbing Edie, wanting to shake her hand, get her autograph, and take selfies with her. She loved the attention, but it wasn't the ideal atmosphere for us to be able to focus. The lawyers' lounge would be quieter, but Edie and her friend could not go in there since they were not lawyers, so we weren't sure where we could go to get some peace and quiet. Fortunately, one of the many kind Supreme Court employees offered to take us to the clerk's office, where Edie was "protected" from her legions of fans.

Pam, James, Jaren, and I were soon ushered into the lawyers' lounge, where the lawyers appearing before the Court traditionally wait before argument. I had been there a few weeks earlier, when I had gone to see a Supreme Court oral argument, so I was familiar with the instructions that General William Suter, the Clerk of the Supreme Court, regularly gave to the lawyers. As General Suter informed everyone in the lawyers' lounge that the Court had extra pencils, cough drops, and sewing kits available for counsel, I remember thinking to myself, *What in the world would I do with a sewing kit right now?* Even if I had lost a button on my blazer, I'm pretty sure that if I tried to sew it on right before standing up to argue in front of the Supreme Court, I would probably take off a finger in the process. Another friend who had argued before the Court had advised me to put on my makeup in the lawyers' lounge, but I didn't do that either, convinced that if I tried, I would end up looking like Chuckles the Clown from *The Mary Tyler Moore Show.*

After the formal presentation by General Suter, I started to pace. In those moments before heading into the courtroom, I couldn't help but think back to the argument I had made, and lost, for marriage equality in New York in 2006. Seven years had passed since then, and in that time, the world had changed dramatically. At the New York Court of Appeals, my message to the judges was *Be brave. Do the right thing, even if it's hard*. Today, my message to the justices would be: *Already married, already gay*. In other words, in 2006, the burden was on our side to explain why gay people should be allowed to marry. By 2013, the burden had shifted, and it was up to the other side to explain why the otherwise legal marriages of gay couples should be categorically disrespected under federal law.

Walking into the courtroom, I actually felt pretty calm. Pam, James, Jaren, and I took our seats at the counsels' table, and as I glanced around the room, I saw that the Court officers had done everything in their power to squeeze as many people into the courtroom as possible. I noticed (while trying very hard not to notice) that a whole slew of Washington, DC, celebrities, such as White House advisor Valerie Jarrett, Democratic Leader Nancy Pelosi, and our own congressman, Jerrold Nadler, walked up to pay their respects to Edie, who was sitting in the second row with Rachel and Viola. My goal was to do my best to ignore all the commotion and focus on my argument, but I was pleased to notice that my hair was at least blown out in the same fashion as that of Nancy Pelosi. As usual, Pam had been correct.

We all rose as the nine justices entered, and at 10:18 a.m., Chief Justice John Roberts opened the proceedings with the words, "We will hear argument this morning in Case 12-307, *United States v. Windsor*, and we will begin with the jurisdictional discussion." As my Paul, Weiss mentor Marty London had exhorted in his text to me months ago, "on to the Show."

The justices began with the jurisdictional arguments, which involved a very technical discussion of federal statutes and case law about the authority (or lack thereof) of the Supreme Court to hear the case. Vicki Jackson did a superb job, as did Sri Srinivasan, who argued for the Department of Justice. Paul Clement argued for BLAG, and I was struck by how fast he talked. My whole career, no one has ever believed I'm from Cleveland, assuming that I'm a native New Yorker because I tend to speak so quickly. Throughout my career, people have been telling me that I needed to speak more slowly. But as I sat there listening to Paul Clement, I realized that this may be the one place on the planet where speaking quickly was definitely an advantage.

During the jurisdictional arguments, I had *shpilkes*, or "ants in my pants," since I had tons of nervous energy and was impatient to stand up and get the show on the road. When the jurisdictional arguments concluded, Chief Justice Roberts called for a short break, and then—at long last—it was time for the arguments on the merits. Paul Clement would go first for thirty minutes, then Solicitor General Don Verrilli for fifteen, and then it would be my turn. I would be the last lawyer, and the first and only gay person, to argue in the entire two days (or almost three hours) of oral argument in the *Perry* and *Windsor* cases combined.

Paul Clement opened by telling the justices that "the legal question on the merits before this Court is actually quite narrow." The federal government, he said, has the "choice to adopt a constitutionally permissible definition" of marriage, rather than having to submit to follow the pro–LGBT equality choices of states like New York.

Justice Ginsburg was the first to interject, speaking in her usual neutral but determined tone:

> Mr. Clement, the problem is if we are totally for the States' decision that there is a marriage between two people, for the Federal Government then to come in to say no joint return, no marital deduction, no Social Security benefits; your spouse is very sick but you can't get leave; people—if

that set of attributes, one might well ask, what kind of marriage is this?

I was thrilled that Justice Ginsburg dove right in with what, after all, was one of our main themes—the sheer breadth of DOMA and how it unjustly discriminated against married gay couples in so many different ways. We had always been worried that enumerating the government benefits that married gay couples were being denied under DOMA would look bad, since it might look like our only goal was to seek what is often derogated as an entitlement, rather than a constitutional right. In other words, although we really wanted this point to be made, I preferred not to be the person to make it. Now that Justice Ginsburg had just made it herself, we were off to a very good start.

A few minutes later, Justice Kennedy made the same point, but interlaced with elements of the federalism argument that had been circulating recently among conservative thinkers. He observed that DOMA

applies to, what, 1,100 Federal laws . . .

[W]hen it has 1,100 laws, which in our society means that the Federal Government is intertwined with the citizens' day-to-day life, you are at real risk of running in conflict with what has always been thought to be the essence of the State police power, which is to regulate marriage, divorce, custody.

Paul responded by saying that "the very fact that there are 1,100 provisions of Federal law that define the terms 'marriage' and 'spouse' goes a long way to showing that Federal law has not just stayed completely out of these issues," and then asserting that "the fact that DOMA involves all 1,100 statutes at once is not really a sign of its irrationality. It is a sign that what it is, and all it has ever purported to be, is a definitional provision . . . all it does is define the term [marriage] wherever it appears in Federal law in a consistent way."

So far, the questions the justices had asked were more helpful for our side, but Paul Clement was more than holding his own, answering their questions with his usual fluency and confidence. A few minutes later, however, came an exchange with Justice Ginsburg that would redefine the notion of marriage equality in the post-*Windsor* era:

PAUL CLEMENT: No State loses any benefits by recognizing same-sex marriage. Things stay the same. What they don't do is they don't sort of open up an additional class of beneficiaries . . . that get additional Federal benefits. But things stay the same. And that's why in this sense—

JUSTICE GINSBURG: They're not a question of additional benefits. I mean, they touch every aspect of life. Your partner is sick. Social Security. I mean, it's pervasive. It's not as though, well, there's this little Federal sphere and it's only a tax question.

It's—as Justice Kennedy said, 1,100 statutes, and it affects every area of life. And so he was really diminishing what the State has said is marriage. You're saying, no, State said two kinds of marriage: the full marriage, and then this sort of skim milk marriage.

Suddenly, there was a lot of appreciative laughter coming from the audience, but because Justice Ginsburg speaks so softly, I wasn't sure that I actually had heard what she had said, so I turned to Pam. When Pam told me that Justice Ginsburg had just coined the phrase "skim milk marriage," I had to use all my self-control not to pump my fist in the air in elation. We had spent countless hours on our team debating how best to express the point that under DOMA, gay married people were being treated as second-class citizens. We had gone around and around trying to find a phrase that would best sum it all up. By characterizing Edie's marriage under DOMA as a "skim milk marriage," Justice Ginsburg had, in a span of thirty seconds, crystallized what our case was really about.

Justice Ginsburg had also used the phrase "as Justice Kennedy said," which was a sign that she understood that the winning side needed his vote. The fact that she had made this point so forcefully, and had attached Justice Kennedy's name to it, could be read to indicate that she, too, thought we were in good shape.

Justice Kagan was the next to interject:

> Mr. Clement, for the most part and historically, the only uniformity that the Federal Government has pursued is that it's uniformly recognized the marriages that are recognized by the State. So, this was a real difference in the uniformity that the Federal Government was pursuing. And it suggests that maybe something—maybe Congress had something different in mind than uniformity.
>
> So we have a whole series of cases which suggest the following: Which suggest that when Congress targets a group that is not everybody's favorite group in the world, that we look at those cases with some . . . rigor to say, do we really think that Congress was doing this for uniformity reasons, or do we think that Congress's judgment was infected by dislike, by fear, by animus, and so forth?
>
> I guess the question that this statute raises, this statute that does something that's really never been done before, is whether that sends up a pretty good red flag that that's what's going on.

Paul calmly segued into his response:

> When you look at Congress doing something that is unusual, that deviates from the way they have proceeded in the past,

you have to ask, Well, was there good reason? And in a sense, you have to understand that, in 1996, something's happening that is, in a sense, forcing Congress to choose between its historic practice of deferring to the States and its historic practice of preferring uniformity.

Up until 1996, it essentially has it both ways: Every State has the traditional definition [of marriage]. Congress knows that's the definition that's embedded in every Federal law. So that's fine. We can defer.

Okay. 1996—

Paul seemed ready to move on, but Justice Kagan wasn't done:

Well, is what happened in 1996—and I'm going to quote from the House Report here—is that "Congress decided to reflect an honor of collective moral judgment and to express moral disapproval of homosexuality."

Is that what happened in 1996?

There was another pronounced collective gasp throughout the courtroom. I had seen Paul Clement argue several times, and I'd never seen him even remotely shaken. But this question understandably threw him off. His answer confirmed that he was on shaky ground:

Does the House Report say that? Of course, the House Report says that. And if that's enough to invalidate the statute, then you should invalidate the statute. But that has never been your approach . . .

I have been privileged to observe many excellent cross-examinations in my career (including many by my partners Ted Wells and Marty London), but this was surely at the top of the list.

The way that Justice Kagan built her questioning in layers, leading to her final question, should be taught in a class on trial skills. And she seemed to enjoy every second of it.

From the very beginning of the case, our goal had been to describe DOMA as exactly what it was—a radical departure from how Congress had always treated married people and an effort to "fence off" gay people from the rest of federal law and recognition. Paul Clement's strategy was to try to characterize DOMA as just an ordinary statute, passed by Congress with overwhelming majorities and signed by President Clinton as if he were simply reauthorizing a federal program as relatively uncontroversial as the National Park Service or the U.S. Postal Service.

In our brief, we had included numerous vitriolic quotes from the 1996 congressional debate over DOMA—that homosexuality was "based on perversion" or "inherently destructive." In footnote 3, we showed that such animus was still alive and well in the amicus briefs, which used language such as "immoral," "radically disruptive to society," and "a vector of injury and disease" when describing gay people. We had specifically included those quotes in the hopes of provoking precisely the exchange that had just taken place between Justice Kagan and Paul Clement, to show that DOMA was something extraordinary, even for 1996.

The moment Paul uttered the words "if that's enough to invalidate the statute, then you should invalidate the statute," I thought, *We just won.* This point was our whole case: the only reason for treating gay marriages differently than straight ones is what is referred to in constitutional terms as "animus." We had specifically written our brief (including the checklist section in the middle that I rewrote dozens of times) so that the justices on our side could take this information and run with it. All along we had believed that this was the argument that had the best chance of persuading Justice Kennedy. And once again, another justice had just made our point for us.

WHEN PAUL'S TIME was up, Solicitor General Verrilli stepped up to the lectern. By this point, I was feeling pretty confident about our chances, but as the solicitor general started his oral argument, my feelings turned to a mild state of panic. My anxiety was not the result of how the arguments were going but stemmed instead from the fact that the solicitor general was making the exact same point that I had planned to make during my opening.

DOMA, he explained to the justices, "exclude[s] from an array of Federal benefits lawfully married couples. That means that the spouse of a soldier killed in the line of duty cannot receive the dignity and solace of an official notification of next of kin." In my opening, which we had written and rewritten hundreds of times trying to make it as powerful and concise as possible, the second sentence was "[W]hen a married gay soldier is killed in the line of duty, military officials must notify the dead soldier's parent, instead of the spouse."

Although we had worked with the DOJ on general strategy, we hadn't exchanged notes with them on our openings. I'm not sure that the solicitor general would have shared his opening with me even if I had asked, since DOJ lawyers tend to play things like this close to their chest. The fact that both the solicitor general and I wanted to open with the military argument speaks to how powerful that argument really was. Now, however, I had to change my opening, and fast.

Sitting there at the lawyers' table, I quickly crossed out my original opening and started jotting notes for what I might say instead. In the meantime, I obviously had to keep listening closely, in case there were any notable exchanges during the solicitor general's argument that could be helpful for mine.

Chief Justice Roberts was the first to interject, turning immediately to the subject of federalism. This was arguably dangerous territory for BLAG because it gave the justices another independent reason—one unrelated to the equality of gay people under the law—to strike down DOMA. In other words, if Justice Kennedy wasn't entirely convinced about our equal protection argument, the federalism theory might still persuade him to vote our way. And Justice Kennedy had already intimated, through the comments he'd made during Paul Clement's oral argument, that he was at least interested in the federalism issue.

In the moment that Chief Justice Roberts asked Solicitor General Verrilli about federalism, two things were immediately clear. First, as the solicitor general of the United States, Don Verrilli had no choice but to say that federalism was not a reason to find DOMA unconstitutional. The federal government's view of its own powers is necessarily expansive, and as one of the highest-ranking federal officials, the solicitor general was not about to argue that Congress had overstepped the limits of its authority. It was his job (and his duty) to argue precisely the opposite.

Second, the chief justice undoubtedly knew that the solicitor general would respond the way that he did. By getting the solicitor general to state plainly that the U.S. government disavowed the federalism argument, the chief justice was presumably hoping to take that argument off the table. In fact, he didn't just ask the federalism question of the solicitor general once, he asked it three separate times.

CHIEF JUSTICE ROBERTS: [Y]ou don't think it would raise a federalism problem either, do you?

SOLICITOR GENERAL VERRILLI: I don't think it would raise a federalism problem . . .

CHIEF JUSTICE ROBERTS: So, just to be clear, you don't think there is a federalism problem with what Congress has done in DOMA?

VERRILLI: We—no we don't, Mr. Chief Justice . . .

CHIEF JUSTICE ROBERTS: You don't think federalism concerns come into play at all in this, right?

As I listened, my sense was that Chief Justice Roberts may have believed that Justice Kennedy was leaning toward striking down DOMA on federalism grounds, which may have explained why the chief justice was eager to neutralize that argument. However, if Justice Kennedy was actually persuaded by the equal protection argument, then the federalism argument would not really matter. Regardless of his strategic thinking, the chief justice kept pressing the issue.

The exchanges on the topic of federalism continued until Justice Sotomayor stepped in to change the subject. She asked what level of scrutiny the justices should apply in this case, and from that point on, the solicitor general's argument stayed on equal protection. He managed to work in one uninterrupted, powerful statement toward the end of his time, making several crucial points:

> If anything, Section 3 of DOMA makes Federal administration more difficult, because now the Federal Government has to look behind valid state marriage licenses and see whether they are about State marriages that are out of compliance with DOMA.
>
> It's an additional administrative burden. So there is no administrative advantage to be gained here by what Congress sought to achieve. And the fundamental reality of it is, and I think the House report makes this glaringly clear, is that DOMA was not enacted for any purpose of uniformity, administration, caution, . . . any of that.
>
> It was enacted to exclude same-sex married, lawfully married couples from Federal benefit regimes based on a conclusion that was driven by moral disapproval.

Soon thereafter, Solicitor General Verrilli's time was up. Now, it was my turn.

FOR MOST OF the day, I had been surprisingly calm. The questioning had gone very well for our side, and although I was very aware of the gravity of the case and the intensity of the feelings in the courtroom and throughout the nation, I felt ready. The moment I stepped up to the lectern, however, my nerves suddenly kicked in. "Mr. Chief Justice, and may it please the court," I said, my voice slightly shaky. I then went right into the new opening that I had hastily scribbled down during the solicitor general's argument.

> I'd like to focus on why DOMA fails even under rationality review. Because of DOMA, many thousands of people who are legally married under the laws of nine sovereign states and the District of Columbia are being treated as unmarried by the Federal Government solely because they are gay.
>
> These couples are being treated as unmarried with respect to programs that affect family stability, such as the Family Leave Act, referred to by Justice Ginsburg. These couples are being treated as unmarried for purposes of Federal conflict of interest rules, election laws and anti-nepotism and judicial recusal statutes.
>
> And my client was treated as unmarried when her spouse passed away, so that she had to pay $363,000 in estate taxes on the property that they had accumulated during their 44 years together.

This is where Chief Justice Roberts interjected, but I was happy that I'd been able to get across at least these three points about DOMA at the outset without interruption, going from the universal negative impact DOMA was having on many thousands of gay people to its particular adverse impact on my client, Edie Windsor. Although initially I had been reluctant to bring up the issue of the benefits being denied to married gay couples under

DOMA, once Justice Ginsburg had brought it up herself during Paul Clement's argument, I knew I could attribute the observation to her, which I happily did.

When Chief Justice Roberts started to speak, it was again on his preferred subject of federalism. "Could I ask you the same question I asked the Solicitor General?" he said. "Do you think there would be a problem if Congress went the other way . . . [if] Congress said, we're going to recognize same-sex couples—committed same-sex couples—even if the State doesn't, for purposes of Federal law?"

This was a bit of a twist: Chief Justice Roberts was giving me a hypothetical, but he was turning it around to ask me to imagine a situation where the federal government actually insisted on providing recognition to gay couples, no matter what the individual states had to say. I was at first a bit uncertain as to where the Chief Justice was going with this, so I tried to pivot back to equal protection.

ME: Obviously, with respect to marriage, the Federal Government has always used the state definitions. And I think what you're proposing is to extend—the Federal Government extend additional benefits to gay couples in States that do not allow marriage, to equalize the system.

CHIEF JUSTICE ROBERTS: I'm just, I'm asking whether you think Congress has the power to interfere with the—to not adopt the State definition if they're extending benefits. Do they have that authority?

ME: I think the question under the Equal Protection Clause is what the distinction is.

CHIEF JUSTICE ROBERTS: No, no. I know that.

You're following the lead of the Solicitor General and returning to the Equal Protection Clause every time I ask a federalism question.

Is there any problem under federalism principles?

The chief justice appeared to be annoyed. He clearly seemed to want me to answer, as the solicitor general had before me, that I did not believe that the reason why DOMA was unconstitutional was because of federalism. I wasn't inclined to give a simple no answer to the question, however, and unlike Solicitor General Verrilli, I didn't have to.

Not only was I disinclined to hand anyone any ammunition for persuading Justice Kennedy to vote to uphold DOMA, but I actually believed that the answer was far more complicated. Here's why: if a couple, one of whom is a U.S. citizen and one of whom is not, wants to get married, all they have to do is go to the city clerk's office and fill out the necessary forms. The couple doesn't go to the federal office building across the street because only the states, not the federal government, can marry people. But if the now-married noncitizen husband wants to get his green card, he has to go to the federal Department of Homeland Security. There, the federal officials are perfectly entitled to ask him things like the color of his new wife's toothbrush in order to determine whether he entered into a "real" marriage, meaning the marriage was not fraudulently entered into for the purpose of obtaining a green card.

So the question is where—on this continuum between the federal government not marrying people and the federal government being able to ask someone applying for a green card whether his marriage is real—does the Tenth Amendment draw the line? There certainly was no clear answer in the Constitution or the case law. This was the complexity that I was trying to suggest in my answers. When I said as much, though, Justice Scalia seemed to get irritated as well.

ME: For the reasons Justice Kagan mentioned, we think the federalism principles go toward a novelty question. I think whether or not the Federal Government could have its own definition of marriage for all purposes would be a very closely argued question.

JUSTICE SCALIA: I don't understand your answer. Is your answer yes or no? Is there a federalism problem with that, or isn't there a federalism problem?

ME: I think the Federal Government could extend benefits to gay couples to equalize things on a programmatic basis to make things more equal. Whether the Federal Government could have its own definition of marriage, I think, would be—it'd be very closely argued whether that's outside the enumerated approach.

JUSTICE SCALIA: Well, it's just—all these statutes use the term "marriage," and the Federal Government says in all of these statutes when it says marriage, it includes same sex-couples, whether the State acknowledges whether it would work?

[Laughter] I don't care if it works.

Does it create a federalism problem?

I was adamant about not giving the one-word answer that the justices sought. I was also concerned that a win on federalism grounds alone would hurt plaintiffs in the next big case (if there wasn't a victory on the merits in *Perry*) because states like Florida, Texas, and Mississippi would be able to argue that states had a right under the Tenth Amendment not to allow or recognize the marriages of gay couples. (And, as it turns out, that's exactly what Florida, Texas, and Mississippi have been arguing in the courts since *Windsor*.) My game plan all along was to try to pivot away from the federalism question if the justices raised it, but we did not expect them to go after it so insistently and for so long.

Justice Alito was the next to jump in, and he redirected the argument back to equal protection.

JUSTICE ALITO: If the estate tax follows State law, would not that create an equal protection problem similar to the one that

exists here? Suppose there were a dispute about the—the State
of residence of your client and her partner or spouse. Was it
New York, was it some other State where same-sex marriage
would not have been recognized? And suppose there was—
the State court said the State of residence is a State where it's
not recognized.

Would you not have essentially the same equal protection
argument there that you have now?

ME: Well, let me answer that question very clearly. Our position
is only with respect to the nine States—and I think there are
two others that recognize these marriages. So if my client—if
a New York couple today marries and moves to North Carolina, which has a constitutional amendment, a State constitutional amendment [prohibiting gay marriage]—and one
of the spouses dies, they would not—and estate taxes determine where the person dies, they would not be entitled to the
deduction.

That is not our claim here.

This response irked some in the LGBT rights community, but
it was absolutely the right answer to give at that time. My job was
to win Edie's case, which was about one woman and one estate
tax bill, not to make broader arguments about what position the
Obama administration would or should take with respect to states
like North Carolina that did not then have marriage equality if
we won our case. I also wanted to take the opportunity to differ-
entiate our case from *Perry*, which I suspected (based on the arguments the day before) had less chance of winning on the merits
than *Windsor* did. The next exchange with Justice Alito allowed
me to do exactly that.

JUSTICE ALITO: What if the hypothetical surviving spouse, partner
in North Carolina, brought an equal protection argument,

saying that there is no—it is unconstitutional to treat me differently because I am a resident of North Carolina rather than a resident of New York. What would be—would that be discrimination on the basis of sexual orientation? What would be the level of scrutiny? Would it survive?

ME: That would be certainly a different case. It would be more similar to the [*Perry*] case I think you heard yesterday than the case that we have today. We certainly believe that sexual-orientation discrimination should get heightened scrutiny. If it doesn't get heightened scrutiny, obviously, it'd be rational basis, and the question would be, what the State interests were in not allowing couples, for example, in North Carolina who are gay to get married.

No one has identified in this case, and I don't think we've heard it in the argument from my friend [Paul Clement], any legitimate difference between married gay couples on the one hand and straight married couples on the other that can possibly explain the sweeping, undifferentiated and categorical discrimination of DOMA, Section 3 of DOMA.

And no one has identified any legitimate Federal interest that is being served by Congress's decision, for the first time in our nation's history to undermine the determinations of the sovereign States with respect to eligibility for marriage. I would respectfully contend that this is because there is none.

Rather, as the title of the statute makes clear, DOMA was enacted to defend against the marriages of gay people. This discriminatory purpose was rooted in moral disapproval, as Justice Kagan pointed out.

I had felt a little nervous at the beginning, but by now I was in the zone. I was completely focused on getting out my strongest points to the exclusion of everything else. Whenever a justice asked me a question, I would look directly at him or her and answer. Because Justice Thomas never asks questions during arguments, I don't think I looked his way even once.

Of all the exchanges I had with the justices, the one that happened next was probably the most substantive. It involved the question of uniformity, which is really the primary argument that DOMA's defenders were still pushing at that point. Under the uniformity argument, Congress was justified in passing DOMA in 1996 because it enabled the government to have uniformity with respect to the marriages (or potential future marriages) of gay couples.

This was BLAG's core argument, and when Paul Clement had been up at bat, Justice Breyer had asked him about it.

JUSTICE BREYER: All right. So you're saying uniform treatment's good enough no matter how odd it is, no matter how irrational. There is nothing but uniformity. We could take—no matter. You see what I'm—where I'm going?

CLEMENT: No, I see exactly where you're going, Justice Breyer.

JUSTICE BREYER: All right. [LAUGHTER] . . .

CLEMENT: Well, again, if we're—if we're coming at this from the premise that the States have the option to choose, and then we come at this from the perspective that Congress is passing this not in a vacuum, they're passing this in 1996. And what they're confronting in 1996 is the prospect that one State, through its judiciary, will adopt same-sex marriage, and then by operation of the full faith and credit law, that will apply to any—any couple that wants to go there.

And the State that's thinking about doing this is, Hawaii, it's a very nice place to go and get married. And so Congress is worried that people are going to go there, go back to their home jurisdictions, insist on the recognition in their home jurisdictions of their same-sex marriage in Hawaii, and then the Federal Government will borrow that defini-

tion, and therefore, by the operation of one State's State judiciary, same-sex marriage is basically going to be recognized
throughout the country.

And what Congress says is, wait a minute. Let's take a time-
out here. This is a redefinition of an age-old institution. Let's
take a more cautious approach where every sovereign gets to
do this for themselves. . . .

Given his skills as an oral advocate, Paul Clement had almost
managed to make this sound reasonable. The problem with his
argument, however, is that the federal government under DOMA
was not actually treating Americans' marriages uniformly. In fact,
what Congress was doing was accepting the marriages of straight
couples and rejecting the marriages of gay couples. Indeed, historically, the federal government had uniformly always treated marriages the same way, regardless of significant differences among
the states as to who (and at what age) people could marry. Thus,
the only uniformity promoted by DOMA was with respect to its
treatment of gay people. Gay people were in fact being treated
uniformly under DOMA—that is, they were being uniformly
disadvantaged. But that's not uniformity, that's discrimination.

Justice Breyer gave me a chance to answer the same question.

JUSTICE BREYER: What—what do you think of his—the argument that I heard was, to put the other side, at least one part
of it as I understand it said, look, the Federal Government
needs a uniform rule. There has been this uniform one man,
one woman rule for several hundred years or whatever, and
there's a revolution going on in the States. We either adopt the
resolution—the revolution or push it along a little, or we stay
out of it. And I think Mr. Clement was saying, well, we've
decided to stay out of it.

ME: I don't—

JUSTICE BREYER: And the way to stay out of it is to go with the traditional thing. I mean, that—that's an argument. So your answer to that argument is what?

ME: I think it's an incorrect argument, Justice Breyer, for the—

JUSTICE BREYER: I understand you do, I'd like to know the reason.

[LAUGHTER]

ME: Of course. Congress did not stay out of it. Section 3 of DOMA is not staying out of it. Section 3 of DOMA is stopping the recognition by the Federal Government of couples who are already married, solely based on their sexual orientation, and what it's doing is undermining, as you can see in the briefs of the States of New York and others, it's undermining the policy decisions made by those States that have permitted gay couples to marry.

States that have already resolved the cultural, the political, the moral—whatever other controversies, they're resolved in those States. And by fencing those couples off, couples who are already married, and treating them as unmarried for purposes of Federal law, you're not—you're not taking it one step at a time, you're not promoting caution, you're putting a stop button on it, and you're having discrimination for the first time in our country's history against a class of married couples.

Already married, already gay! I finally got to make our argument. In the nine states where gay people were then allowed to marry, there hadn't been chaos as a result—we hadn't seen any breakdown or disruption of the social order. Gay marriage wasn't tearing the fabric of the nation. Whatever reason anyone had for thinking that gay people shouldn't be allowed to marry, we had a response.

Justice Sotomayor followed my answer on uniformity by asking, "Do you think there's a difference between that discrimination [against gay married couples] and the discrimination of States who say homosexuals can't get married?" I responded by saying again that *Windsor* and *Perry* were different cases, but her question gave me a chance to stress once again the real reason why Congress had passed DOMA:

> The answer can't be uniformity as we've discussed. It can't be cost savings, because you still have to explain then why the cost savings is being wrought at the expense of married couples who are gay; and it can't be any of the State interests that weren't discussed, but questions of family law in parenting and marriage are done by the States, not the Federal Government.
>
> The only conclusion that can be drawn is what was in the House Report, which is moral disapproval of gay people, which the Congress thought was permissible in 1996 because it relied on the Court's *Bowers* decision, which this Court has said was wrong, not only at the time it was overruled in *Lawrence*, but was wrong when it was decided.

Chief Justice Roberts then jumped in to ask me whether the "84 senators based their vote on moral disapproval of gay people?" With that, he gave me the opening that I'd been looking for, the chance to win my bet with our team by quoting Justice Kennedy's own words directly.

ME: I think what is true, Mr. Chief Justice, is that times can blind, and that back in 1996 people did not have the understanding that they have today, that there is no distinction, there is no constitutionally permissible distinction—

CHIEF JUSTICE ROBERTS: Well, does that mean—times can blind. Does that mean they did not base their votes on moral disapproval?

ME: No; some clearly did. I think it was based on an understanding that gay—an incorrect understanding that gay couples were fundamentally different than straight couples, an understanding that I don't think exists today and that's the sense I'm using that times can blind. I think there was—we can all understand that people have moved on this, and now understand that there is no such distinction. So I'm not saying it was animus or bigotry, I think it was based on a misunderstanding on gay people . . .

The moment I said "times can blind," Chief Justice Roberts—and all the other justices—knew exactly what I was doing. Those words are probably the most quoted phrase from Kennedy's opinion in *Lawrence v. Texas*, and they speak precisely to the point I was trying to make. In 1996, lots of people thought gay people were different, not to mention strange and scary, but in 2013, that wasn't the case anymore.

Were people homophobic bigots in 1996? No, they were blinded by the times they lived in. What cured the blindness of prior generations in failing to see that their gay brothers, sisters, colleagues, and neighbors have the same human need for love and commitment as everyone else?

In large part, the reason for this sea change in attitudes toward gay people is the fact that until recently, many Americans simply did not realize that they knew anyone who was gay. Because of the sting of social disapproval and the persistence of discrimination in nearly every facet of everyday existence, for most of the twentieth century and continuing even today, many gay people have lived their lives in the closet so as not to risk losing a job, a home, or the love and support of family and friends. Without the benefit of knowing and understanding the lives of gay people living openly and with dignity in their communities, many Americans failed to see that gay people and their families have the same aspirations to life, liberty, and the pursuit of happiness as everyone else.

Perhaps the paradigmatic example of this phenomenon is the experience of the senator from my home state of Ohio, Rob Portman, who supported the Ohio marriage bans at issue in this case based on his "faith tradition that marriage is a sacred bond between a man and a woman." However, shortly before the oral arguments in *Windsor*, he changed his mind upon learning that his own son is gay.

Justice Scalia asked me next how many states currently permit "gay marriage," and I answered nine. "So, there has been this sea change between now and 1996," he said. I couldn't really tell whether Justice Scalia expected me to respond with a yes, or a no, but I readily agreed, "I think with respect to the understanding of gay people and their relationships there has been a sea change, Your Honor." This gave Chief Justice Roberts the idea for his next question.

CHIEF JUSTICE ROBERTS: I suppose the sea change has a lot to do with the political force and effectiveness of people representing, supporting your side of the case?

ME: I disagree with that, Mr. Chief Justice, I think the sea change has to do, just as was discussed in *Bowers* and *Lawrence*, was an understanding that there is no difference—there was [no] fundamental difference that could justify this kind of categorical discrimination between gay couples and straight couples.

CHIEF JUSTICE ROBERTS: You don't doubt that the lobby supporting the enactment of same-sex marriage laws in different States is politically powerful, do you?

ME: With respect to that category, that categorization of the term for purposes of heightened scrutiny, I would, Your Honor.

I knew where the chief justice was going with this. As we had argued before the Second Circuit, one of the four characteristics that the courts have looked to in deciding whether a particular minority group should receive heightened scrutiny is a lack of political power. The chief justice was implying that gay people now had more than enough political power to protect themselves from discrimination through the political process, but I disagreed. "Really?" he asked. I responded, "Yes." (My mother, who was sitting with my father in the courtroom, later told me that when I gave this answer to the chief justice, she panicked, convinced that a bunch of federal marshals were going to walk over, put me in handcuffs, and escort me away.)

Then the chief justice said, "As far as I can tell, political figures are falling all over themselves to endorse your side of the case." (Here was the unforeseen consequence of President Clinton's op-ed that I had worked so hard to get.)

My face flushing for the first and only time, I responded:

> The fact of the matter, Mr. Chief Justice, is that no other group in recent history has been subjected to popular referenda to take away rights that have already been given or exclude those rights the way gay people have, and only two of those referenda have ever lost. One was in Arizona; it then passed a couple of years later. One was in Minnesota, where they already have a statute on the books that prohibits marriage between gay people.
>
> So I don't think—and until 1990, gay people were not allowed to enter this country. So I don't think that the political power of gay people today could possibly be seen within that framework.

Throughout our entire case, I had succeeded in keeping my personal feelings at bay. As a lawyer, my duty is always to my client, and for four years, I had kept my focus relentlessly on Edie Windsor and the facts of her case. But DOMA wasn't just a law that I wanted to see struck down as an attorney. It was a law that adversely affected me, my wife, and my son. I wanted to win this case for Edie, but I wanted DOMA struck down for my own family, too.

As the only gay lawyer who had argued in either *Windsor* or *Perry*, I was acutely aware that I needed to keep on an even keel, even more so than the other lawyers. I could not appear to be emotionally invested, even though I was. But in the moment that Chief Justice Roberts used the phrase "falling all over themselves," years of my own injured feelings came rushing to the surface. Being told by a nurse that I couldn't take Jacob home. Having a social worker ask what we would tell Jacob when he "grieves the loss of the father." And I was one of the lucky ones. Many more gay people—too many to count (including Edie)— had suffered far worse indignities in their sometimes too-short lives, and many more would continue to do so, no matter how much political power Chief Justice Roberts believed we had.

My voice had cracked slightly with emotion as I answered, but as the chief justice began to respond, I quickly regained my composure. "[Y]ou just referred to a sea change in people's understandings and values from 1996, when DOMA was enacted," he said, "and I'm just trying to see where that comes from, if not from the political effectiveness of groups on your side of the case."

I knew I was nearly out of time, and this would be my last substantive response before my argument was over. At that moment, a thought popped into my head that we hadn't mooted or ever discussed, but it was far too late to ask anyone else what they thought. I know it sounds crazy, but I honestly believe that God, a higher power, or whatever else you want to call it helped to put it there. In an instant, I decided to trust my instincts and forge ahead.

> To flip the language of the House Report, Mr. Chief Justice, I think it comes from a moral understanding today that gay people are no different, and that gay married couples'

relationships are not significantly different from the relationships of straight married people.

In the hundreds of hours we had spent preparing, we had never
come up with this idea of flipping the phrase "moral disapproval"
from the legislative history of DOMA to a "moral understanding" of gay people today. The minute it came into my head and
out of my mouth, however, I knew that it was exactly the right
thing to say. There was little the chief justice could really say in
response and we were out of time anyway, so that's how my argument ended.

Paul Clement stood up to do his three-minute rebuttal, and
while I sat down next to Pam, my brain still spinning, I leaned
toward her and whispered, "I think my answers were okay."

"They were great!" she whispered back.

I hadn't screwed it up. I had done right by Edie. And I honestly
felt in that moment that I wouldn't have changed a single word in
the answers I had given. What an enormous relief.

AS LONG AS I am still alive and breathing, I will never forget those
next few moments when we walked out of the Supreme Court
building onto the steps after the oral argument that day. Our
whole team had gathered in the lobby, where we were met by
Edie, Rachel, Jacob, Rachel's mom, Rachel's sister, our nephew
Ari, and Pam's partner, Viola. We could hear the crowd outside
yelling and cheering, and in that moment I flashed back to the
Court employee's offer a few weeks earlier to help us slip out the
back way. I had to smile. There was no way I would miss this
moment for anything in the world.

Hilary Rosen and Emily Giske were already there, wearing
dark Ray-Bans and looking like Secret Service agents, helping to
orchestrate the scene. "Is everybody ready?" Hilary asked. "Here
we go." As we started walking out, I could feel Hilary's hand on

my back, pushing me to the front of the group. (Emily later told me that they had joked that they never would have guessed in a million years that they would be doing "advance" for Robbie Kaplan.)

We stepped out into the brilliant sunshine, and it took a moment for my eyes to adjust. I had figured that there would be a crowd, but I never expected it to be as big as it was: there were literally hundreds of people. As soon as they saw Edie, they erupted into a wild roar. Looking radiant in a gray suit and bright pink scarf, wearing the circular diamond pin that Thea had given her for their engagement almost a half century before, Edie held her arms wide, as if to embrace the entire crowd. Responding to a reporter's question about the reasons for the "sea change" in attitudes toward gay people at the press conference on the courthouse steps, Edie explained, "Some brave person woke up one morning and said, 'I'm gay' . . . and then another person did it, and then another . . ."

Edie's answer was perfect, as good as any I had given the justices that day. I looked at her and thought, *We did it*. We did it—for ourselves, for our families, for the millions of gay people whose lives would be changed for the better.

We did it, both Edie and I, for all of us—and for Thea.

16

EQUAL DIGNITY

The "Guide for Counsel," published by the Supreme Court the same year that our case was decided, explains as follows: *"Opinions may be handed down at any time after the argument. The only information the Clerk or his staff can give you in this regard is that cases argued during the Term are usually decided before the end of June."* Because *Windsor* had been argued at the end of March, we knew that the justices would most likely hand down their decision sometime in June. In other words, we were going to have to wait about three months (or twelve weeks, or eighty-four days, or 2,016 hours) before learning whether all of our work had paid off.

I tried very hard during that waiting period not to think about the fact that, at any given moment, the justices might be deciding Edie's case or even writing their opinions. But succeeding in not thinking about things that worry me is not one of my talents. Rachel and I decided to go on vacation in April in what proved to be a futile attempt to take my mind off the case. Both Edie and I were stressed out and edgy, desperate for the decision to be handed down.

The justices of the Supreme Court don't give advance notice of the day on which they will release any particular decision; they simply announce that on certain dates they will hand down whichever opinions happen to be ready. So once again, as we had done back when we were waiting to hear whether the Court would grant certiorari, we gathered with all of our Internet browsers on SCOTUSblog.com and hit *refresh, refresh, refresh*.

Instead of meeting in a conference room at Paul, Weiss, however, this time we decided to gather at my apartment, since it was a lot closer to Edie's apartment than our offices. We hoped that it would be a little easier on her since she wouldn't have to come to Midtown. So Rachel, Edie, and the Paul, Weiss team crowded around my dining room table on June 13 to learn which decisions the Supreme Court had released that day. We stared at our open laptops, hitting *refresh, refresh, refresh* on the SCOTUSblog website. The Court issued three decisions that day, but none of them were in the *Windsor* case.

The same thing happened on at least two more occasions (June 17 and 24). Each time, we were disappointed. Ariel Levy, who was then working on a profile of Edie for *The New Yorker*, was there with us in my apartment. In her piece, "The Perfect Wife," Levy accurately captures the mood during our vigil: "Kaplan was frustrated, too. She rubbed her forehead. 'This is worse than waiting for a jury.'" I put my head down on my forearms, according to Levy, and "moaned I've got to take up smoking or something."

Finally, there was only one day left. On Wednesday, June 26, the Court would issue its remaining decisions for the term, which we knew would include not only our case, but the *Perry* decision as well.

This was it—the culmination of three and a half years' work, not to mention the aspirations of countless Americans. As we all sat there sweating in the New York City summer heat, we were looking for three key signals that we believed would tell us whether we had won or lost the case. The first was which justice had written the opinion. Given his historic legacy of writing the two prior major gay rights decisions *Romer* and *Lawrence*, we believed that if Justice Kennedy wrote the majority opinion for *Windsor*, it would bode well for our prospects.

Second, we were looking at the order in which the opinions would be released. Knowledgeable SCOTUS watchers had already concluded, based on the number of opinions that each justice had already authored during the term, that for *Windsor* and *Perry*, it was likely that Chief Justice Roberts would write one of the two opinions and that Justice Kennedy would write the other. If that happened, SCOTUS protocol dictated that Justice Kennedy's opinion would be read in the courtroom first. Accordingly, if the *Windsor* decision was being handed down before the *Perry* decision, that would be a very good sign as well.

And the third and final thing we were looking for—the one that would truly guarantee either a victory or a defeat—was which justice or justices had written dissents. We were pretty confident that if Justice Scalia had written a dissent in our case, we probably wouldn't need to read any further. We would know for certain that we had won.

Refresh, refresh, refresh. Finally, the news flashed up on our screens: *Windsor* was the first decision of the day; majority opinion by Justice Kennedy; dissent by Justice Scalia. Even before reading a single word of the decision, we knew we had won—Section 3 of DOMA had been found unconstitutional.

At that point, pandemonium broke out in my apartment. Everyone was crying, shouting, jumping with joy, or all of the above. As I hugged Rachel, she said through her streaming tears, "Everything will be different for Jacob now."

While I was overwhelmed, I somehow managed to keep my tears in check and spent my time screaming and then rushing to my small home office where it was quiet to read the opinion and dissents. But I do remember that I laughed as I looked over at Ariel Levy, who was crying harder than almost anyone else. So much for objective journalism—though to be honest, I'm not sure any sentient human could have been completely objective in our apartment that day.

IN *UNITED STATES V. WINDSOR*, the Supreme Court voted 5–4 to strike down DOMA, with Justice Kennedy writing the majority opinion and Chief Justice Roberts, Justice Scalia, and Justice Alito each writing their own separate dissents. In *Hollingsworth v. Perry*, the Prop 8 case, the justices voted 5–4 not to rule on merits, concluding that the defenders of Prop 8 lacked standing to appeal. Essentially, in *Perry*, the justices decided not to decide, which meant that the district court's decision would stand and marriages of gay couples would resume in California.

In those three months (which felt like three years) between the Supreme Court oral argument and when *Windsor* was decided, I was guardedly optimistic that we would win Edie's case. I was pretty worried, however, about the grounds on which the Court would ultimately rule. I wanted *Windsor* not only to strike down Section 3 of DOMA but to do so using legal reasoning that would help to win future cases about the legal equality of gay people. Thus, it was very important that *Windsor* not be decided based on Tenth Amendment or federalism grounds that arguably applied to DOMA but would not apply to the many other state laws that discriminate against LGBT people.

While the Court agreed with us about DOMA's "unusual deviation from the usual tradition of recognizing and accepting state definitions of marriage," the *Windsor* decision was not grounded in federalism. Justice Kennedy made this point explicitly three separate times in his opinion when he stated, for example, that "state laws defining and regulating marriage, of course, *must respect the constitutional rights of persons.*" Indeed, in his dissent, Justice Scalia noted that the *Windsor* majority "formally disclaimed reliance upon principles of federalism."

What the *Windsor* opinion is about is human dignity and equality. Justice Kennedy wrote that "interference with the equal dignity of same-sex marriages was more than an incidental effect of DOMA. It was its essence." He observed that "DOMA writes inequality into the entire United States Code," commenting that DOMA "touches many aspects of married and family life, from the mundane to the profound." And, noting that the 1996 House Report expresses moral disapproval of homosexuality, Justice Kennedy suggested that that alone calls DOMA's constitutionality into question. According to the Supreme Court, DOMA was "invalid, for no legitimate purpose overcomes the purpose and effect to disparage and to injure those whom the State, by its marriage laws, sought to protect in personhood and dignity."

Justice Kennedy used the word *dignity* ten times in his twenty-six-page opinion for the Court in *Windsor*. According to the *Oxford English Dictionary*, the word *dignity* means "the state or quality of being worthy of honor or respect." Sometimes it's the simplest and most obvious things that say the most. The "state or quality of being worthy of honor or respect" is exactly what our case was all about.

Although Justice Kennedy did not directly address the debate about gay parents in his opinion, he did write that DOMA "humiliates tens of thousands of children now being raised by same-sex couples. The law in question makes it even more difficult for the children to understand the integrity and closeness of their own family and its concord with other families in their community and in their daily lives."

It is almost impossible to overemphasize the significance of this statement. For decades, gay people and their relationships have been vilified as threats to children. In fact, Edie, who adores children, had explained to me at one point that one of the reasons why she and Thea never adopted kids was in large part because of these negative attitudes. As recently as the Proposition 8 campaign in California in 2008, gay people were maligned as perverts and pedophiles. At the very least, their suitability as optimal parents has been repeatedly questioned. Having the Supreme Court not even acknowledge these negative views about gay people as parents in *Windsor* was stunning. Instead, what mattered now was the humiliation that the kids of gay parents would feel if their parents couldn't be married.

In writing our brief for the Supreme Court, I had been adamant that we never use the terms "same-sex," or "opposite-sex," or "homosexual," or "heterosexual." I believe that people who are comfortable with gay people don't refer to them using these terms. If, like so many Americans today, you have a neighbor, friend, colleague, or family member who is gay, you most likely don't refer to that person as "a homosexual." You certainly don't refer to their husband or wife as a "same-sex spouse."

While Justice Kennedy's opinion did, in fact, use the phrase "same-sex," I was delighted to see that it did not include any language from the Court's prior opinions in *Lawrence* and *Romer*, which assumed that gay people were somehow different from straight people. Indeed, even in Justice Scalia's dissent in *Windsor*, rather than attacking the gay *Kulturkampf*, as he did in *Romer*, or the "homosexual agenda," as he did in *Lawrence*, Justice Scalia reserved his ire for the other justices instead. Referring to the majority opinion as "legalistic argle-bargle," he asserted, "There are many remarkable things about the majority's merits holding. The first is how rootless and shifting its justifications are . . . Some might conclude that this loaf could have used a while longer in the oven. But that would be wrong; it is already overcooked. The most expert care in preparation cannot redeem a bad recipe."

Justice Scalia went on to predict, as he had in 2003, that the inevitable result of the *Windsor* decision would be nationwide marriage equality in all fifty states:

> It takes real cheek for today's majority to assure us, as it is going out the door, that a constitutional requirement to give formal recognition to same-sex marriage is not at issue here . . . I promise you this: The only thing that will "con-

fine" the Court's holding is its sense of what it can get away with. . . .

How easy it is, indeed how inevitable, to reach the same conclusion with regard to state laws denying same-sex couples marital status.

AFTER LEARNING THAT we had won, Edie immediately declared that she wanted to go to Stonewall, where we knew crowds of people would be gathering to celebrate our victory. But before we could think about going anywhere, the phone rang. I had a pretty good idea of who would be calling since the White House LGBT liaison, Gautam Raghavan, had asked me where we would be when the decision came down and how to reach us in case we won. "Edie," I said, "it's for you," handing her the telephone.

"Hello?" Edie shouted into the receiver, squinting as she tried to hear; there was obviously a lot of commotion in my apartment. "Who am I talking to? Oh, Barack Obama?" She then went on, as if getting a call from the president of the United States that Wednesday morning was the most natural thing in the world. "I wanted to thank you. I think your coming out for us made such a difference throughout the country." A moment later, she looked upset and confused. "Oh God. I think I just hung up on the president," she said. Fortunately, the telecommunications issue was not our fault and President Obama was soon able to call back and finish the conversation, even though he was on Air Force One on his way to Africa.

Before heading to Stonewall, we had a couple of stops to make. Edie, Rachel, Jaren, Julie, Alexia, and I climbed into an SUV and drove two blocks to the LGBT Community Center on West 13th Street, the very same place where we had first introduced Edie and her lawsuit three years before.

On that day, back in the fall of 2010, we had held our press conference in a small room with just a few rows of chairs, many of which were empty. Now the entire building was literally bursting at the seams. There were crowds of people crammed into every nook and cranny, cheering, shouting, reaching out to touch Edie, and snapping photos of us as we walked by.

I again introduced Edie to the crowd: "DOMA was the last law on the books that mandated discrimination against gay people by the federal government simply because they are gay." Echoing Justice Ginsburg's statement from oral argument, I noted that "the days of skim milk marriages for gay people are now over."

Edie had asked us to help prepare three different speeches for her that day, knowing that she was going to have to respond to whatever decision was handed down. One was called "Total Win," one was entitled "As Applied" (in case the Supreme Court had ruled narrowly in Edie's favor, but did not extend its ruling to cover other married gay couples), and the third was labeled "Loss." As Edie pulled the "Total Win" speech out of her pocket and stood in the front of the sweltering room facing a wall of cameras and reporters, she observed, "If I had to survive Thea," she said, "what a glorious way to do it."

Edie spoke for several minutes, and then reporters started peppering her with questions. Steven Thrasher of the Daily Beast had a great one: "Ms. Windsor, you can probably answer this better than anyone in America right now. What is love?"

"Love is a million things," Edie replied. "What was love with me and Thea? It started with tremendous respect for each other, and with two mantras. Mine was 'Don't postpone joy,' and Thea's was 'Keep it hot!'" The room erupted into laughter. Now that we had won, our three rules for the case had expired and Edie could say whatever she liked. And she certainly wasted no time in doing so.

Moving to a more serious note, and obviously suffused with memories of Thea, Edie then quoted the following lines from W. H. Auden's poem "The Prophets," which she knew by heart:

For now I have the answer from the face
That never will go back into a book
But asks for all my life, and is the Place
Where all I touch is moved to an embrace,
And there is no such thing as a vain look.

Looking out at so many faces, I couldn't help compare the euphoria in that room with the fairly muted response to our original press conference in 2010. It was, as James later put it, "like night and day."

We left the LGBT Center press conference and made a pit stop at Paul, Weiss to regroup. As we drove uptown, dozens of people ran up to our car to shake our hands and take photos. As Edie was walking down the hallway at the firm, she ran into Brad Karp, chair of Paul, Weiss. He immediately got down on his knees to bow before her, which delighted Edie to no end. It was a perfect symbol of the respect that Paul, Weiss had felt and accorded Edie from the very beginning.

Edie had one more place to go before Stonewall. Feeling confident in our chances, Hilary Rosen had arranged for Edie to tape an interview with Diane Sawyer for ABC Nightly News, the two women with probably the best blond bobs in all of New York City. Calling Edie an "unlikely gladiator," Diane Sawyer asked what the Supreme Court's decision meant for her personally. Edie responded by saying that "my country is now giving dignity to this beautiful person I was with." When asked what she would say to Thea if she were still alive, Edie responded that she would say: "Honey, it's done."

Our next stop was Stonewall. Hundreds of people had gathered in front of the bar in the West Village, the place where the modern era of gay-rights activism began one sweltering night in June 1969 when a group of young gay men and drag queens decided to fight back against the police who had come there to arrest them.

Earlier that evening in 1969, Edie and Thea had just returned from a trip to Italy. When Edie went out later to buy some milk, she remembered the odd silence in the streets that night. Learning about the riots that had just occurred ultimately changed the way that Edie felt about the "queens," many of whom hung out at Stonewall and who dressed flamboyantly in drag. Before Stonewall, like many other middle-class gay people, Edie had been more than a little ashamed and embarrassed by them. As she explained to Chris Geidner of BuzzFeed, "Until then, people who wanted to march and protest did it very carefully in proper suits and ties, and the women dressed in dresses. You were asked to leave if you hadn't come dressed properly. But, [the queens] existed. And they cared." But after Stonewall, Edie justifiably saw them as heroes, and Stonewall became a special place not only for Edie but for thousands of LGBT people across the country.

Alexia tells a great story about what happened when we were driving with Edie to Stonewall that day:

> When Edie and I were pulling up to Stonewall, everyone was very worried about security. Everyone was really tense and we were in this SUV with tinted windows, trying to drive close enough that we could get Edie to the stage that had been set up by the LGBT community groups without her getting run over by the crowd, and Edie kept rolling down the window to wave at people and touch people's hands. There was just so much love for her and she was so excited. I was getting increasingly hysterical about safety and it basically got to this point where she would roll down the window, I'd roll it up, she'd roll it down, I'd roll it up. It perfectly captures how gleeful we all were.

When Edie stepped out of the car, the crowd, which had packed the streets and sidewalks, went crazy. She waved her hands and blew kisses, beaming with joy as people clapped, cheered, and screamed her name. This was our hometown, after all, so there were dozens of old friends and elected officials at the rally that day who were gay or lesbian, including many (Emily Giske, Christine Quinn, Brad Hoylman, Danny O'Donnell, and Amy Rutkin) who had worked on LGBT equality for so long. But I was most touched by the fact that my friend and rabbi, Jan Uhrbach, had driven three hours into the city to introduce me. When I saw Jan there at Stonewall, I finally burst into tears myself.

When speaking that day at Stonewall, I began by noting that "the meaning of the decision by the United States Supreme Court is truly overwhelming, even for me, as the lawyer who argued the case, standing here, where so many others for so many years marched and protested and fought to get us to this very moment." Keeping with our motto that "it's all about Edie," I explained: "It is important to recognize that our victory against DOMA never would have happened without the tenacity of a five-foot-tall, 100-pound lady by the name of Edie Windsor. The events of this week remind us why it is that we have a Constitution—to bind us together as citizens of one nation each of whom is entitled to equal protection of the law. There is no person and no case that better demonstrates that core concept of equal protection than *Edith S. Windsor v. the United States of America.*"

In a perfect serendipity of the calendar, the culmination of the annual gay pride celebration in New York City was taking place that weekend. On Friday night, Edie, Rachel, and I attended a packed Shabbat service at Congregation Beit Simchat Torah, the same synagogue where Rachel and I had first met fourteen years earlier. I delivered a *drash*, or sermon, on that week's Torah portion (Parshat Pinchas; Numbers 25–30), which told the story of five brave Jewish sisters (the daughters of Zelophehad) who had challenged Moses and thereby changed Jewish law so that they could receive their father's inheritance. To a congregation of

LGBT friends and allies filled with an almost unbelievable sense of joy, I explained my understanding of the importance of change within Judaism:

> Perhaps the dominant view in our popular culture today is that religion, or belief in God, is inimical to the concept of change. The very idea that I, as a woman, not to mention a lesbian, am standing on this bimah talking to you tonight would be utterly inconceivable to many.
>
> But what I hope to be able to demonstrate to you is that this is not the only way to be religious or to believe in God. The notion that Jewish law is fixed in stone, unbending and unyielding and not subject to change is simply not consistent with the story of Zelophehad's daughters. After all, it is God himself who changes his own prior rule when God sees the inherent justice in the daughters' argument.

I concluded my *drash* with the words of the great rabbi Abraham Joshua Heschel, who had escaped the Holocaust and marched with Martin Luther King at Selma in March 1965: "All it takes is one person . . . and another . . . and another . . . and another . . . to start a movement." (When Rabbi Heschel returned to New York from Selma, someone asked him what it had been like, and he characteristically responded with poetry: "I felt my legs were praying.")

The next night, we celebrated our victory by throwing a huge dance party in honor of Edie and Thea's love of dancing. We invited dozens of people—friends, attorneys, anyone who had supported Edie's case in one way or another. It was like the combined gay bat mitzvah/prom that none of us had ever had, with lots of food and drinks, a great DJ playing classic disco hits, and everyone dancing. The crowd even lifted James Esseks and me up in chairs amid the dancing throngs.

The next day, Sunday, June 30, the celebration continued with the Gay Pride Parade in Manhattan. Edie was the Grand Marshal. Twenty-two years earlier, on June 30, 1991, my mother had seen the New York City Pride Parade while coming to visit me at my apartment. That day, I had revealed to her my secret that I was a lesbian, and her response had not been ideal. But my mother and I had come a very long way since then. And now, on the anniversary of that incredibly difficult moment, I found myself sitting with Edie, my wife, Rachel, and my son, Jacob, in an open convertible bedecked with rainbow flags, waving to cheering, screaming, ecstatic crowds. It felt like the final, glorious moment of my own coming-out story.

JUSTICE SCALIA'S FORECAST in his *Windsor* dissent turned out to be remarkably prescient. In the two years following *Windsor*, dozens of courts released decisions allowing gay couples to marry in states as different as Utah, Oklahoma, Texas, and Florida, all citing *Windsor*. The number of states permitting marriage equality soared from thirteen at the time of the decision to thirty-seven. By May 2015, a Gallup poll showed that a record high, or 60 percent, of Americans supported recognizing marriages between gay couples. When Gallup had first asked this question in 1996, 68 percent of Americans had been opposed to recognizing marriages between persons of the same sex. In fact, the impact of *Windsor* was so great that Harvard Law professor Laurence Tribe told a reporter, "I can't think of any Supreme Court decision in history that has ever created so rapid and broad a lower-court groundswell in a single direction as *Windsor*."

As amazing as all this was, however, those of us fighting for LGBT equality still had, to paraphrase Jimmy Cliff, a few more rivers to cross. We still had to secure the right to gay marriage in all fifty states. Lawyers began filing suits in courts across the country. When I got a call in October 2014 from some lesbians I had met in Asheville, North Carolina (Diane Walton, Meghann Burke, and Jasmine Beach-Ferrara, who run the Campaign for Southern Equality), about filing a case on behalf of gay couples in Mississippi, I jumped at the chance. (And yes, for those of you who don't know it yet, there really is such a thing as the "lesbian mafia.")

Rebecca (Becky) Bickett and Andrea Sanders live on the coast in southern Mississippi and have been a couple since meeting in the aftermath of Hurricane Katrina in 2005. They are the parents of twin one-year-old boys. Carla Webb and Jocelyn (Joce) Pritchett of Jackson, Mississippi, were legally married in Maine in 2013, though the state of Mississippi did not recognize their marriage. They also have two children, a boy and a girl. In November 2014, we filed suit in the U.S. District Court for the Southern District of Mississippi on behalf of these two couples.

As we had done with Edie, we pressed for an aggressive schedule in the Mississippi case. I wanted to get our case to the appellate level at the Fifth Circuit Court of Appeals as soon as possible since I knew that two other cases (one from Texas and one from Louisiana) had been decided at the district court and were already on appeal to that court. We drafted our initial motion papers seeking a preliminary injunction in a New York minute, filing them with the court within a week of taking the case.

Less than a year and a half had passed since the *Windsor* decision, but the differences in terms of legal precedent were profound. For one thing, nearly every single case we cited was a post-*Windsor* decision that had explicitly relied on *Windsor*. Despite the rush, I honestly don't think I ever had so much fun drafting a brief in my entire life. For a law geek like myself, it was like recording our own post-*Windsor* greatest hits album. We opened the brief with a description of what had happened since June 2013:

Since *Windsor*, more than forty federal district courts and four circuit courts have held that the U.S. Constitution requires that gay people be allowed to marry; only one federal circuit court and two district courts have held to the contrary. This remarkable degree of consensus among the courts is no coincidence—it is mandated by the logic and language of *Windsor*, which enshrine and repeat the unique protections our Constitution affords minority groups from discriminatory treatment.

The Mississippi case was assigned to Judge Carlton Reeves. Appointed by President Obama in 2010, Judge Reeves was only the second African American federal judge in Mississippi. His father was in the military, and the family moved often before Judge Reeves was born. In 1968, the family moved back to their original home in Yazoo City, Mississippi, where Judge Reeves attended public school.

Although I very much hoped that Judge Reeves would see discrimination against gay people as a civil rights issue, I continued to be wary of trying to make any direct comparisons between the struggle of African Americans and the struggle of LGBT Americans. There were too many significant differences, including the obvious facts that gay Americans had never been denied the right to vote or had to endure Jim Crow. As I explained to Judge Reeves at oral argument: "Thurgood Marshall when he litigated these cases as a young man was literally worried every day he was going to get killed. I'm not aware of any attorney litigating any LGBT civil rights case who has faced anything like that."

But as it turned out, I need not have worried since Judge Reeves was happy to make the point for me. At the oral argument on November 12, 2014, he brought up the landmark Supreme Court decision of *Brown v. the Board of Education*:

What's your response to *Brown v. Board of Education* and the Supreme Court putting a proviso in that . . . [the] states . . . would [have to] implement *Brown* with "all deliberate speed?"

(The Supreme Court, concerned about the reaction in the states, had used this phrase "all deliberate speed" to send a message to the states that they did not have to rush toward integration.)

At the time of Judge Reeves' query, I actually misunderstood where he was going. I thought he was concerned about what would happen in Mississippi if a federal judge ordered the state to allow gay couples to marry. For that reason, I responded:

> That was clearly done by the Supreme Court at the time out of a fear, whether legitimate or not, probably legitimate, that there would be so much social unrest. . . .
>
> In this context, there's no issue. Gay people have been married in Massachusetts now for ten years. Now, I concede that the Commonwealth of Massachusetts is different from the state of Mississippi. But there's been no rioting on the streets of Massachusetts. There's been no social unrest in the state of Massachusetts. Indeed, as we cited in our reply brief, rates of divorce in Massachusetts have gone down over the last ten years.

It soon became clear, however, exactly what Judge Reeves meant by his reference to "all deliberate speed," and it was the opposite of what I had been thinking. In a moving description of his own experiences growing up as an African American public school kid in the Mississippi Delta, Judge Reeves came back to the issue later in the oral argument when Justin Matheny, one of the attorneys representing the state of Mississippi, was at the podium:

> [I]t was 1954 that *Brown* was enacted and in Mississippi it was 1970 before my first-grade class was integrated . . .
>
> So doesn't the court have some responsibility to maybe not wait and see? Because we may be here in 2031. We may

be here in 2131. . . . [W]hat guarantee is there that the political process would work its way through in what I might
consider or what the courts might consider to be a timely
fashion?

This may have been the most powerful question I have ever
heard from a judge at an oral argument. Listening to Judge Reeves,
I couldn't help but think how extraordinary it was to be sitting
there in that courtroom in Mississippi, where so many civil rights
battles had been fought, listening to an African American federal
judge describe his own experience with the consequences of the
Supreme Court's action (or inaction). But as Judge Reeves later
explained in his decision (quoting William Faulkner), "The past is
never dead. It's not even past. That is as true here as anywhere else."

As a practical matter, none of the arguments we were making
or that were being urged by the state of Mississippi were different
from the arguments that James Esseks and I had made in the New
York marriage case a decade before. I made the same argument
about my clients that I had in Albany in 2006:

My clients Becky Bickett and Andrea Sanders, Joce Pritchett
and Carla Webb are all here today with their families. All
they want is to be treated like everyone else. What they
want for themselves and their children is a right that most
people take for granted. By treating straight families one
way and gay families another way as if they were inferior or
second class, the State of Mississippi discriminates against
gay people and their families; and the consequences of that
discrimination are profound.

For example, if, God forbid, one of my clients were to get
critically sick tomorrow, it is not at all clear that her spouse
or partner would be able to visit her in the hospital or to
make important medical decisions about her treatment if she

is unable to do so. When it comes time for my clients to pay their taxes, they have to go to the trouble and expense of preparing two sets of returns. And they cannot get, of course, the tax deductions that are available to straight married couples in Mississippi.

And perhaps most obviously and most importantly, Becky and Andrea's 15-month-old twin boys and Joce and Carla's children, a six-year-old girl and a two-year-old boy, do not have two legal parents who are married under the laws of the state in which they live. That's important because of the many concrete rights and benefits that children enjoy when their parents are married.

But it's also important in another sense, namely, in the sense that the dignity and self-worth of these kids is demeaned or, in the words of Justice Kennedy, humiliated daily by having to grow up in a state that tells them through its laws that their family is inferior. To use a fancy legal phrase from New York City, that's just plain wrong.

When Judge Reeves released his decision, it became clear that what had truly changed in the intervening years since our 2006 loss was not the arguments of counsel, or even the way that we articulated them, but the ability of judges to hear them.

In reviewing the arguments of the parties and conducting its own research, the court determined that an objective person must answer affirmatively to the following questions:

Can gay and lesbian citizens love?

Can gay and lesbian citizens have long-lasting and committed relationships?

Can gay and lesbian citizens love and care for children?

Can gay and lesbian citizens provide what is best for their children?

Can gay and lesbian citizens help make their children good and productive citizens?

Without the right to marry, are gay and lesbian citizens subjected to humiliation and indignity?

Without the right to marry, are gay and lesbian citizens subjected to state-sanctioned prejudice?

Answering "yes" to each of these questions leads the court to the inescapable conclusion that same-sex couples should be allowed to share in the benefits, and burdens, for better or for worse, of marriage.

Judge Reeves handed down his seventy-two-page opinion (more than two times longer than our brief) late in the afternoon on the Tuesday before Thanksgiving. In it, he powerfully surveys the history of discrimination against African Americans in Mississippi, the history of such discrimination against LGBT Americans, and the distinctive nature of homophobia. Judge Reeves discusses at some length the story of longtime civil rights organizer Bayard Rustin, who helped guide the Montgomery bus boycott and who was specifically targeted for being gay. As Judge Reeves explains:

The most interesting part of Rustin's story, though—and the reason why he merits more discussion here—is that he was subjected to anti-gay discrimination by both white and black people, majority and minority alike. . . . Rustin's story speaks to the long tradition of Americans from all walks of life uniting to discriminate against homosexuals. It did not matter if one was liberal or conservative, segregationist or civil rights leader, Democrat or Republican; homosexuals were "the other."

Judge Reeves's decision was released as we were in our car fighting our way through the pre-Thanksgiving traffic on I-95 to get to

Rachel's mother's house in Rhode Island for the holiday. Because I was driving, Rachel read the entire opinion to me from her iPhone. Not only did we fully comply with the applicable antitexting laws, but it was probably the best four-hour drive of my life.

AS EXPECTED, THE state of Mississippi immediately appealed Judge Reeves's decision, and our case moved up to the Fifth Circuit, where Mississippi obtained a stay. Two other gay-marriage cases, one from Texas and one from Louisiana, would be heard by the Fifth Circuit on the same day as ours, before a panel of three judges: Judge Jerry Smith, a conservative whose vote we knew we most likely couldn't get; Judge Patrick Higginbotham, a Reagan appointee who had been on the bench for more than three decades, and Judge James Graves, who, like Judge Reeves, was also an Obama-appointed African American judge from Mississippi. Oral arguments were scheduled for Friday, January 9, at the federal courthouse in New Orleans.

Josh Kaye and I flew to Houston in advance of the argument to meet with attorneys in the Texas case, *De Leon v. Perry*, and compare notes. Not wanting to miss an opportunity to go on an eating tour of the Deep South, we drove from Houston to New Orleans in a rental car, stopping along the way to sample the local cuisine of crab étouffée and fried catfish, not to mention the almost superhuman number of oysters consumed by Josh. As we drove, Josh and I used the time to prepare for what I knew would probably be the last marriage equality argument of my career by "mooting" the case. Josh would ask me the hardest questions he could think of and we worked to practice my answers, as Louisiana Cajun country whizzed by.

The Fifth Circuit would hear arguments in each of the three cases separately, with Louisiana going first, followed by Mississippi, and then Texas. As I listened to the three judges asking questions during the Louisiana oral argument, it seemed pretty clear to me that, as expected, Judge Smith was not likely to vote our way. But the other two judges seemed far more open to the marriage equality arguments that the Lambda attorney, Camilla Taylor, was making.

When it was my turn to argue, I felt none of the jitters I had experienced when I began my argument at the Supreme Court. This was not my first time arguing before a circuit court and I certainly knew this area of the law. While I still didn't want to make any direct analogies to the civil rights movement, I kept thinking about the crucial role that had been played by judges in this very courthouse. I really couldn't help myself. So I confidently walked up to the podium and said, "Good morning, Your Honors. May it please the court. I am delighted to be down here in New Orleans. I apologize for bringing our cold weather with us. And it's an honor to be arguing *this* case in the *John Minor Wisdom* courthouse."

I had chosen these words carefully. In 1994, the Fifth Circuit courthouse was renamed to honor John Minor Wisdom, a judge who served on the court from 1957 until his death in 1999. Judge Wisdom was one of the "Fifth Circuit Four," renowned for his landmark decisions implementing desegregation in the wake of *Brown v. Board of Education*. During the 1960s, despite sometimes violent opposition, Judge Wisdom courageously issued opinions ordering integration at the University of Mississippi, eliminating racial discrimination in jury selection, and striking down barriers to voter registration in Louisiana. As the *New York Times* reported on his death at age ninety-four in 1999, Judge Wisdom was one of a "handful of remarkable men who prevailed by meeting the demands of the times with an innovative and creative judicial response that restructured an unjust social order and helped shape the nation in a second reconstruction and left a permanent imprint on American history."

By opening with a reference to Judge Wisdom, I was obviously drawing a link between the historic struggle of civil rights for African Americans and the current struggle for the rights of gay people. And I'm pretty sure that the judges understood exactly what I meant.

Much of the argument at the Fifth Circuit focused on the 1972 case of *Baker v. Nelson*, in which the Minnesota Supreme Court had ruled that a law restricting marriage to opposite-sex couples was constitutional, and the Supreme Court had dismissed the appeal as not even raising a substantial issue. When Judge Smith brought up that decision, I responded with the following:

ME: The world was a very different place in 1972 when *Baker* was decided. . . . There has certainly been a sea change not only in the law, but in the way gay people live in our society. In 1972, . . . [i]f they wanted to keep a job or be civil to their neighbors, most gay people lived in the closet. We have a very different world today, where there are gay people, like my clients, living openly with their children. . . .

JUDGE SMITH: Why do you suppose, though, that in light of the specific reasoning and holding in *Baker*, the Supreme Court said . . . there's no problem here, nothing to see here.

ME: Why did they say that in 1972?

JUDGE SMITH: Yeah.

ME: Because times can blind, Your Honor. In 1972, . . . it was criminal to be gay in most states in this country.

"Times can blind." No matter how many times or how many ways I used Justice Kennedy's words, it would never be enough. I felt particularly vindicated when, during the oral argument in the Texas case that followed ours, Judge Graves joked, "All this talk about *Baker* and the seventies is making me nostalgic for my Afro and my 8-track tapes." It's hard to imagine a better way to illustrate how dramatically the times had changed than that.

At one point during my argument, Judge Smith brought up the legacy of *Windsor*, which led to the following humorous exchange:

JUDGE SMITH: What do you think it is in *Windsor*, and of course I know you're intimately familiar with *Windsor* because you tried that case and argued that case.

ME: I've heard of the case, Your Honor. Yes.

[LAUGHTER]

JUDGE SMITH: And congratulations to you for your good work there.

This led Judge Smith to ask me why I believed that the decision in *Windsor* dictated a pro-equality ruling at the Fifth Circuit. I had spent a lot of time thinking about why so many courts had struck down bans on marriages between gay couples in so many states in the wake of *Windsor*, so I answered:

I don't often find myself agreeing with Justice Scalia on this issue, in this area, but here I have to say I agree with him completely. While the holding of *Windsor* clearly does not apply to the right of couples to marry under state law under the Fourteenth Amendment, the logic of *Windsor* does. Because the logic of *Windsor* . . . says that gay people have dignity that's equal to everyone else. And once you accept that gay people have the same kind, are equal to everyone else, then all these reasons really make no sense. That's why you're seeing this . . . enormous groundswell in the federal courts. Not because it's a popularity contest, but because when you look at the logic of *Windsor*, it's hard to imagine treating gay people in such a discriminatory manner, if you accept the fact that they're the same as everyone else.

During my Fifth Circuit argument, I was again very reluctant as a New Yorker to criticize the state of Mississippi:

ME: I'm not from Mississippi, but Judge Reeves below certainly was, and he was not as optimistic as Judge Sutton in the Sixth Circuit that the democratic process in Mississippi could be relied upon to give gay people their rights under the Fourteenth Amendment. You can read that yourselves. He's much more of an expert on that than I am.

JUDGE GRAVES: Well we got an amicus brief from members of the Mississippi legislature, didn't we in this case?

ME: We did. It didn't predict, if I recall correctly, that they intended to pass equal rights for gay people any time soon.

[LAUGHTER]

Once again, the judges had made my arguments for me. When my time was up, the attorney for the state of Mississippi, Justin Matheny, stood up for his rebuttal. He was at the podium only a brief time, but it involved what was probably the best exchange of the entire day. Matheny argued that time, rather than judicial intervention by the court, would ultimately resolve the issue of discrimination against gay people and that the courts should not step in: "Saying that Mississippi will never change its mind, or it's not likely to, is not a reason to take away the state's ability to decide things."

Judge Higginbotham paused for a moment, ran his hand through his leonine white mane of hair, and, leaning back in his chair, looked down at Matheny from the bench. He then intoned, "Those words, 'will Mississippi change its mind?' have resonated in these halls before."

With this comment, Judge Higginbotham, who had first been appointed to the bench when John Minor Wisdom was still presiding over cases at the Fifth Circuit, clearly and firmly connected African American civil rights and gay rights. Justin Matheny did not reply but simply closed his rebuttal by saying, "The state asks that the court reverse the district court's preliminary injunction below," before quickly taking his seat.

After the oral arguments, we all went out for lunch at Herb-saint, a restaurant across Lafayette Square from the courthouse where we gorged on mint juleps, fried oysters, and gumbo. Our clients Carla and Joce were thrilled to be able to meet "Miss Edie" by cell phone when I called to tell her about the argument. On her Facebook post later that day, Joce recalled, "So, we're sitting at lunch. And Roberta Kaplan says 'Let's call Edie! She'll want to know how it went.' I'm sitting there in awe watching the incredible Robbie Kaplan tell Edie Windsor that today was all about her name. And then Robbie says, 'You wanna talk to my Mississippi plaintiff?' And hands me the phone."

I was proud to have argued this case in a place where so much civil rights history had been made. Now all we could do was wait and see whether we had persuaded the Fifth Circuit to continue making history.

EPILOGUE

As it turned out, the Fifth Circuit never got a chance to rule. Only a week after our oral arguments in New Orleans, the Supreme Court announced that it would take up the issue of marriage equality once and for all. The justices agreed to hear a group of four cases coming out of the Sixth Circuit, with oral arguments at the end of April.

Although there had been a tidal wave of district and circuit court opinions affirming the equality of gay people under the law as a result of *United States v. Windsor*, the Supreme Court often chooses not to decide issues for which there is no disagreement among the circuit courts. So even though marriage equality was not yet a reality in all fifty states, the Supreme Court, in October 2014, had declined to grant certiorari in cases from the Tenth, Fourth, and Seventh Circuits covering states such as Utah, Oklahoma, Virginia, and Indiana, since all those courts had agreed that limiting marriage to straight couples violated the Constitution.

The next month, however, the United States Court of Appeals for the Sixth Circuit (covering Kentucky, Michigan, Ohio, and Tennessee) became the first and only circuit court to uphold laws that banned marriages between gay and lesbian couples. I was particularly disappointed when that decision came down, since it involved a case brought by a man named James Obergefell who lived in my home state of Ohio. The silver lining, at least, was that now the Supreme Court had a case to resolve.

Echoing the story of Edie and Thea, *Obergefell v. Hodges* is also the story of a relationship that spanned decades, a cruel neurological condition, an eventual marriage, and an untimely and heartbreaking death. Jim Obergefell and his longtime partner, John Arthur, had been together for many years, living in Cincinnati, Ohio. Later, Arthur became terminally ill with Lou Gehrig's disease, or ALS. The couple wanted to be married so badly that they chartered a medical plane to get married in Maryland on July 11, 2013, since they couldn't then do so in Ohio. Shortly thereafter, Arthur died. Obergefell sued to require Ohio to recognize him as Arthur's husband on the death certificate.

This was it: the final inning in the struggle for marriage equality in the United States of America. Depending upon how the Supreme Court ruled, either we would have full marriage equality in all fifty states or we would not, which would be a major setback, to say the least.

Behind the scenes, a group of activists connected with HRC, including Chad Griffin and Hilary Rosen, were discussing what we could do to help the new Supreme Court case, *Obergefell v. Hodges*. Capitalizing on the power of modern technology, Hilary came up with the inspired idea of submitting an unprecedented form of amicus brief to the Supreme Court, the People's Brief, to be read and signed online by members of the public.

In working on the People's Brief with law professors Dale Carpenter and Steve Sanders, I couldn't help but flash back to writing the briefs for the New York marriage case in 2006 and for *Windsor* in 2013. Although we had come so far, we still had at least one more river to cross. We began with the 1972 case *Baker v. Nelson*. And then Jaren had another brilliant idea: using *Baker v. Nelson* on offense, rather than playing defense. As we explained to the Supreme Court: "Forty-five years ago in Minneapolis, two gay men sought a license to marry each other. Not surprisingly, their request was denied. To everyone but them, the recognition that they sought was utterly unthinkable at the time." Our brief surveyed the dramatic sea change that had occurred since *Baker,* not only in American society but in the Supreme Court's own jurisprudence. For example, in the 1986 *Bowers v. Hardwick* case brought by a "practicing homosexual," the Supreme Court held that the argument that it was unconstitutional to criminalize sexual relations between gay people was "at best facetious." Seventeen years later, in *Lawrence v. Texas,* the Supreme Court held that "*Bowers* was not correct when it was decided, and it is not correct today." By 2013, Justice Kennedy observed in *Windsor:* "It seems fair to conclude that, until recent years, many citizens had not even considered the possibility that two persons of the same sex might aspire to occupy the same status and dignity as that of a man and woman in lawful marriage."

We wanted to show that there really was only one reason to explain why Ohio insisted on disregarding Jim Obergefell's marriage to his late husband:

> It is not insignificant that petitioner James Obergefell from Ohio merely seeks to have the state correct the facts asserted on the death certificate of his late spouse, John Arthur. The two men were, in fact, married under the law of Maryland where their marriage was performed. It is absurd to contend that refusing to certify that a decedent was "married" to his spouse at the time of his death could possibly influence child rearing, or the willingness of straight couples to marry, or even offend tradition. But actions speak louder than words. Ohio insists that there must be a blank space on Mr. Arthur's death certificate where Mr. Obergefell's name should be. Not content to deny these men the equal protection of the law in life, it also seeks to deny them dignity even in death.

The People's Brief, submitted to the Supreme Court on March 6, 2015, garnered 207,551 signatories from people in all fifty states.

Edie Windsor was the first person to sign. Not surprisingly, two
of the states that had the most signatures, Ohio and Texas, were
states where gay couples were not yet permitted to marry. When
we printed out the final document, it was 3,500 pages long. Making the required fifty copies to be delivered to the Supreme Court
took four solid days of printing, and the resulting mountain of
paperwork filled nineteen boxes, which were delivered by HRC
and Jim Obergefell to the Supreme Court on March 6.

A few weeks later, on April 28, 2015, I sat in a packed Supreme
Court courtroom to hear the oral arguments in *Obergefell*. It felt
like old home week for LGBT civil rights advocates at the Supreme
Court. Paul Smith (who had argued *Lawrence* at the Supreme
Court) was there, as were Columbia law professor Suzanne Goldberg (who worked on *Lawrence* while at Lambda), James Esseks,
Evan Wolfson, Freedom to Marry campaign director Marc Solomon, Chad Griffin, Fred Sainz of HRC, Ted Olson, Pam Karlan,
and many others. Sitting next to each other a few rows behind
me were Gavin Newsom, the former mayor of San Francisco who
led the way in marrying gay couples in 2004, and Margaret Marshall, the former chief justice of Massachusetts, who first ruled in
Goodridge v. Department of Public Health that the core constitutional
principles of due process and equal protection mandate that gay
couples be permitted to marry. As a fitting culmination to what
she had started more than a decade before, Mary Bonauto argued
the case for our side on the question of whether all fifty states
were required to allow gay couples to marry, and experienced
Supreme Court advocate Doug Hallward-Driemeier argued that
out-of-state marriages between gay couples had to be recognized
in all fifty states.

As I sat there listening to the arguments of John Bursch, the
former solicitor general of Michigan, I remember thinking that
if these were the only arguments our adversaries were still willing to advance in court, then there was little chance that we were

going to lose. Bursch, for example, asserted assuredly to the justices that the "view on the other side here is that marriage is all about love and commitment. And as a society, we can agree that that's important, but the State doesn't have any interest in that." As I often find myself saying to my son, "Wait a minute." The government doesn't have any interest in the love and commitment of married couples? Not only was that news to me and almost everyone else in the courtroom, but it was inconsistent with the lived experiences of most Americans.

Whatever lingering doubts I had that we might lose were dispelled after the following exchange between Bursch and Justice Kennedy:

BURSCH: And what they are asking you to do is to take an institution, which was never intended to be dignitary bestowing, and make it dignitary bestowing . . .

JUSTICE KENNEDY: [J]ust in fairness to you, I don't understand this not dignity bestowing. I thought that was the whole purpose of marriage. It bestows dignity on both man and woman in a traditional marriage.

BURSCH: It's supposed to—

JUSTICE KENNEDY: It's dignity bestowing, and these parties say they want to have that—that same ennoblement.

BURSCH: Sure.

JUSTICE KENNEDY: Or am I missing your point?

BURSCH: I think you're missing my point. If we go back to that world where marriage doesn't exist and the State is trying to figure out how do we link together these kids with their biological moms and dads when possible, the—glue are benefits and burdens, but not necessarily dignity. You know, dignity may have grown up around marriage as a cultural thing, but the State has no interest in bestowing or taking away dignity from anyone, and certainly it's not the State's intent to take

dignity away from same-sex couples or—or from anyone based
on their sexual orientation.

JUSTICE KENNEDY: Well, I think many States would be surprised,
with reference to traditional marriages, they are not enhanc-
ing the dignity of both the parties.

But perhaps the most dramatic and critical moment at the oral
arguments that day turned out not to be what any of the justices or lawyers had to say. Approximately thirty minutes into
the arguments, a man in the back of the galley started screaming violently that all "gays" were going to hell. While his words
don't show up in the official transcript, the heckler, who was soon
removed from the courtroom and arrested, kept shouting, "If you
support gay marriage, you will burn in hell" and "Homosexuality
is an abomination," as he was being dragged out of the building.
Even though the courthouse was full of federal marshals that day,
the experience was frightening. On the other hand, it's hard to
imagine a more powerful demonstration of the kind of irrational
hatred and prejudice against a minority group that in the past has
caused our nation's highest court to step in to enforce the man-
dates of our Constitution.

After the argument ended, the waiting game began again.
Although not as torturous for me as it was in 2013, it wasn't
exactly relaxing, either. However, when on June 22 the Supreme
Court added June 26 as a new date for the Court to release decisions for the term, I knew that we had won. There was no way
that the Supreme Court was going to issue a decision harmful
to the rights of gay people on June 26—the anniversary of both
the *Lawrence* and the *Windsor* decisions. So when the decision
came out on June 26, as I sat in San Francisco, away on business,
on a conference call with Edie, Rachel, and the rest of the Paul,
Weiss team, I felt an almost indescribable sense of exhilaration,

one that only became stronger when I read Justice Kennedy's opinion itself.

To the extent that there had been any remaining uncertainty as to whether the *Windsor* decision had stood for the equal dignity of gay people, *Obergefell* made that point explicitly. In words bound to be read by officiants at weddings for many years to come, Justice Kennedy wrote:

> No union is more profound than marriage, for it embodies the highest ideals of love, fidelity, devotion, sacrifice, and family. In forming a marital union, two people become something greater than they once were. As some of the petitioners in these cases demonstrate, marriage embodies a love that may endure even past death. It would misunderstand these men and women to say they disrespect the idea of marriage. Their plea is that they do respect it, respect it so deeply that they seek to find its fulfillment for themselves. Their hope is not to be condemned to live in loneliness, excluded from one of civilization's oldest institutions. They ask for equal dignity in the eyes of the law. The Constitution grants them that right. . . .
>
> *It is so ordered.*

This was it—all that we had ever hoped and worked for. Immediately, gay and lesbian couples began marrying throughout the country. Even in Mississippi, after some initial hemming and hawing by Governor Phil Bryant, the Fifth Circuit ruled as follows on July 1, 2015: "*Obergefell* . . . is the law of the land and consequently, the law of this circuit and should not be taken lightly by actors within the jurisdiction of this court." Our Mississippi clients Andrea Sanders and Becky Bickett were finally married in their hometown of Pass Christian on July 5, 2015, with their twin sons there as witnesses. Rather than try to describe their feelings for them, here are Andrea's own words: "OK. For those of you who have been wondering when it is happening . . . we are getting married this Sunday. After 11 years, it is finally happening!" Since we couldn't be there in person, and to reciprocate for all the great Southern food we had shared together, we sent them a gift basket of food from Zabar's on the Upper West Side.

THERE WERE MANY times during the summer after *Windsor* was decided when I felt like the guy in the Chagall painting, floating high above the world in a state of exultation. Rabbi Heschel has referred to this as a "sense of the ineffable." But we obviously can't live every day in the clouds. While we all have to return to the ground, I still experience those Chagall moments at times. That certainly happened on June 26, 2015, when the Supreme Court handed down its decision in *Obergefell v. Hodges*. I also experience that feeling whenever I encounter something that is completely ordinary today that would have been completely extraordinary only a couple of years ago. Perhaps the best example of this is when our then-seven-year-old son Jacob asked us, after we had watched the movie *My Fair Lady*, whether it was an old-fashioned movie since it was made "before men could marry men."

In the end, "it's all about Edie" is really only another way of saying that it's all about dignity. While cases, precedents, and constitutional doctrine matter, so do the lives of the people targeted by discriminatory laws. I had to recognize my own dignity as a lesbian before I could be truly effective as an advocate. Those brave queens at Stonewall had to fight back in 1969 so that they would no longer be subject to arrest simply for being gay. Evan Wolfson, while still a student at Harvard Law School, had to have the vision to write a paper in 1983 entitled "Samesex Marriage and Morality: The Human Rights Vision of the Constitution." Mary Bonauto had to bring those first cases in Vermont and Massachusetts when many thought she was being reckless, crazy, or both. Edie Windsor had to stand up and sue the United States of America to honor her marriage to Thea Spyer. Jim Obergefell in Ohio and Carla Webb and Joce Pritchett in Mississippi had to go to court to have their marriages legally acknowledged. Countless other gay men and lesbians had to step forward and demand that their dignity be recognized by their families, neighbors, colleagues, and finally their own government. And, together, we changed the world.

ACKNOWLEDGMENTS

There is really only one thing that I know for sure: no human being knows what life has in store for them. Edie Windsor surely didn't. As a young woman growing up in Philadelphia during the Depression and World War II, she obviously had no idea what the future would hold. The same, of course, is true for me. As a closeted lesbian in high school in Cleveland, Ohio, in the early 1980s, as a closeted college student at Harvard in the mid 1980s, or as a slightly less closeted law student at Columbia Law School in the late 1980s, *if* you had told me that that one day, as an out litigation partner at Paul, Weiss, I would marry a woman, have a child, and then win a landmark civil rights case before the United States Supreme Court, I would have told *you* that you were certifiably insane. But neither Edie nor I got to this place on our own. As a result, while I am not someone who is easily intimidated, I have to admit that I found writing the acknowledgements for this book intimidating, not because of writer's block or the amount of work involved, but out of a realistic concern that there are so many people to thank.

First and foremost, I need to thank my partners at Paul, Weiss LLP, most particularly our firm chair, Brad Karp, who supported me in this endeavor from the very beginning. The very first paragraph in our Statement of Firm Principles, written by Judge Simon Rifkind four years before I was born, states that "Our objectives are, by pooling our energies, talents and resources, to achieve the highest order of excellence in the practice of the art, the science and the profession of the law; through such practice to earn a living and to derive the stimulation and pleasure of worthwhile adventure; and in all things to govern ourselves as members of a free democratic society with responsibilities both to our profession and our country." Doing pro bono cases like *United States v. Windsor* is part of the embedded DNA of our law firm, which is one of the many reasons that I am so proud to be a Paul, Weiss partner. A special thanks (and more) is due to the "core members" of the Paul, Weiss team (Craig Benson, Andrew Ehrlich, Julie Fink, Jaren Janghorbani, Joshua Kaye, Colin Kelly, Alexia Koritz, Nila Merola, Melissa Monteleone, and Walter Rieman) as well as all the many other current and former Paul, Weiss lawyers who made significant contributions to *Windsor* and our case in Mississippi (Amy Beaux, Janna Berke, Rick Bronstein, Zachary Dietert, Jimmy Fleming, Sarah Foley, Ryan Goldstein, Alan Halperin, Rachel Harris, Jacob Hupart, Lauren Janian, Carol Kaplan, Neil Kelly, Michael Nadler, Ralia Polechronis, Davin Rosborough, Jacobus Schutte, Warren Stramiello, and Alexandra Walsh). What *United States v. Windsor* means is that what we as lawyers do every day, as part of what I still believe to be a noble profession, matters a lot. And we could not do what we do without the unbelievable talent and work ethic of our staff here at Paul, Weiss, including Marc Arena, Dan Conniff, John Hearn, John Hodder, Kate McCartin, Terry Moot, Danyale Price, and Axel Rudolph, and most of all my fabulous assistants Laurie Morris and Claudette Wilson.

I next have to thank Pam Karlan, her co-director Jeffrey Fisher, and her brilliant students at Stanford Law School (Michael Baer, Elisabeth Dooley, Bailey Heap, and Nico Martinez). There are a lot of smart people in the world and Pam is surely among the smartest. But what amazes me most about Pam is not her off-the-charts IQ but her fundamental decency as a human being. While I have met a lot of smart people in my life, I have met precious few who are as fundamentally kind as Pam. In a speech she delivered at Stanford, Pam gave her students the following advice: "Do pro bono work because it's the right thing to do and because what you're doing will make the world better, not because someone is watching. Pick projects that promote justice or freedom or fairness or peace or dignity or a cleaner environment, not just projects that promote you. The point is to connect and not to look good to the crowd." I cannot think of a single person who better personifies those words than Pam Karlan.

I also owe a huge debt of gratitude to James Esseks and the Windsor team at the ACLU (Joshua Block, Leslie Cooper, Rose Saxe, and Steve Shapiro). I am so grateful to James for having the imagination to ask me to work with him on the New York marriage equality case more than a decade ago and for putting up with me ever since. In a piece James wrote after the death of Judge Robert Carter, for whom James clerked, James quotes the following passage written by Judge Carter about his attempt to integrate the swimming pool at his New Jersey high school in the early 1930s: "I could not swim at the time, but at every gym class, choked up and near tears with emotion and defiance, I would get in the pool at its shallow end and cling to the side of the pool until the period ended. None of the white boys used the pool with me in it, so there I was clinging to the side of the pool for dear life until the period ended." As James concludes, "We can see in the adolescent Bob Carter the man who would have the temerity to fight an accepted wrong, the fortitude to persevere over decades, and the courage to transform his own life as a means of changing other people's lives and eventually the entire country." What James Esseks wrote about Judge Carter could just as easily and accurately be said about James himself.

A further thank-you is in order to the other members of Team Windsor, including Mary Bonauto, the Italian American superwoman (sans spandex) from New England who helped walk us all down the aisle, and her colleague Gary Buseck of the Gay &

Lesbian Advocates & Defenders. Professor Suzanne Goldberg of Columbia Law School and Alan Morrison of George Washington Law School were incredibly generous with their time, enduring countless phone calls where they offered their ideas, edits, and advice. Hilary Rosen, Olivia Alair, and the rest of their team at SKD Knickerbocker; Lisa Green here at Paul, Weiss; as well as my friends Anthony Hayes and Valerie Berlin provided the best possible counsel and support in dealing with the torrent of the media surrounding the Supreme Court argument and decision. And it has been a pleasure and an honor to work with Chad Griffin and Fred Sainz of HRC as well as Professor Dale Carpenter of the University of Minnesota Law School and Professor Steve Sanders of Indiana University Maurer School of Law on The People's Brief.

Twenty-two years ago, I was assigned to work on a case with Colleen McMahon, the first Paul, Weiss woman litigation partner, who is also from Ohio and who had also arrived at the firm by way of an Ivy League law school almost two decades before me. That was probably the best assignment I ever received. And the next-best assignment I received was three years later, when I got a call from Marty London asking me to fly to Tokyo because of something having to do with trading in copper. There are few phrases I wrote in the *Windsor* brief without first thinking to myself, *"How would Marty/Colleen put it?"* They both taught me what it means to be a lawyer. Fortunately, I didn't have to imagine any such hypotheticals for Marty Flumenbaum, since his office is next to mine. I am so lucky to have so many old and new friends among my Paul, Weiss partners, like Allan Arffa, Bob Atkins, Lynn Bayard, Dan Beller, Bruce Birenboim, Chris Boehning, Jay Cohen, Kelley Cornish, Michael Gertzman, Claudia Hammerman, Brian Hermann, Michele Hirshman, Merrie Kane, Alan Kornberg, Dan Kramer, Valerie Radwaner, Walter Ricciardi, Richard Rosen, Jacqui Rubin, Liz Sacksteder, Bob Schumer, Moses Silverman, Eric Stone, Maria Vullo, Ted Wells, Beth Wilkinson, and Julia

Wood. The same is true for Judge Judith S. Kaye and Judge Mark L. Wolf, who taught me that judges can be faithful to the law, true to the Constitution, and loyal to our better selves.

This book never would have happened had Lisa Dickey not come to me a year ago and proposed to help me chronicle our journey on the *Windsor* case. I am so grateful to her for creating order out of disorder and for helping me to find my voice. Amy Cherry looks, sounds, and acts like the platonic ideal of a book editor—she and her team at W. W. Norton are the real deal. And last but certainly not least, Gail Ross is an incredible agent, always there with wise and cogent advice.

Thanks as well to my parents, Richard and Bess Kaplan, who always encouraged me in my crazy dreams, and who still faithfully take the trip from Cleveland to New York several times a year, although I suspect that may now have more to do with seeing their grandson, Jacob. Since marrying Rachel, my family has grown in wonderful ways. In addition to my own brother, Peter, I now have the big family I always wanted, and I am so grateful for all the brilliant ideas and edits on this book offered by my sister-in-law, Rebecca Lavine; my brother-in-law, Adam Lavine; his wife, Aiko Lavine; and my mother-in-law, Gladys Lavine. Our nephews and niece—Shingo Lavine, Ayano Lavine, and Ari Lavine—have provided me with the best help of all—an unconditional and constant cheering section. While I am grieved that neither Rachel's father, David Lavine, nor my grandmother Belle Horwitz of blessed memory lived to see *United States v. Windsor*, they helped to inspire every single gutsy move I made.

Edie is right that as gay people, we choose our own families. I am so blessed to have such a wonderful extended family of friends like Emily Giske, Annie Washburn, Karen Keogh, Emma Dryden, Anne Corvi, Deborah Glick, Leslie Sharpe, Nina Morrison, Terrence McNally, Tom Kirdahy, Amy Rutkin, Bruce Anderson, Daniel Maury, Andrew Sendall, Sharon Nelles, and

Monica Graham, many of whom made the trek to Washington, DC, or New Orleans for my arguments. I am so grateful for the amazing community we have at the Conservative Synagogue of the Hamptons, led by Stacey Menzer, Michael Summa, and our amazing rabbi and my dear friend, Jan Uhrbach. This list must also include Edward DeBonis and Brendan Fay, who had the crazy idea of acting as "Edie–Robbie" matchmakers in the first place, as well as Jacob's beloved nanny, Ellie Alvarez, Lizzy Peters, and Jacob's incredible teacher Terry Trent, who have become members of the extended Kaplan-Lavine clan.

Thanks to my clients in the Mississippi case, Rebecca "Becky" Bickett, Andrea Sanders, Jocelyn "Joce" Pritchett, and Carla Webb; and the Campaign for Southern Equality, as well as Jasmine Beach-Ferrara, Meghann Burke, Diane ("Dizy") Walton, Aaron Sarver, Paula Garrett, Donna Reed, Harvey Pfizer, Rob McDuff, and Sibyl Byrd, who taught me what Southern hospitality really means. Because of them, I finally got a chance to drive through Texas, Louisiana, and Mississippi listening to Lucinda Williams songs, making (all too) frequent stops for fried chicken, etouffee, and barbecue.

Thanks to Edie, of course, for being everything she is, was, and will be. And thanks to Thea Spyer for being there for me when I really needed her.

Finally, and most importantly, even as someone who really likes to talk, I don't have words to express the love and gratitude I feel for my wife, Rachel Lavine, and our son, Jacob Philip Kaplan-Lavine. For me, Rachel and Jacob truly are, to borrow Jacob's now not-so-secret password, "the greatest things in the world." Without Rachel, my *bashert* or soulmate, not only would I never have had the guts to take on the fight for the civil rights of LGBT Americans, but this book would have been a much less compelling (and honest) read. And without Jacob, I never would have had so much joy in my life.

INDEX

ABC Nightly News, 297
"activist judges," 55
adoption, 33–39, 63, 64,
    74, 80–84. *See also*
    parenthood
African American civil rights
    movement, 145–46, 300,
    303–5, 307, 309–10, 312
AIDS epidemic, 20, 29, 30,
    49
Alito, Samuel, 187, 255, 275–
    77, 292
Alvaré, Helen, 208
Alvarez, Ellie, 258–59
Amazon, 212
Amedure, Scott, 40
AMERICAblog, 143–44
American Civil Liberties
    Union, 30, 56, 65–67, 80,
    118, 206
  awards Roger Baldwin
    Medal of Liberty to Edie,
    160, 162–63

Windsor and, 123–25, 126–
    30, 132, 143, 232
American Pediatric Associa-
    tion, 72
American Psychiatric Asso-
    ciation, 72, 190
American Psychological
    Association, 190
amicus briefs, 72, 206–9,
    210–14, 234, 316–18. *See
    also specific cases*
antiapartheid movement, 53
antigay arguments, 72–73.
    See also homophobia; *spe-
    cific categories of arguments*
antisodomy laws, 51–52, 64,
    72, 185
Apple, 212
Aravosis, John, 143–44
Arkansas, 80
Arkansas Supreme Court,
    80
Arthur, John, 316, 317

Auden, W. H., "The Prophets," 296–97

Baehr, Ninia, 30
Baer, Michael, 206
Baker v. Nelson, 196–97, 310, 316–17
Baker v. Vermont, 50
Banta, John, 65–66
Barnett, Randy, 244
Barr, Bob, 40
Beach-Ferrara, Jasmine, 301–2
Beaux-Arts City Hall building, San Francisco, California, 55
Belkin, Aaron, 24, 151
Beller, Daniel, 210
Benson, Craig, 169
Bickett, Rebecca (Becky), 302, 305–6, 321–22
Biden, Joe, 176–77
bigotry. *See* discrimination
Bipartisan Legal Advisory Group (BLAG)
  Edith Schlain Windsor v. the United States of America and, 148–52, 155–61, 165–70, 172–73, 181–82, 192–93, 196, 200, 206, 212, 218–19, 221, 223–24, 233, 241

United States v. Windsor and, 264, 270–71, 279–80
Bishops of the Episcopal Church, 209
Blackmun, Harry, 185
Blatt, Lisa, 237–38
Boies, David, 117–18, 132, 200
Bonauto, Mary, 47, 129–30, 208, 252, 318, 322
  amicus briefs, on behalf of *Perry*, and, 234, 235
  amicus briefs, on behalf of *Windsor* and, 201, 206
  as architect of marriage equality movement, 179
  Gill v. Office of Personnel Management and, 132, 143, 189
  GLAD and, 48–50, 76, 113, 129, 144
  Goodridge v. Department of Public Health and, 51, 53–55, 76
  Pedersen v. Office of Personnel Management and, 178
Boston Marathon bombing, 207
Bowers v. Hardwick, 51, 185, 246, 282, 284, 317
Braschi v. Stahl Associates, 49
Breyer, Stephen, 119, 187, 279–81
Brownstone, Harvey, 103, 104–5

Brown v. Board of Education, 234–35, 303–4, 309
Bryant, Phil, 321
Burke, Meghann, 301–2
Bursch, John, 318–20
Buseck, Gary, 144
Bush, George W., 54–55, 117–18, 144, 148, 236–37
BuzzFeed, 93, 298

California, 55
    marriage equality in, 117–18, 132, 178, 200, 234, 236, 253–55, 292–93 (*see also Hollingsworth v. Perry*)
    Proposition 8 in, 117–18, 132, 178, 200, 234, 236, 253–55, 292–93 (*see also Hollingsworth v. Perry*)
Campaign for Southern Equality, 301–2
Canada, 51
    marriage equality in, 51, 57, 63, 103–4
Canales, Viola, 205–6, 252, 263, 287
Carpenter, Dale, 316
certiorari, definition of, 183
Chagall, Marc, 322
Chauncey, George, 157

Chicago, Judy, 22–23
children, marriage and, 71–72, 74–75, 79–80 (*see also* adoption)
Christian Coalition, 40
Christian Right, 40
Christie, Chris, 178
Ciprack, Carmen, 68, 69
Citigroup, 212
City of Cleburne v. Cleburne Living Center, 228–29
Civil Marriage Trail Project, 103
civil rights, 30. *See also* African American civil rights movement; LGBT rights movement
civil rights cases, generation of, 120–21
civil unions, 50
Cleburne, Texas, 228–29
Cleburne Living Center (CLC), 228–29
Clement, Paul, 148–51, 155, 158, 192–93, 241, 264–71, 274, 278–80, 287
Cleveland, Ohio, 22
Clinton, Bill, 30, 40, 144, 215, 285
    Defense of Marriage Act and, 39, 40, 231–33, 246, 269
    Don't Ask, Don't Tell policy, 39

Clinton, Bill (*continued*)
  "It's Time to Overturn
    DOMA," 232–33
closetedness, 24–31, 34,
    36–37, 43, 93–96, 119–20
Coalition for the Protection
    of Marriage, 208
Coles, Matt, 56, 64, 66–67
Columbia University, 28, 29
coming out, 19–20, 25, 28–30,
    43, 45, 119–20
Commentary magazine,
    245–46
community, marriage and,
    46–47
Concerned Women for
    America, 208
Congregation Beit Simchat
    Torah, 41–42, 191–92,
    299–300
Connecticut, 190
  challenges to DOMA in,
    129–30, 178
  marriage equality in,
    129–30
Conservative Judaism,
    209–11
"A Conservative Rabbi's
    Case for Marriage Equal-
    ity" (Uhrbach), 210–11
conservatives, 39–40, 54–55,
    245–46
Cooper, Charles, 253–55

Cooper & Kirk, 254
Coplan, Jill Hamburg, 160–61
Cott, Nancy, 157–58
culture wars, 40
Cuomo, Andrew, 165
cynicism, 145–46

Dancel, Genora, 30
"Dayenu," 252
death penalty, 68–69
DeBonis, Eddie, 114, 202
Defense of Marriage Act, 30,
    39, 40, 57, 111–12, 114,
    120, 132, 162
  1996 debate over, 217–18
  amicus briefs filed in defense
    of, 206–7, 218–19
  breadth of, 265–66, 292–93
  challenges to, 113, 123–28,
    131–52, 155–61, 164–68,
    178–79, 181–83, 189–90,
    192–201, 203–41, 291 (*see
    also specific cases*)
  Clinton and, 39, 40, 231–33,
    246, 269
  Dictionary Act and, 219–20
  as discriminatory, 216–17, 269,
    278–82, 285, 292–93
  ethics law and, 189–90,
    212
  federal employees and,
    189–90
  impact of, 213–14, 219–20

Obama administration's
decision not to defend,
144–47, 148, 160, 205, 224
Obama's calls to repeal, 144
passage of, 212, 246–47,
267–69, 279–80
repeal of Don't Ask, Don't
Tell and, 212–14
Section 3, 111, 181, 193, 224,
272, 281, 291, 292
states' rights and, 220, 244–
46, 292
striking down of, 292
unconstitutionality of, 220–
21, 241, 244–47, 257, 271,
275, 291, 292–93
De Leon v. Perry, 308
Delery, Stuart, 192–94
Diamond, Lisa, 207–8
Sexual Fluidity: Understanding Women's Love and
Desire, 168–70
dignity, 292–93, 319–20, 322
discrimination, 30, 49–50,
170–73, 195–96, 216–17,
269, 278–82, 285, 292–93,
307
dishonorable discharges, from
U.S. military, 30
"DOMA Infringes on States'
Rights" (Will), 244–45
domestic partnership, 46–47,
56–57, 101

Don't Ask, Don't Tell policy,
24, 151–52
Clinton, Bill, 39
repeal of, 212–14
Dooley, Elizabeth, 206
Droney, Christopher, 194
Duane, Tom, 43
due process, 12, 66–67, 73,
246–47

Edie & Thea, 122, 126, 130
debut of, 110–11
as evidence, 112–13
shooting of, 106–7
Edith Schlain Windsor v. the
United States of America,
11, 131–47, 148–49, 152–
61, 165, 170–74, 179–88,
192–94, 196–99, 284–85.
See also United States v.
Windsor
amicus briefs filed in, 189–
90, 201, 206–14, 218–19,
234
business brief for, 212
Circuit Court decision in,
195–98
considered for certiorari
before the Supreme Court,
203–22, 223–41, 250
jurisdictional issue, 205–6,
223, 224
merits arguments for, 223

Edith Schlain Windsor v. the United States of America (*continued*)
  merits brief, 206, 214–22
  oral argument for, 192–94, 223, 240
Ehrlich, Andrew, 67, 119, 144, 165, 201–2, 242, 252
elections, 1994 midterm, 39–40
Empire State Pride Agenda, 171, 208
Episcopal Church, 209
equal protection, 12, 245, 271–72, 274, 299
Esseks, James, 66, 80, 123–26, 129–30, 182, 186, 226, 228, 230–31, 235, 252
  Edith Schlain Windsor v. the United States of America and, 132–33, 143–44, 157, 179, 200–202
  United States v. Windsor and, 262–63, 297, 300, 305, 318
estate taxes, 111–12, 117–18, 124–26, 166–68, 193–94
ethics law, 189–90, 212
Evangelical Lutheran Church, 209

Facebook, 212, 245
fact, establishing, 166–68
Family Equality Council, 208
Family Research Council, 208
Fantasy Island, 239–40
Faulkner, William, 305
Fay, Brendan, 102, 103, 104, 106, 114, 202
FBI, 171, 172–73, 187, 216
federal employees, 189–90
federalism, 246, 265, 270–72, 274, 275–77, 292
Federalist Society, 68–69, 121, 191, 193
Fink, Julie, 119–20, 136, 146–47, 162–63, 186, 201–2, 230, 239, 242, 295
Fisher, Jeffrey, 234
Florida, marriage equality in, 301
Flumenbaum, Marty, 140
Francis, James, 155, 156–57, 166–68
Frank, Barney, 48
Freedom to Marry campaign, 208, 318

Gallup poll on popular support for marriage equality, 301
Gay & Lesbian Advocates & Defenders (GLAD), 48, 49–50, 113, 118, 123–24, 129–30, 132, 144, 208

of Massachusetts, 76

Gay & Lesbian Independent
    Democrats, 43

Gay Pride Parade, New York,
    18

gay sexual relationships, pub-
    lic opinion about, 29

Geidner, Chris, 93, 298

Gibson Dunn, 236

*Gill v. Office of Personnel Man-
    agement*, 123–24, 129–30,
    132, 143, 178–80, 183,
    187–89, 197, 201

Gingrich, Newt, 39–40

Ginsburg, Ruth Bader, 187,
    199–200, 235, 241, 264–
    67, 274, 296

Giske, Emily, 164, 201–2, 252,
    261, 287–88, 299

Glick, Deborah, 43

Goldberg, Suzanne, 318

Goldman Sachs, 212

Goldstein, Tom, 253

*Golinski v. Office of Personnel
    Management*, 178, 180, 183,
    187–90

GO magazine, 160–61

*Goodridge v. Department of
    Public Health*, 51, 53–55,
    76, 318

Graffeo, Victoria, 73

Graves, James, 308, 310

Gregory, David, 176–77

Griffin, Chad, 235, 316, 318

Hallward-Driemeier, Doug, 318

Harris, Rachel, 119

Harvard University, 24, 25,
    28

Hawaii, 30, 39
    Commission on Sexual Orien-
        tation and the Law, 40
    Department of Health, 30
    marriage equality in, 40,
        279–80
    Supreme Court of, 39

Hawaii Supreme Court, 30

Hays, Robert Jr., 149

health insurance, 46

Heaps, Bailey, 206

heightened scrutiny, 141–42,
    145–46, 194–95, 219, 220,
    278, 285

"Here Comes the Groom"
    (Sullivan), 48–49

Hernandez v. Robles, 67, 163–
    65, 196, 263, 305–6, 316
    decision in, 77–81, 84, 85
    oral argument for, 70–77,
        115–16
    Rosenblatt's recusal from,
        69–70

Heschel, Abraham Joshua,
    300, 322

Higginbotham, Patrick, 308, 312

Holder, Eric, 139, 144–45, 146

Hollingsworth v. Perry, 200–201, 234–36, 238, 250, 252–55, 277–78, 282, 286

decision in, 290, 291, 292

legal team from, 236–38

oral argument for, 253–57, 264

homophobia, 28, 44, 63, 171–73, 283–84. *See also* discrimination

Horwitz, Belle (Grandma Belle), 22–23, 45

Horwitz, Benjamin (Benjie), 22

Howe, Amy, 253, 254

Hoyer, Steny, 148

Hoylman, Brad, 299

Human Rights Campaign (HRC), 114, 118, 150, 235, 245, 316, 318

Huntsville, Texas, 68

Indiana, marriage equality in, 315

"It's Time to Overturn DOMA" (Clinton), 232–33

Jackson, Vicki, 223–24, 250

Jacobs, Dennis, 121, 190–91, 193, 195–97

Janghorbani, Jaren, 119, 149, 161–62, 184, 186, 191, 195, 201–2, 242, 252, 257, 262–63, 295

Jarrett, Valerie, 263

The Jenny Jones Show, 40

Jewish congregations, 209, 210

Jewish Conservative Movement groups, 209–10

Jewish holidays, 191–92, 250

Jewish Theological Seminary (JTS), 60, 209, 210

Johnson, Donna, 213–14

Johnson, Jeh, 151–52

Johnson, Magic, 29

Jones, Barbara, 134, 136, 138, 140, 155, 158, 174, 179, 181–82, 186, 187, 193

Jury Project, 32–33, 194–95

Kagan, Elena, 179–80, 183, 187–88, 197, 201, 203, 255, 267–69, 275, 278

Kaplan, Roberta

childhood of, 22–23

clothing for court, 243–44

competitive spirit of, 181–82

marriage of, 59–61, 63, 68, 209, 285–86

before moot courts, 225–
30, 231, 233–34, 236–38,
249
parents of, 22, 29, 34,
45–46, 59, 301
sermon at Congregation
Beit Simchat Torah,
299–300
speech at Stonewall site,
299
before the Supreme Court,
273–87
Kaplan-Lavine, Jacob, 21–22,
135, 137, 162, 180–81,
221–22, 286, 287, 322
birth of, 61–62, 67
Edith Windsor and, 175–
76
Ellie and, 258–60
New York City's Pride
Weekend and, 301
Roberta's adoption of,
80–84
Karlan, Pam, 223–25, 230–31,
233, 242, 249, 252–53, 258,
318
Edith Schlain Windsor v. the
United States of America
and, 184–88, 198, 201,
203–7, 217
United States v. Windsor,
261–63, 266, 287
Karp, Brad, 115, 204–5, 297

Kaufman, Elaine, 86
Kaye, Joshua, 186, 201–2,
240, 241, 308
Kaye, Judith, 32–38, 40, 49,
68–69, 76–77, 79–80,
194–95, 242
Kelly, Colin, 119, 242
Kelly, Neil, 149
Kennedy, Anthony, 187–88,
207, 220, 229, 269, 310,
317
Lawrence v. Texas and,
51–53, 246–48
Obergefell v. Hodges and,
319–21
opinion in Windsor, 292–93,
294
previous decisions written
by, 290
United States v. Windsor and,
265–67, 271–72, 275, 282–
83, 291
King, Martin Luther Jr.,
300
King & Spalding, 148, 149–
50, 152, 155, 212
Koritz, Alexia, 93, 161, 201–
2, 239, 242, 295
Koufax, Sandy, 191

Lagon, Pat, 30
L.A. Law, 29
Lamb, Michael, 157

Lambda Legal Defense and
    Education Fund, 30, 65,
    67, 69, 112–13, 118, 124,
    132, 208, 309, 318
Lavine, Ari, 287
Lavine, David, 136–37
Lavine, Rachel, 114, 135–37,
    162, 164–65, 181, 201–2,
    221–22, 259–61, 263, 286,
    290–91, 295
  birth of Jacob and, 62–63,
    81–84
  early relationship with
    Roberta, 41–45, 56–59
  honeymoon of, 67
  marriage of, 59–61, 63, 68
  mother of, 287, 308
  New York City's Pride
    Weekend and, 301
  Passover Seder and, 250–52
  sister of, 287
  victory celebration after
    decision, 299–300
  wedding of, 209
  at Yom Kippur services,
    191–92
Lawrence v. Texas, 51–54, 64,
    229, 246–48, 256, 282–84,
    290, 294, 317–18, 320
Leahy, Patrick, 179
legislation. See also specific
    : legislation
  antisodomy laws, 51–52

against gay sexual relation-
    ships, 20
Levin, Kramer, 210–11
Levine, Howard, 36–37
Levi Strauss, 212
Levy, Ariel, 291
  "The Perfect Wife," 290
LGBT activists, 30, 31, 43, 48–49
LGBT Center, 131–33, 171,
    295–97
LGBT churches, 208
LGBT Film Festival, 110
LGBT people, changing atti-
    tudes toward, 28–29, 29,
    151, 301
LGBT rights movement,
    48–49, 113, 114, 145–46,
    151, 303–5, 307. See also
    Don't Ask, Don't Tell
    policy; marriage equality;
    parenthood
  in New York, 64–65
Lin, Jean, 138
London, Martin, 40–41, 202,
    263
Louisiana, marriage equality
    in, 308–9
Loving v. Virginia, 66

Maraweck, Virginia, 261
marriage. See also marriage
    equality
  adoption and, 33–34

children and, 71–72, 74–75,
    79–80
community and, 46–47
in Hawaii, May 1, 1991, 30
interracial, 66
procreation and, 71–72,
    74–77, 79–80
Marriage Act of Ontario, 105
marriage equality, 39, 46–49,
    51–53
in all fifty states, 294–95,
    301–2, 315–22
in California, 117–18, 132,
    178, 200, 234, 236, 253–55,
    292–93 (see also Hollings-
    worth v. Perry)
in Canada, 51, 57, 63, 103–4
in Connecticut, 129–30
in Florida, 301
in Hawaii, 40, 279–80
in Indiana, 315
in Louisiana, 308–9
in Maryland, 178
in Massachusetts, 53–55, 64,
    76, 178, 304, 318, 322
in Michigan, 318–20
military members and,
    212–14
in Minnesota, 310
in Mississippi, 302–13,
    322–23
in New Hampshire, 132
in New Jersey, 178

in New York, 64, 65–68,
    69–81, 84, 85, 122–29,
    163–64, 277–78
in Ohio, 315–22
in Oklahoma, 301, 315
popular support for, 151–52,
    301
rapid developments
    between 2011 and 2015,
    151
significance of, 50
states' rights and, 220, 244–
    46, 275–77, 280–81
symbolism of, 50, 58
in Texas, 301, 308–9, 318
U.S. government and,
    212–14
in Utah, 301, 315
in Vermont, 132, 322
in Virginia, 315
in Washington, DC, 132
in Washington state, 178
Marriage Equality Act,
    163–64
Marshall, Margaret, 53–54,
    303, 318
Martinez, Brian, 144
Martinez, Nico, 206
Maryland, marriage equality
    in, 178
Massachusetts, 51
challenge to DOMA in,
    113, 123–24, 132

Massachusetts (*continued*)
  marriage equality in, 64,
    76, 178, 304, 318, 322
Massachusetts Supreme Judi-
  cial Court, 51, 53–55
Matheny, Justin, 304–5, 312–13
Matter of Alison D., 34
Matter of Dana, 33, 35–39, 64,
    74, 80–81
Matter of Jacob, 33, 35–39, 64,
    74, 80–81
McCarthyism, 173, 187
McHugh, Paul, 207–8
McMahon, Colleen, 32–33,
    34, 194–95, 222
McMillen, Constance,
    160
McNally, Terence, 222
Meet the Press, 176–77
Melillo, Joseph, 30
Mercury, Freddie, 29
Messinger, Ruth, 18–19
Methodist churches, 209
Michigan, marriage equality
  in, 318–20
Microsoft, 212
military members
  LGBT people as, 212–14
  marriage equality and,
    212–14
Milk, Harvey, 55
Milligan, David, 261

Minnesota, marriage equality
  in, 310
Minnesota Supreme Court, 310
Mississippi, marriage equality
  in, 302–13, 322–23
Montgomery bus boycott,
    307
moot courts, 225–30, 231,
    233–34, 236–38, 249
"moral disapproval," 286
"moral understanding,"
    286–87
Morrison, Alan, 189–90, 212,
    230
Morrison, Nina, 189
Murray, Mary, 243
Muska, Susan, 106, 110, 122

Nadler, Jerrold, 263
NARTH, 168–69
National Association of
  Evangelicals, 208
National Organization for
  Marriage, 208
National Union of South
  African Students, 53
New Hampshire, marriage
  equality in, 132
New Jersey, marriage equal-
  ity in, 178
New Orleans, Louisiana, 308,
    309

New Republic, 48–49

Newsom, Gavin, 55, 318

New York, 55–56, 64–65, 190

leadership of, 74

marriage equality in, 64,
65–68, 69–81, 84–85, 122–
29, 163–64, 277–78

state legislature in, 163–64

New York, New York,
23–24, 47

Clerk's Office, 46

domestic partnership in,
101

Pride Weekend in, 165,
299–301

New York Court of Appeals,
32, 34–39, 49, 56, 64–69,
73–74

The New Yorker, 235, 290

New York Post, 177

New York Times, 50, 105–6

editorial "In Defense of
Marriage, for All," 144

New York University, 171–72

alumni magazine of, 161

North Carolina, 277–78

NPR, 155, 243

Obama, Barack, 139, 140, 143–
46, 148, 160, 187, 205, 295

decision not to defend
DOMA, 224

judicial appointments by,
303 (*see also* Kagan, Elena;
Sotomayor, Sonia)

statement in support
of marriage equality,
177–78

Obama administration, 177–78

Obergefell, James, 315, 317,
318, 322–23

Obergefell v. Hodges, 315–22

amicus briefs, on behalf of,
316–18

decision in, 320–21

the People's Brief, 316–18

O'Connor, Sandra Day, 22

O'Donnell, Daniel, 65–66,
164, 299

O'Donnell, Rosie, 65

Ohio, 284

marriage equality in, 315–22

Oklahoma, marriage equality
in, 301, 315

Olafsdottir, Greta, 106, 110,
122

Olson, Theodore, 117–18, 132,
200, 236–38, 255–57, 318

Ontario, Canada, 51

Oracle, 212

Orwell, George, 208

Ouellette, Alicia, 36–37

Out magazine, 160–61

Outserve-SLDN, 213–14

parental rights, 61–62

parenthood, 33, 34–39, 57–59, 61–62, 63, 64, 74, 78–80, 80–84, 293–94. *See also* adoption

Parents and Friends of Ex-Gays & Gays (PFOX), 208

Partnership for New York City, 190

Passover, 250–52

Paterson, David, 164

Paul, Weiss, Rifkind, Wharton & Garrison, 31, 32–33, 40–41, 43, 56, 194, 242, 252

   complaints written by, 126–27

   Edith Schlain Windsor v. the United States of America and, 118, 121–22, 185–86, 199–202

   gay partners at, 68–69, 119–20

   pro bono cases and, 115

   United States v. Windsor and, 203, 206, 221–22, 290, 297, 320

   Pedersen v. Office of Personnel Management, 178, 188, 189

Pelosi, Nancy, 55, 148, 263

Penry, Johnny Paul, 68

the People's Brief, 316–18

People v. Onofre, 64, 72

Peplau, Letitia Anne, 157

"The Perfect Wife" (Levy), 290

Phelps, Margie, 206, 207

polygamy, 71, 158

Portman, Rob, 284

Pregil, Antoinette, 30

Presbyterian churches, 209

Pritchett, Jocelyn (Joce), 302, 305–6, 312, 323

procreation, 71–72, 74–75, 76–77, 79–80, 255

"The Prophets" (Auden), 296–97

Proposition 8, in California, 117–18, 132, 178, 200, 234, 236, 253–55, 292, 293 (*see also Hollingsworth v. Perry*)

pulp fiction, 92

Quaker churches, 209

Quinn, Christine, 43, 299

Rabbinical Assembly, 210

Raghavan, Gautam, 295

"rainbow coalition," 65–66

rational basis, 139–43, 181, 186, 254

Reagan, Ronald, 144, 236, 254

Reed, Ralph, 40

Reeves, Carlton, 303–4, 306–8, 311

Reform Jewish organizations, 209

Rehnquist, William, 254

religious organizations, amicus briefs on behalf of *Windsor* filed by, 209

Religious Right, 20

Republican Revolution, 39–40

Republicans, 39–40

requests for admissions, 166–68

Reuters, 184

Rieman, Walter, 252

right to marry, 30

Roberts, John, 187, 254–55, 263–64, 270–74, 282–86, 291–92

Roberts, Robin, 177–78

Robinson, Gene, 209

Rodrigues, Tammy, 30

Roe v. Wade, 235

Romer v. Evans, 229, 246, 247–48, 290, 294

Rosen, Hilary, 235, 287–88, 297, 316

Rosenblatt, Albert, 69–70

Russian Revolution, 42–43

Rustin, Bayard, 307

Rutkin, Amy, 41–42, 299

Sainz, Fred, 318

Salt Lake Tribune, 168–69

"Samesex Marriage and Morality: The Human Rights Vision of the Constitution" (Wolfson), 322

Sanders, Andrea, 302, 305–6, 321–22

Sanders, Steve, 316

Sandy Hook Elementary School shootings, 207

San Francisco, California, 55

San Francisco County Clerk, 55

Sawyer, Diane, 297

Scalia, Antonin, 52–54, 187, 255–56, 275–76, 284, 291 dissent in *Windsor*, 292, 294–95, 301, 310

Schonfeld, Julie, 210

SCOTUSblog, 199, 253, 290

Segura, Gary, 158–59

Selma, Alabama, March, 1965, 300

Sexual Fluidity: Understanding Women's Love and Desire (Diamond), 168–70

Shepard, Matthew, 207

siblings, 73–74

Signorile, Michelangelo, 29–30

"skim milk marriage," 266–67, 296

slippery-slope arguments, 73–74

"slutty heterosexuals" argument, 74–75, 78–79, 196

Smith, George Bundy, 68, 69, 75–76, 77

Smith, Jerry, 308, 310–11

Smith, Paul, 318

Smith, Robert, 68–69, 71–72, 77–79, 80, 196

Solomon, Marc, 318

Sommer, Susan, 67, 70–72

Sotomayor, Sonia, 187, 254, 272, 281–82

Spyer, Thea, 20–22, 60, 85, 112–15, 122, 124–28, 152–55, 162, 166–68, 171, 202, 288, 300

death of, 109, 131, 135, 174, 216

domestic partnership and, 101–2

engagement of, 91–92

love story of, 215–16

marriage of, 103–5, 111–12, 122–23, 126–30, 226–28, 239, 293, 322

MS and, 96–101, 103–5, 107–9, 216, 249

Stonewall and, 298

wedding announcement of, 105–6

Srinivasan, Sri, 187, 188, 198, 264

Stanford Supreme Court Litigation Clinic, 185, 233–34

Starbucks, 212

states' rights. *See also* federalism, marriage equality and, 220, 244–46, 275–77, 280–81, 292

Stonewall, 295, 297–99, 322

Straub, Chester, 190–91

Sudbay, Joe, 143–44

Sullivan, Andrew, "Here Comes the Groom," 48–49

Suter, William, 262–63

Sylvia Samuels et al. v. New York State Department of Health, 65–67

Tauro, Joseph, 132

Taylor, Camilla, 309

television, first lesbian kiss broadcast on, 29

terminology, 294

Texas, marriage equality in, 301, 308–9, 318

Thomas, Clarence, 187, 279

Three Women, 92

Thurgood Marshall Courthouse, 192–93

Thurmond, Strom, 255

Time magazine, 40, 187–88

"Times can blind," 247, 282–83, 310

Titone, Vito, 49

Toobin, Jeffrey, 235

Totenberg, Nina, 155, 243–44

Trachtman, Jeffrey, 210–11

Tribe, Laurence, 301

Twitter, 245

UBS, 212

Uhrbach, Jan, 60, 209–11, 299

"A Conservative Rabbi's Case for Marriage Equality," 210–11

uniformity argument, 181, 279–80

United Church of Christ, 209

United States Conference of Catholic Bishops, 209

United States Court of Appeals for the Sixth Circuit, 315

United States v. Windsor, 11, 263–87, 322. See also Edith Schlain Windsor v. the United States of America

5–4 vote in, 292

certiorari in, 184, 186, 188, 201

decision in, 289–301, 310, 320–21, 322

dissents in, 292, 294–95, 301

impact of, 301–13, 315

jurisdictional arguments, 263–64

meaning of, 299

press conference after decision, 295–97

University of Chicago National Opinion Research center, 29

University of Mississippi, 309

U.S. Congress, 144, 148. See also U.S. House of Representatives; U.S. Senate

1994 midterm elections, 39–40

1996 debate over DOMA, 217–18

amicus briefs on behalf of Windsor filed by members of, 211–12

DOMA and, 39, 40, 267–69, 279–80

repeal of Don't Ask, Don't Tell, 151–52

Tenth Amendment, 275–76

U.S. Constitution, 51, 55, 66, 120, 220–21, 246–47, 299

federalism, 292

U.S. Constitution (*continued*)
Fifth Amendment, 221
Fourteenth Amendment, 310
Tenth Amendment, 244–45
U.S. Court of Appeals for the Fifth Circuit, 179, 181–82, 302, 308–13, 315, 321
U.S. Court of Appeals for the First Circuit, 143
U.S. Court of Appeals for the Fourth Circuit, 315
U.S. Court of Appeals for the Ninth Circuit, 178, 188, 200, 292
U.S. Court of Appeals for the Second Circuit, 120, 129–30, 140–41, 149, 182, 185–86, 188–90, 195–98, 202, 263, 284–85, 315
U.S. Court of Appeals for the Sixth Circuit, 315
U.S. Court of Appeals for the Tenth Circuit, 315
U.S. Department of Defense, 151–52
U.S. Department of Justice, 138–48, 155, 160, 179, 187, 192–93, 200, 205, 224, 264
　United States v. Windsor and, 270–72

U.S. District Court for the Southern District of Mississippi, 302
U.S. District Court for the Southern District of New York, 120
U.S. House of Representatives, 148, 190
　1996 House Report, 293
　amicus briefs on behalf of *Windsor* filed by members of, 211–12
　Bipartisan Legal Advisory Group (BLAG), 148–52, 155–61, 165–70, 172–73, 181–82, 192–93, 196, 200, 206, 212, 218–19, 221, 223–24, 233, 241, 264, 270–71, 279–80
U.S. military
　dishonorable discharges from, 30
　Don't Ask, Don't Tell policy, 24, 30, 39
　LGBT people in, 30
U.S. Senate, amicus briefs on behalf of *Windsor* filed by members of, 211–12
U.S. Supreme Court, 51–54, 120, 148–49, 184, 315
　Baker v. Nelson, 196–97, 316–17
　Bowers v. Hardwick, 246, 247–48, 282, 284, 317

Brown v. Board of Education,
234–35, 303–4, 309
cases considered by,
198–200
challenges to DOMA at,
178–81, 182, 183, 187–89,
197–201, 203–22, 223–41
*City of Cleburne v. Cleburne
Living Center*, 228–29
conferences at, 198–99
decision to hear *Windsor*,
205–6
"Guide for Counsel," 289
Hollingsworth v. Perry,
234–38, 250, 252–57, 264,
277–78, 282, 286,
290–91
jurisdictional issues, 205–6,
224
justices on, 187–88
Lawrence v. Texas, 64, 229,
246–48, 256, 282–84, 290,
294, 317, 318, 320
Loving v. Virginia, 66
Obergefell v. Hodges, 315–22
Reuters report examining
cases, 184
Roe v. Wade, 235
Romer v. Evans, 229, 246,
290, 294
United States v. Windsor,
203–22, 223–41, 250, 263–
64, 320

Utah, marriage equality in,
301, 315

Vermont, 50, 190
marriage equality in, 132, 322
Vermont Supreme Court, 50
Verrilli, Donald Jr., 182, 183,
187, 264, 270–72, 271,
274, 275
Village of New Paltz, New
York, 55–56, 65
Villechaize, Hervé, 239–40
Virginia, marriage equality
in, 315
visitation rights, 34

Walton, Diane, 301–2
Washburn, Annie, 202, 238
Washington, DC, marriage
equality in, 132
Washington Post, 210, 232–33,
244–45
Washington state, marriage
equality in, 178
Waters, John, 49
Webb, Carla, 302, 305–6, 313,
323
weddings, 58, 59–60
West, Jason, 55–56
West, Tony, 139–40, 144–45,
146
Westboro Baptist Church,
206–7, 218

White, Byron, 229

White, Jeffrey, 178

Will, George, "DOMA Infringes on States' Rights," 244–45

Williams, Pete, 29–30

Windsor, Edith. *See Edith Schlain Windsor v. the United States of America*; *United States v. Windsor*, 17, 21–22, 60, 85, 189, 191–92, 199–204, 229–31, 238–39, 249–50, 313, 322

appeal of as a plaintiff, 188

awarded Roger Baldwin Medal of Liberty, 160, 162–63

certiorari in, 200–201, 205–6

discrimination against, 171–73, 216

domestic partnership and, 101–2

engagement of, 91–92

estate taxes and, 112–15, 124–28

first marriage of, 152–55, 168–69

as Grand Marshal in Gay Pride Parade, 300–301

health issues of, 134–36, 138–39, 174–76

illness of, 109–10

love story of, 215–16

marriage of, 103–5, 111–12, 122–23, 126–30, 226–28, 239, 293, 322

New York City's Pride Weekend and, 301

Obergefell v. Hodges and, 318

oral argument for, 264

in the press, 160–61, 245–46, 290

press conference after decision, 295–97

Stonewall and, 297–99

United States v. Windsor and, 252, 261–62, 273, 285–88, 290

victory party for, 300

wedding announcement of, 105–6

Windsor decision and, 295–97, 299–300

worklife of, 93–96, 106

Wisdom, John Minor, 309–10, 312

Wolf, Mark, 30–31, 48, 53

Wolfson, Evan, 30, 235, 318

"Samesex Marriage and Morality: The Human Rights Vision of the Constitution," 322

Yom Kippur, 191–92

Young, Ernest, 244

Zelophehad's daughters, 299–300